Islamic Exodus
Into the freedom of Christ

Sobhi Malek

Order this book online at www.trafford.com
or email orders@trafford.com

Most Trafford titles are also available at major online book retailers.

Print information available on the last page.

ISBN: 978-1-4120-8415-4 (sc)

Trafford rev. 06/25/2019

 www.trafford.com

North America & international
toll-free: 1 888 232 4444 (USA & Canada)
fax: 812 355 4082

DEDICATION

To

Jonathan & Joel
Two Mentors in the Art of Raising a Father!

And to

All the Muslims, in many countries
and from all walks of life,
in whose path God has put me,
who have made the exodus into the freedom
of Christ, the only Lord and Savior.

CONTENTS

PART FOUR: CHALLENGE AND OPPORTUNITY

ACKNOWLEDGMENT

Without her editorial abilities, her closer touch with humanness,
her love for Jesus and her sacrifice for Muslims,

This book would be merely a set of rigid lectures!

For that,
I am very grateful to

JERI

My wife, my friend and my editor!

INTRODUCTION

I want to help you be a part of what God is doing today on a small scale and will do soon in an unprecedented fashion—bringing Muslims into the freedom of Christ.

Islam today presents a challenge not only to Westerners but to all peoples around the globe, including Muslims themselves! In fact, many Muslims would prefer to offer the world a picture of Islam that is quite different from the one painted by them and about them in recent years.

Non-Muslims see in this religion and way of life a vivid and contrasting mosaic—politically, socially, and economically. Islam occupies vast geographic areas and has a grip on great numbers of adherents. Their numbers vary widely, depending on who is counting! But it would not be far from reality to state that about 1.3 billion people call Islam their religion. Muslims can be found not only in the Middle East where Islam originated, but also in virtually every large city on every continent.

I love Muslims. I have two primary goals in writing this book. First, I want to help the reader gain a realistic understanding of Islam and an interest in Muslim peoples. Second, I want to help equip Christian witnesses to communicate sensitively and intelligently with Muslims so as to win them to Christ and plant the Church among them.

The desire to share the gospel with Muslims does not mean that Christians feel superior. No, we do not think we are better than Muslims or any other people. Rather, we believe that, like all others, we are fallen human beings. Yet, God's grace has lifted us up and set us free to live for Him. That grace has also granted us a biblical grasp of the truth and a divine mandate to bring other fallen human beings into God's Kingdom.

As I said earlier, I love Muslims. It is because of my biblical grasp of the truth that I desire that they make this exodus into the freedom of Christ—this is my prayer and my calling.

PART ONE

The Man, the Book, the Traditions

1 | *Muhammad*

The scene is Mecca in central Arabia. The date is A.D. 570. The incident: a boy is born!
If birth certificates had existed then, one like the following would have been issued:

Name of child	**Muhammad**
Sex	**Male**
Place of birth	**Mecca, central Arabia**
Tribe	**Quraysh**
Family	**Beni Hashem**
Grandfather	**Abdul Muttaleb**
Father	**Abdullah, deceased**
Mother	**Amena, housewife**

It was a momentous occasion, for with the birth of Muhammad events were set in motion that resulted in the appearance of a new world religion—Islam. "There is no God except Allah, and Muhammad is the Apostle of Allah," the devout Muslim declares.

There are no written documents of the history of Muhammad or of Islam that were recorded earlier than A.D. 800. So the earliest records available were put down in writing about 170 years after the death of Muhammad. To put this into perspective, imagine that all historical accounts of World War II (1939–1945) depended on oral sources and would have waited until the year 2115 to be recorded.

CHILDHOOD AND YOUTH

Muhammad's early life was filled with tragedy and loss. A few months before he was born his father died. When he was six his mother also died, and the boy was placed under the care and guardianship of his grandfather. Two years after his mother's death his grandfather died as well. So Abu-Taleb, one of Muhammad's uncles, became responsible for rearing him.

Muhammad was Semitic by race. He belonged to Quraysh, one of the many Arab tribes in the region. Some Arabs are descendants of Joktan (Genesis 10:26), the brother of Peleg from whom the Hebrews descended; some come from Ishmael, Abraham's son; others are descendants of Abraham through his wife Keturah. Tradition says that Muhammad was a vigorous man of medium height with a light brown complexion, black eyes, a thick beard, rough hands and feet, and a ruddy face.

Mecca, Muhammad's birthplace, was on a trade route and had become an important commercial city. Its merchants dealt with Persians, Byzantines, and Abyssinians (Ethiopians). Mecca was also one of the greatest religious centers of the region. Its people were very proud to have the Ka'aba, the most prestigious Arabian shrine, in their city.

As a young man, Muhammad entered the service of Khadija, a wealthy widow. He led her trade caravans, traveling to places outside his homeland and visiting Syria and Palestine repeatedly. He gained a good reputation as an honest merchant—and so won Khadija's admiration. This personal achievement eventually led to their marriage.

MARRIAGE AND FAMILY

Upon Muhammad's return from one of his business trips, he and Khadija were married. She was forty years old and had already had two husbands, while Muhammad was twenty-five and had never been married. The union proved to be a happy one. Khadija's wealth gave Muhammad prestige among his fellow Meccans. Several children were born to the couple, but only four daughters reached adulthood. During Khadija's life Muhammad did not marry any other women.

After Khadija died, Muhammad felt free to take other wives. There are conflicting reports as to how many women he actually married throughout his life. Some say nine, others say many more. A number of these marriages were political and won for him the allegiance of particular families or tribes.

According to the Qur'an (Sura 33:37–38), God permitted the Prophet to wed his daughter-in-law, Zaynab, after his adopted son, Zaid, had divorced her. When Muhammad married Aysha, the daughter of his best friend Abu-Bakr, he was fifty-three and she was about nine years old. She became his most favored wife. It was not an uncommon practice in those days for daughters to be contracted in marriage at an early age and presented as a gift or a sign of alliance. According to the Qur'an a man should have no more than four wives at a time. However, Muhammad was exempted from that rule and had several wives at the same time.

Muhammad's wives were supposed to be veiled in the presence of other men as a sign of modesty, a custom that was similarly practiced by the Jews of his time. As could be expected, jealousy and bickering caused heated arguments among his wives and he had to arbitrate. Aysha, his youngest wife said:

> I was jealous of the women that gave themselves to the Apostle of God. I used to say, "A woman giving herself to a man?" But then God gave Muhammad the verse, "You may put off any of your wives as you please, and you may take to bed any of them as you please" (Sura 33:51). So, I said to him, "Your God is always in a hurry to respond to your whims!"[1]

VISIONS AND A NEW RELIGION

Meccans worshiped idols which they kept in their houses and in the Ka'aba. Because it was such an important religious temple, the Ka'aba housed many idols representing gods, one of whom was Allah, "the God." The Arabs claimed that Abraham himself had built the Ka'aba. Each year, Arabic tribes from other parts of the region made a pilgrimage to Mecca to march in ritual around it.

Arabs also feared trees, wells, winds, and hills, believing them to be the dwelling places of good and evil spirits.

Muhammad hated the idolatrous religion of his community. He was troubled by that and often went to a cave to be away from people and meditate alone. On one of these occasions, he had the first of his intense, fearful experiences. His whole frame shook. He became frightened and went into a trance. Then he thought he heard a voice commanding him:

Read, in the name of your Lord who has created,
Created man from a clot of blood,
Read, and your Lord is the most generous,
Who has taught by the pen,
Taught man what he did not know.
(Sura 96:1–5)

At this, Muhammad fell into extreme distress and darkness of mind. He consulted with his wife Khadija, her cousin, and some other friends, seeking help. No more revelations came for about two years. Then suddenly, while he was going through a period of depression that made him contemplate suicide, Muhammad reportedly had another vision that sent him home trembling.

At first, Muhammad himself thought that he was possessed by jinn (spirits) which were commonly believed to possess Arab poets and soothsayers. Then he thought that what he saw and heard was the Supreme Allah himself. However, others convinced him that he had seen Jibril (the angel Gabriel), sent from Allah, to announce that he, Muhammad, had been selected to be a prophet. During the course of these visions, he received the Qur'an. From that time on, revelations came with increasing frequency, and Muhammad announced them to people.

For three years after his first revelation, Muhammad had only a few converts—some family members, a few close friends, and his slaves. Meccans considered Muhammad's teachings a threat to their religion. They said that he had visions and heard voices because he was possessed by evil spirits. He proclaimed one God; they believed in several deities. He claimed to be a messenger sent from Allah; they thought he was only a soothsayer. He said that God was giving him new revelations; they insisted that he was merely repeating ideas and information available to the people of centuries past.

When Muhammad tried to widen the scope of his outreach and convince other Meccans that his claims were valid, he met with bitter opposition. The animosity of Meccans toward him grew even stronger after the deaths of his much-esteemed wife, Khadija, and his influential uncle, Abu-Taleb. They reviled and mocked him, and the persecution became intense. Finally, they plotted to kill him.

Muhammad, again in a state of depression, had another experience. One night, he claimed to have traveled from Mecca to Jerusalem, where angels and prophets met him. Then he ascended through the seven heavens to the divine throne and the presence of God. During this period of depression and persecution, Muhammad escaped from Mecca. This is called the *Hijra*, or emigration.

EMIGRATION AND CONQUESTS

The *Hijra* took place in the summer of A.D. 622. Along with his sixty followers, the Prophet escaped to Yathreb, about 450 kilometers (280 miles) north of Mecca. Yathreb came to be known later as Medina, "the City." The Jewish leaders of Yathreb advised both the Jews and the pagan Arabs to welcome Muhammad to their city.

The *Hijra* marked Islam as an identifiable religion and became the official beginning of the Muslim calendar. Starting with the year of the *Hijra*, Muslims count time by using lunar years and add "A.H." (Anno Hegirae, "in the year of the *Hijra*"). For Muhammad, the escape from Mecca signaled the end of about thirteen years of persecution and mistreatment by the Meccans. In Medina, he had more freedom to spread his new religion. There he became the respected, revered head of state, the supreme military commander, and the genius founder of Islam. The city became his headquarters until his death ten years after the *Hijra*.

During Muhammad's first year in Medina, he organized his followers and planned tactics. He called everyone to submit to God as the only Deity and to believe in His prophets, angels, and the Day of Judgment. This obedience is called Islam, which means "submission" in Arabic. A person who submits and yields his life to God according to Islam is called a Muslim.

By 627 A.D., Muhammad and his devotees had forced two of the three Jewish tribes in Medina to leave the city and had slaughtered the third.[2]

Muhammad's followers built homes in their new community. Gardens and farms surrounding Medina provided them with sufficient food. But soon the tremendous influx of immigrants caused a food shortage. So they decided to raid Meccan caravans for supplies and thus get revenge for their mistreatment. During the second year of the *Hijra*, Muslims attacked a Meccan caravan of about one thousand camels. The Muslims defeated the Meccans and took a lot of spoils.

From that time until his death, Muhammad and his followers waged about seventy-six military campaigns against neighboring and distant tribes and towns and traveling caravans. Some of these battles were aimed at converting people to Islam, while others were to obtain food and goods for the Muslim community in Medina. In response, Meccans and other tribes organized several campaigns to destroy Muhammad and his followers. Quraysh, his own tribe, vowed to wipe out his religion. But in most of the battles, Muhammad and his followers gained victory over their enemies, slew them, and seized their property and supplies.

Toward the end of his life, Muhammad was able to conquer Mecca. Triumphant, he entered the city of his birth with his forces. He went to the Ka'aba and destroyed all the idols and pagan altars, preserving only the "Black Stone."[3]

Muhammad declared the Ka'aba to be the most holy shrine in Islam and reserved it for the worship of Allah alone. He established the hajj, the Muslim pilgrimage to the Ka'aba, to replace the pagan Arab pilgrimage there.

Muhammad lived two years after the conquest of Mecca. He died at the age of sixty-two on 8 June A.D. 632, and was buried in Medina. A Jewish woman called Zaynab B. al-Harith is said to have poisoned him. Muhammad Pickthall states that

> A Jewess prepared for the Prophet poisoned meat, of which he only tasted a morsel without swallowing it, then warned his comrades that it was poisoned. One Muslim, who had already swallowed a mouthful, died immediately, and the Prophet himself,

from the mere taste of it, derived the illness which eventually caused his death.[4]

Today after Muslim pilgrims visit the Ka'aba in Mecca, they travel to Medina to pay their respects to Muhammad at his tomb.

After Muhammad died, his position of leadership was occupied by a long line of caliphs. Caliph is an Arabic word which means "deputy" or "successor." In a broader sense the term refers to mankind as God's agents on earth. But as a title, it means Muhammad's successor as the religious and political head of the community of Muslims. Many caliphs, including the first four who came to power, met violent deaths.

REFLECTION AND EVALUATION

Muhammad presents many contrasts. He had many of the qualities of a great leader and statesman. He often defended the cause of the poor, the widow, and the orphan. He brought a lot of social reform to the Arabs. One of his important accomplishments was to ban the pagan Arab custom of killing baby girls. But there is another side to both his personal life and public career.

Muhammad was often vicious and cruel. Islamic history includes many stories that tell of his revenge against his enemies. Sometimes whole families or even whole tribes were wiped out. Atrocities were committed even when there was little provocation. Muhammad rejected criticism of his actions. Throughout history Muslims have defended such acts, saying that whatever Muhammad did was right because he was the Prophet.

After Muhammad's death, an important phenomenon occurred which showed that many of his converts were not truly convinced of his claims. Several tribes which had been coerced into adopting Islam during his lifetime returned to their former religions. But through a series of battles still known as the "Wars of Reverting," they were forced to remain Muslim.

Like other human beings, Muhammad committed sin and made mistakes. Several verses in the Qur'an indicate that he needed forgiveness for things he did. For example, he was asked to call upon Allah for pardon (Sura 40:55; 47:19; 48:1, 2). The Hadith quotes Muhammad as saying: "I ask God to forgive me and I repent more than seventy times a day."[5]

Not only did Muhammad need forgiveness, but at times he had to be rebuked. Drawing on Sura 80:1–11, Muslim tradition says that a blind beggar came to Muhammad in need, but the Prophet turned him down. Allah rebuked him.

Muhammad also had encounters and dealings with jinn (Sura 46:29). In addition, the Qur'an indicates that he was subject to satanic thoughts and influences and was therefore to seek refuge in Allah from the mischief of darkness, of jealousy and of those who practice "secret arts" (Sura 7:199, 200; 113:1–5; and 114:1–6). When he died, it was reportedly a jinn in the form of a dog that announced Muhammad's death to Persia.[6]

Muhammad never performed a miracle. To those who demanded that he produce a miraculous sign to prove that Allah had commissioned him, he replied that he was not sent to do signs because earlier generations did not believe them and that his gift of the Qur'an was his miracle (Sura 17:59, 90–94; 29:50). Muslims believe that the Qur'an is the greatest of all miracles.

Muhammad was instructed that it was futile to intercede for those who do not believe in God and in the Prophet himself: "Whether you ask for them to be forgiven or not, even if you ask seventy times, God will never forgive them" (Sura 9:80).

It is estimated that as many as 100 million people are called Muhammad or one of its variants. This makes it the name most used in the world. That is one of the ways Muslims perpetuate and immortalize the memory of their prophet whom they consider the best of God's creation, the seal of the prophets and the lord of every servant.

2 | *The Qur'an*

سورة الناس

بِسْمِ اللَّهِ الرَّحْمَنِ الرَّحِيمِ

قُلْ أَعُوذُ بِرَبِّ النَّاسِ (1) مَلِكِ

النَّاسِ (2) إِلَهِ النَّاسِ (3) مِنْ شَرِّ الْوَسْوَاسِ

الْخَنَّاسِ (4) الَّذِي يُوَسْوِسُ فِي صُدُورِ

النَّاسِ (5) مِنَ الْجِنَّةِ وَالنَّاسِ (6)

(Verses from the Arabic Qur'an)

N ow we turn our attention to the Qur'an, the sacred book of Islam. For the Muslim, the Qur'an is far more than a collection of religious ideas, stories, and beliefs. It is the actual words of Allah given to Muhammad. Devout Muslims believe that the very recitation of its verses in the original language of Arabic brings blessing and puts them in contact with the divine.

We will look at the Qur'an from several viewpoints, examining its relationship to Muhammad, its literary features, its claim of divine inspiration and the conspicuous contradictions between the verses of Mecca and those of Medina.

ISLAMIC VIEW OF THE QUR'AN

Muslims consider the Qur'an to be the supreme and final revelation of God to humans. They believe it was "sent down" from God through the angel Gabriel "on" Muhammad. They hold that it is entirely divine and that there is nothing human in it. According to their teaching, Muhammad received every word and every letter from the angel. Some say that even the ink and the paper used to print the Qur'an become divine because they are used to express the words of God.

Most Muslims maintain that the Qur'an is eternal, not created. They state that its original form was pre-existent as an entity before the world was made, present in eternity past even before it was given to Muhammad. The divine original, called the "Mother of the Book," is written on golden tablets that are preserved in heaven. Some even go so far as to say that the Qur'an is the alpha and the omega, the beginning and the end of all knowledge. This knowledge, they claim, is contained in essence in the Qur'an. It is potentially like a seed. The mystery of God, the order of the world, the principles of life, and so forth are all found in the Qur'an. Everything is to be understood, explained, and evaluated in light of the Qur'an.

This Islamic view of the Qur'an has far-reaching implications and raises serious questions. For instance, if the Qur'an is eternal and not created, then it must be God. But Muslims proclaim the absolute oneness of God with no multiplicity of persons. Then, how is it possible that the Qur'an is inseparable from God, as Muslims say, yet it is not God? Also Muslims assert that the Qur'an is a necessary attribute that is fixed in the essence of God. What does all that mean?

It seems that Islamic orthodoxy here claims for the Qur'an what biblical Christianity believes the Logos (the Word) to be (John 1:1–14). In other words, it is not a book in the ordinary sense; it is God's very words. It is the expression of God's will. Thus, in a sense, the Qur'an has the same place in Islam as Jesus has in Christianity. So the "Mother of the Book" in Islamic belief has been given the biblical attributes of the Word of God.[1]

Arabic is the language of the Qur'an because it is heaven's language. This belief is an integral part of the Islamic concept of inspiration. Every word is divine. Even the forms of the words and letters as well as their meanings are from God. There is power in reciting the Qur'an, hence the very sounds and utterances that are made enable both the reader and hearer to penetrate the content and be graced by God's book. Therefore, it is important for people to memorize qur'anic verses whether they understand them or not. In Islamic thinking, what the Qur'an says is inseparable from how it says it. The earthly Qur'an in the Arabic language is the point where divinity touches humanity. Thus, when Muslims recite from the Qur'an, they traditionally do so in Arabic, not in translation, even when their own language is not Arabic.

MUHAMMAD AND THE QUR'AN

According to Islamic teaching, the vehicle of the divine message of the Qur'an was the "pure" soul of the prophet Muhammad. Because his soul was pure, God's word was transmitted without any human interference or interpretation; he was a passive and mechanical recipient. If any of his feelings or opinions had been part of the process, the message would have been tainted. But they were not. Thus the Qur'an is untouched by man. Yet Muhammad was present when it was given. What was the nature of his involvement?

Islamic tradition says that the Qur'an is the collection of statements Muhammad heard while in a trance. The Prophet went through traumatic experiences while receiving various portions of the qur'anic revelation. He would be gripped by a seizure and a feeling of pain; or he would hear noises like the jingling of bells, lose consciousness and perspire profusely. After recovering from these physical symptoms, he would give a statement that would become a part of the Qur'an.

There have been many attempts to interpret and explain the symptoms that accompanied Muhammad's revelations. Here are five basic interpretations of those symptoms:

1. They were counterfeit. Muhammad pretended he was having the trances and other physical symptoms.

2. They were caused by mental and emotional trauma.
3. They were the result of epileptic seizures.
4. They were produced by demon-possession.
5. They came from God.

Many Muslims conclude, in the light of Muhammad's own statements, that he was not in a normal state of consciousness while receiving the inspiration and that the Qur'an is therefore pure and unadulterated. As a matter of fact, the qur'anic meaning of God's inspiration to Muhammad is an act of spirit-possession that temporarily displaced the normal capacities of the earthly agent. Such beliefs lead us to conclude that the qur'anic doctrine of inspiration is a verbal and mechanical one in the strongest sense. The human agent is passive, totally controlled by the "divine" impulse.

Muslim tradition states that Muhammad could neither read nor write. This means that the miracle of the Qur'an would be great indeed. However, some scholars, both Muslim and non-Muslim, contest this claim. Qur'anic statements such as in Sura 7:157; 29:48; and 62:2 do not necessarily say that the Prophet was unable to read or write, but rather that it was not his custom to do so. In other words, he was not a scholar.

FORM, STYLE, AND TRANSMISSION

The Qur'an was originally written down in Arabic. Vowels or accents in Arabic are signs added above or below the letters. When a word does not have those vowels, it can often be read as a noun, a verb, an adjective or some other part of speech. Even a verb, when written without vowels, can be read either in the active or passive voice. When the Qur'an was compiled, it was written in Kufic, a type of Arabic script which contained no vowels. Later on, when people wanted to add the vowels, a major problem arose. They had to decide whether words were nouns or verbs, and whether the verbs were active or passive. They had to determine the meaning of the word first before adding the vowel signs. An Arabic word without these marks can have several possible meanings. Thus, many different interpretations are possible.

There is no doubt that, without the diacritical points [vowels], the Qur'an is indeed an extremely obscure work and that the possibility of repointing affords virtually limitless opportunities to reinterpret the scripture, in Arabic or in any other language that one chooses.[2]

Here is an example of a word in Arabic script and the various meanings it can have.

This word بعد with these accents:	Means
بَعْدَ	After (preposition)
بَعُدَ	Became remote (verb)
بَعَّدَ	Dismissed (verb)
بُعْد	Distance (noun)

And another example:

This word حمام with these accents:	Means
حَمَام	Pigeons
حِمَام	Death
حَمَّام	Bathroom
حُمَام	Honorable man

To give you an idea of its size, the Qur'an is a little shorter than the New Testament. It contains 114 chapters or suras that vary considerably in length. The chapters are arranged according to size: the longer ones come first, followed by the shorter ones. In the Arabic Qur'an, the chapters are not numbered. Rather, each one has a name such as "The Cow," "Women," and "The Believers." The chapters are subdivided into a total of 6,236 verses.

Muhammad did not write down the suras that were revealed to him. During his lifetime, his followers committed the Qur'an to memory. Only a small portion was recorded, and even that was done haphazardly. Some parts were written on palm leaves, others on stone, and still others on animal bones or any other material. It is reported that after Muhammad's death, his goat ate part of chapter 33 ("The Confederates") that was recorded on a piece of cloth that had been placed under his pillow. Aysha, Muhammad's youngest wife, was the one to whom the chapter had been entrusted and who reported the incident.[3]

Abu-Bakr and Omar, the first two caliphs, worked to collect all the material of the Qur'an. Soon there were four rival versions. When Othman became caliph in A.D. 644, he ordered that all versions except one be destroyed. That is the one that is available now. However, a different edition kept circulating until as late as A.D. 1000.

CLAIM OF DIVINE INSPIRATION

Is God truly the source of the Qur'an without human input or intervention, as Islam believes? If so, we would expect it to be a perfect document in pure Arabic without problems, flaws or contradictions. But that is not the case. Consider the following difficulties.

Stories and Concepts Taken from Other Religions

Let us look into the Islamic claim that the Qur'an was sent directly from God to Muhammad through the angel Gabriel. It is an established fact that Muhammad had cross-cultural experiences beginning in his youth. Thus he was exposed to people of religions other than his own pagan Arab beliefs. One of those religions was Christianity.

According to *The Encyclopedia of Islam*, Christian ideas and the narrative accounts of the Gospels and of the apocryphal books had already spread throughout Arabia by the time Muhammad was born. In fact, a Christian community with close ties to the Ethiopians existed in the Yemen.[4] Muslim tradition states that when Muhammad was about twelve years old, he went with his uncle on a trip to Syria. There he met a Christian monk named Bohayra, who complimented him and made prophetic statements about the young Meccan's future.

Several experts on Islam indicate the strong possibility that one or more people supplied Muhammad with stories and concepts drawn from their own religious background. Thus they helped Muhammad formulate the Qur'an. Waraqua, Khadija's cousin, was a Christian. It is said that he was in the process of translating portions of the New Testament when Muhammad received his first vision. For fifteen years and until his death, Waraqua was very close to Muhammad. Salman, Zayd, Kos and others who were Jews or Christians were close to Muhammad. At least three of Muhammad's wives were acquainted with some biblical teachings and history: Saffiyah and Rayhanah were Jewish, and Mariyah was a Coptic Christian.[5]

Some of Muhammad's opponents accused him of being an imposter. They said that he was offering them mere stories and sayings known of old. They claimed that someone had told him those stories and that he in turn falsely attributed them to a revelation from God (Sura 25:4–6). His only answer to such accusations was that God sent it down on him (Sura 3:3, 7; 5:48; 44:2–4).

Material from other religious sources was used in the Qur'an. Experts on Islam state that major portions of the Qur'an have their roots in writings and beliefs known at the Prophet's time. Some qur'anic stories and concepts must have been drawn from the following sources.[6]

1. *The Bible*. Many ideas, stories, and beliefs in the Qur'an are drawn from the Old and New Testaments. Examples are the Creation and the stories of Adam, Abraham, Moses and so forth. Some of these are close to the biblical accounts, while others are not and would be considered a distortion of the biblical facts. Examples of the latter are the Samaritan who tempts Israel to worship the golden calf, and Mary the mother of Jesus being the sister of Aaron and the daughter of Amram.

2. *Apocryphal and extra-biblical Christian writings*. Stories drawn from these sources include: a) Seven young men sleep in a cave for three hundred and nine years (Sura 18:8–26), taken from a book called *The Glory of the Martyrs* by Gregory of Tours; and b) Jesus creates birds from mud (Sura 3:49), taken from a book called *The Gospel of Thomas the Israelite*.

3. *Rabbinical Jewish writings*. There were many Jews in Arabia at the time of Muhammad. They exerted a strong economic and cultural influence on their Arab neighbors. In Medina, at the time of the *Hijra*, there were three major Jewish tribes. The beliefs, practices, and information contained in their sacred books were available to Muhammad.

One can see striking similarities between these and the Qur'an. Here are two examples: a) Abraham is rescued from the fire into which Nimrod had cast him (Sura 21:52–72), taken from *Midrash Rabbah*; and b) the queen of Sheba meets Solomon who is surrounded by his armies of jinn, humans, and birds (Sura 27:20–45), which is taken from the *Second Targum of the Book of Esther*.

4. *Pagan Arab beliefs and practices.* The Qur'an contains various pre-Islamic Arab folk and religious beliefs and customs. Examples are: a) the pilgrimage to Mecca (Sura 2:196–198); and b) the veneration of the Ka'aba as God's house and the most holy shrine on earth (Sura 5:97).

5. *Ancient Indian and Persian stories.* Muhammad's night journey from Mecca to Jerusalem (Sura 17:1) and its details in the Hadith about his ascension through the seven heavens are strikingly similar to ancient Persian traditions concerning the ascension of the Persian priest called Arta Viraf Namak.

Men Around the Prophet

Some extemporaneous statements made by men around Muhammad were incorporated into the Qur'an. Seyouti, an early Muslim writer, remarks that in several cases qur'anic revelation came through persons other than the Prophet. He cites a contemporary of Muhammad who said:

> Umar used to have an opinion on a certain subject and lo! a revelation came down in accordance with the same.[7]

Also some of Muhammad's scribes or writers stated that they convinced him to change the wording of some qur'anic verses.

Conflicts, Cancellations, and Changes

In the Qur'an there is evidence of inconsistency and conflict. Some of this stems from changes Muhammad claimed God ordered. A. Maged, author of *The Political History of the Arab State*, says: "Muhammad used to cancel verses that he had already dictated [to his writers] and come up with others to replace them."[8]

A remarkable and unique phenomenon in Islam's holy book is Satan's ability to give qur'anic verses.[9] To explain this, Muslim commentaries state that "Satan spoke through the tongue of the Prophet without Muhammad knowing it."[10] We encounter such an incident in "The Chapter of the Star" (Sura 53). Zamakhshari, the Muslim commentator, in his *Kashaf*[11] reports that Muhammad recited this chapter to a group of people which included some of his followers as well as outsiders. As part of his recitation, he swore by three pagan Arab goddesses, praised them, and permitted their intercession, saying:

By al-Lat and al-Uzzah and Manat, the third, the other. They are exalted beings. Their intercession is to be sought after and their kind should not be neglected (Earlier rendering of "The Star," Sura 53:19 and verses following).

The idol worshippers who were listening were very pleased that Muhammad had publicly witnessed to the importance of their gods. However, the incident created an immense problem for him with his followers. They criticized him strongly for teaching idol worship. Muhammad said that Satan had interfered and had given him the verses about the goddesses. In Islamic theology these are called the Satanic Verses. He then declared that he had received another revelation to replace the original. He claimed that Allah spoke, saying:

Whenever we [Allah] sent a messenger or a prophet before you [Muhammad] and he had a strong fancy, Satan came and interjected other thoughts into his fancy. But Allah abolished what Satan had interjected; then Allah confirmed his verses. Allah is knowing and wise (Sura 22:52).

The new rendering of the verses in the "Star" chapter reads as follows:

Have you considered al-lat and al-Uzzah and Manat the third, the other? What! Do you have males, while he [Allah] has females? That would be an unfair sharing. They are but names you and your fathers named; Allah has sent down no authority for them. [Their worshipers] follow only conjecture and what their souls fancy, though guidance has come to them from their Lord (Sura 53:19–24).

Looking at the new version, we notice that Muhammad: a) canceled the oath; b) canceled the part about the exalted beings, claiming instead that they were invented names; c) canceled the part about their intercession and said that God had given them no authority whatsoever; and d) added parts about males, females, conjecture, and so forth.

Professor W. Montgomery Watt, formerly of the University of Edinburgh, comments on this incident, pointing out that one of the most interesting aspects is the light it throws on Muhammad's outlook at the time:

> Even though he sincerely believed that these verses came to him from outside himself, yet he cannot at first have found anything in them that he regarded as contrary to the religion he was preaching.[12]

Several times Muhammad had to retract doctrinal tenets that he had already given as inspired. In each case he insisted that the new tenet or view was also inspired. So the more recent verses were given to cancel or abrogate and abolish the older ones. Thus the Qur'an says:

> Whatever verse we [Allah] abrogate or cause you [Muhammad] to forget, we will come up with a better one or one like it. Do you not know that Allah is able to do all things?" (Sura 2:106; see also 16:101 and 17:86).

There are many such changes. Consider the following examples.
1. Treatment of non-Muslims. Many verses in the Qur'an encourage Muslims to be tolerant toward non-Muslims.

> You will surely find the closest of them in love to the believers are those who say "We are Christians"; that, because some of them are priests and monks, and they wax not proud (Sura 5:82).

However, in a later passage we read:

> Slaughter those who do not believe wherever you find them (Sura 9:5).

"Those who do not believe" is sometimes applied to all non-Muslims. Alfred Guillaume points out that in effect, this later passage "cancelled no less than one hundred and twenty-four verses."[13]
2. The number of Muhammad's wives. In the following passage, the Prophet was given no limit as to the number of wives he could marry:

> O prophet! We have made it lawful for you to have as your wives those women for whom you have paid dowries, and those you

own as loot of war, and the daughters of your paternal and maternal uncles and aunts who emigrated with you, and believing women who offer themselves to the prophet if the prophet desires to marry them. This privilege is particularly for you and not for other believers (Sura 33:50).

Then two verses later, Muhammad was prohibited from taking any more wives or changing any of them:

You are not permitted to marry other women from now on. Nor are you allowed to change your wives for others even though you would be attracted by their beauty (Sura 33:52).

In spite of Muhammad's efforts to remove the reproach of contradictions by adopting the "cancellation" explanation, there remain many inconsistencies in the Qur'an. The sacred book of Islam states that the acid test for its divine inspiration is the absence of any contradictions, since Allah cannot contradict himself (Sura 4:82). Applying this test, one finds that the Qur'an does not stand up to its own claims.

Related to these issues is the fact that Satan sometimes made Muhammad forget what he was supposed to give as inspiration:

If the devil makes you to forget, then, when you remember, do not sit with those who do wrong (Sura 6:68)

Commentators explain the verse in this way:

Satan may make you [Muhammad] to forget some of the inspiration that came upon you, and so you sit with those who do wrong. When that happens, once you remember that you're not supposed to sit with them, leave their company and do not continue to sit with them![14]

Non-Arabic Words

The Qur'an claims that its language is pure Arabic (Sura 26:193–195; 39:28; 44:58; 16:103). However, it contains scores of words that are not at all Arabic but have been borrowed from other languages such as Persian, Syriac, Hebrew, Nabataean, Ethiopian, Greek and others. Here are some examples:

Jinn, Houri, Fer-daws—Persian
Tawrah, Gehannam, Ahad—Hebrew

Fer-'awn—Ancient Egyptian
Ibrahim—Syriac
Injil—Greek

Besides these terms, some of the names in the Qur'an are not in their Arabic forms. The true Arabic form of the name Ishmael is *Yesma'il,* which starts with the Arabic letter *ya.* In the Qur'an, however, it starts with an *aleph* and is given as *Isma'il.* Apparently, Muhammad drew his information from either Greek or Syrian sources. The same problem is found with many other names, such as *Is-hak* instead of *Yes-hak* for Isaac and *Is-ra-il* instead of *Yes-ra-il* for Israel. Also, *Yunes* is used for Jonah, *Ilyas* for Elijah, and *Isa* for Jesus, all of which most definitely derive from Greek.

If the Qur'an were truly given by God in the Arabic language, why does it contain the Greek or Syriac forms of some names rather than the Arabic ones? No wonder the Meccans persistently accused Muhammad of composing the Qur'an with the help of foreigners who gave him ancient tales of biblical, talmudic, and pagan origins.

Numerous Repetitions

Throughout the Qur'an, it is common to find statements repeated frequently for no apparent reason. For example, Sura 55 contains the question: "Which of your lord's favors do you deny?" This question is repeated thirty-one times in seventy-eight verses. Not only statements, but also whole stories are repeated frequently. The Qur'an has the story of Adam four times, of Noah eleven times, of Abraham nine times, of Lot eight times, of Moses seven times, of Solomon three times, and of Jonah three times.

Errors of Fact

Several errors of fact appear in Islam's holy book. It is reported that "there are more than one thousand historical, scientific and grammatical errors in the Qur'an."[15]

For instance, the Qur'an tells us the following: a) Dhul Qarnain walked to the place where the sun sets and found that it was a muddy well (Sura 18:83–86); b) the earth is balanced and made steady by mountains (Sura 31:10); c) God's revelation to Moses at the burning bush took place not at Mount Horeb, as stated in Exodus 3:1–5, but in the "holy valley of Tuwa" (Sura 20:12); and d) the sun runs to its dwelling place (Sura 36:38).

According to the Qur'an, Haman was prime minister for the pharaoh who ruled Egypt when Moses sought the deliverance of his people (Sura 28:8, 38; 40:36). However, the Bible states that Haman was a top official in the court of Ahasuerus in the kingdom of Persia. Archeological research shows that the Persian kingdom flourished around four centuries before Christ. In contrast, the pharaoh whom Moses confronted lived about fifteen centuries before Christ.

The Qur'an says that the Samaritan made a golden calf for the Israelites and told them to worship it, saying: "This is your god and Moses' god" (Sura 20:85–88). According to the biblical account, a) Aaron was clearly the one who made the golden calf during Israel's wilderness wanderings (fourteenth century B.C.); and b) there were no "Samaritans" until the reign of Omri, king of Israel (eighth century B.C.) after the Israelites had arrived in Canaan and had been well established there for centuries (Exodus 32:1–6; 1 Kings 16:24).

According to the Qur'an, (Sura 19.27, 28; and 66:12), the Virgin Mary was the daughter of Emran (biblical Amram) and the sister of Aaron (consequently a sister of Moses). In the Old Testament, Aaron and Moses did have a sister whose name was Mary (the original Hebrew form was Miriam). However, she was not the mother of Jesus. There was a span of fifteen hundred years between the two Marys.

The Qur'an itself states that if it were to contain inconsistencies, that would indicate that it is not from God:

> Should not they consider the Qur'an! If it were from someone other than God, they would have found many discrepancies in it (Sura 4:82).

Yet, as we have seen above, there are many incongruities.

Questionable Ethics

The teachings of the Qur'an do not display the kind of moral or ethical superiority that one would expect to find in a divinely inspired book. Killing is permitted to force people to convert to Islam (Sura 2:191,193, 216, 244; 4:76; 8:12, 13, 39). Lying is permitted (Sura 5:89; 16:106). Swearing is permitted (Sura 86:1–4; 89:1–5;

91:1–9; 95:1–4). Taking revenge is permitted (Sura 5:45). It is worth mentioning here that Muhammad allowed lying in three cases:

> The prophet of God permitted lying in three cases: in war, to one's wife and to help people.[16]

Drawing on this hadith, ibn Taimiya, the Muslim fundamentalist theologian (1263–1328), advised that Muslims, when in the minority, should lie to Christians and Jews to protect Islam and Muslims.[17]

The Qur'an also gives Muslims permission to hide their true feelings and convictions and pretend to accept an agreement that can be broken later. This is called Taqiya. According to the Muslim holy book, you are allowed to deny your Islamic faith under duress (Sura 16:106). In such a case you need to be sure that you do not enjoy unbelief (same verse as above). Also Muslims can pretend to befriend unbelievers (Sura 3:28),[18] and may eat of forbidden foods (Sura 5:3; 6:119).[19]

DRAMATIC CHANGES IN THE QUR'AN FROM MECCA TO MEDINA

Both Muslim and non-Muslim historians and writers agree that there was a dramatic shift in the content and application of the message of Muhammad between Mecca and Medina. The following chart summarizes this striking change in Muhammad's attitude, purpose and actions as revealed in the Qur'an itself. I will call the Meccan period "the Appeasement Period" because at that time Muhammad was trying to appease others to gain their acceptance. On the other hand, since in Medina force was used and wars were waged, I will call that period "the Military Force Period."

Verses came in:	Mecca *Appeasement Period*	Medina *Military Force Period*
Muhammad	1. Weak and struggling to be accepted. 2. An ascetic. 3. For more than 27 years he has only one wife. 4. A messenger to the Arabs. 5. Argues with the pagans. 6. Invites people to convert to Islam. 7. Acts as a religious reformer.	1. A strong, merciless warrior. 2. Enjoys the good things of life. 3. For 10 years he has several wives at the same time. 4. A messenger to the Arabs as well as others. 5. Argues with "the people of the Book" (Jews and Christians). 6. Leads wars to obtain booty and subjugate people to Islam. 7. Acts as a military commander.
The Qur'an	1. Draws heavily on biblical information; states that it came to confirm the Bible (Sura 35:31) and is the Arabic interpretation of the Bible (Sura 10:37). 2. Uses poetic, rhythmic style. Rhyme prevails. Verses are short, emotional and imaginative.	1. Draws heavily on Arab culture, events in the Muslim community, and Muhammad's personal experiences. 2. Uses prose style. Rhyme and rhythm are found much less. Verses are long with little emotion or imagination.
Islam	A religious reformation movement.	A military and religious establishment with a serious political agenda.

Verses came in:	Mecca *Appeasement Period*	Medina *Military Force Period*
The Muslim Message	1. "Politically correct."	1. Strongly military.
	2. A religious movement.	2. A political/religious movement.
	3. Concerned with religion.	3. Concerned with state.
	4. Name most used for God: The Merciful.	4. Name most used for God: Allah.
	5. Practical issues.	5. Philosophical arguments.
	6. Goal: reforming the status quo.	6. Goal: establishing the new religion/state.
	7. Islam is a set of beliefs to be accepted.	7. Islam is a set of laws to be obeyed.
	8. Name for Israel: the biblical "Children of Israel."	8. Name for Israel: derogatory "Jews."
Opponents of Islam	Treat them with patience and courtesy (Sura 73:10).	Kill them and drive them out (Sura 2.191).
Spreading Islam	Not by force (Sura 2:256).	Kill those who do not accept (Sura 2:193).
Jews and Christians	Treat them in a civil way (Sura 29:45).	Fight them until they convert (Sura 9:29).
Wine	Is allowed to Muslims (Sura 16:67).	Is forbidden (Sura 5:90).

It is worth mentioning that today, when Muslims quote qur'anic verses that talk about peace, they cite the older (Mecca) teachings that, though still in the Qur'an, were canceled by the newer (Medina) ones.

It is interesting to note that in 1985 the Sudanese government executed Muslim theologian Mahmood Muhammad Taha for daring to say that the verses that came to Muhammad in Medina with their emphasis on legalistic issues are obsolete today and that Muslims should follow only the precepts of the spiritual verses of Mecca. Taha was publicly hanged in Khartoum at the age of seventy-six.

3 | *The Hadith*

"Qutaiba said,
that Layth said,
that Okiel said,
that al-Zohari said,
that Obeid-Allah said,
that Abu Hurayrah said,
that Muhammad said,

'I have been directed to fight against people till they say: "There is no god but Allah." And he who professes it Is granted full protection of his property and life.'"

(Hadith, Sahih Muslim, No 29 and http://www.islamweb.net/ver2/archive/readArt.php?id=59047)

It is important to understand that Muslims regard the Qur'an as a verbatim copy of the "Eternal Book" of Allah that is preserved in heaven. In addition, many of their practices and beliefs are based on the *sunna* of Muhammad, or the custom, method and example of the Prophet—his teachings and statements regarding different situations and experiences. The collection of what he said and did, or the tradition of Muhammad, is called the *Hadith*. The word hadith in Arabic means "narrative" or "talk."

In a religious context, *hadith* is used in two ways. First, each individual statement of something that Muhammad said or did or approved of is called a hadith. Second, the collection of such statements is called the Hadith. This is the record of all that the Prophet did and said.

The Hadith fulfills an important function in Islam. For Muslims, Muhammad is their most cherished example. Sayings attributed to him were gathered so that the faithful could follow in his footsteps. Where the Qur'an fails to provide a Muslim with guidance in a certain situation, the Hadith comes to his or her help. In fact, the Hadith is foundational to Islam, second in authority only to the Qur'an.

The Hadith also emerged for another reason. During the early decades of the history of Islam, it seems there was a desire to canonize or Islamize some Christian and Jewish concepts that were appealing and akin to the Muslim faith but not mentioned in the Qur'an. The Hadith was the primary vehicle to achieve this.

Some of the traditions were authentic. However, the Muslim desire to have every detail of life dictated by precedent in the sayings and practices of the Prophet forced a great deal of forgery into the Hadith. Thousands of statements and stories were falsely ascribed to Muhammad. Several collections appeared, many of them containing unwarranted and forged material. Certain statements were made up to prove a personal point or to promote or denigrate a person or an issue. During the formative years of early Islam, a man named Abdel Karim I. A. Awjaa admitted that he had changed 4000 hadiths to allow things that the Prophet had originally forbidden and forbid things that he had originally allowed.[1] It has been freely admitted that when it comes to hadith, even the pious are all too ready to lie.[2]

The result was that there was a hadith for every imaginable detail of Muhammad's life and habits. A leading Muslim scholar in the early history of Islam refused to eat watermelons because he could not find a hadith about how Muhammad ate them. And therefore he himself would not dare eat watermelons!

It became apparent early on that there were vast numbers of spurious hadiths, which prompted the Muslim ruler Caliph Omar II (A.D. 683–720) to order the collection of genuine hadiths. Several compilations were made, but none of them is considered an absolute canon of the Hadith. However, certain compilers were recognized as more trustworthy than others. The two most reliable of these are the two Sahihs (*sahih* means "sound" or "correct.") These are:

1. *Sahih Bukhari*. The Muslim scholar Bukhari was born 180 years after the death of Muhammad. He sifted through 600,000 hadiths and chose only 4,000 that he considered genuine. He arranged the hadiths in his book according to subjects.

2. *Sahih Muslim*. Imam Muslim was a disciple of Bukhari. So, historically he was even further removed from Muhammad's era than Bukhari. He also collected 4,000 hadiths that he considered genuine. These are not all the same as Bukhari's collection. He arranged the hadiths according to the final authority (the "final authority" is the earliest or first witness of the chain, the one closest to Muhammad).

Let us notice three important things:

a) The hadiths were transmitted by word of mouth for more than 150 years before they were collected and committed to writing.

b) The two most reliable collections were compiled more than two hundred years after Muhammad.

c) From the figures given above, we see that out of every 150 hadiths, these men considered only one as genuine and 149 as forged.

Sciences of tradition (*ulum al-hadith*) with special branches to cover the areas of collection, criticism, interpretation, and so forth, developed to filter and evaluate the thousands of hadith.

Each hadith has two major parts. First, there is the *sanad* or authority. The sanad gives the chain of authorities including the final source who are witnesses to the validity and correctness of the hadith. It appears usually at the top or the beginning. Second, there is the *matn* or content. The *matn* is the text, the hadith proper. (*Matn* also has another name. It is called *sunna*, which means an example to be followed.)

As an example, here is a hadith from Bukhari.

Habban told me:

Abdu-llah told us:

Zakariyya b. Is-haq told us on the authority of Yahya b. Abdullah b. Sayfi

that he heard Abu Ma'bad say,

I heard ibn Abbas say:

The Prophet… said:

"You will come upon some of the People of the Book, so the first thing you should do is to call them to state that God is one… then inform them of the five prayers…"[3]

In this hadith, the *sanad* is the chain of authorities, or the names of several individuals who carried the hadith on from the first person who heard Muhammad say it—in this case, ibn Abbas. Ibn Abbas is the "final authority" or "final source" of the hadith. The *matn* is what Muhammad said. But the *matn* is also a *sunna* because Muslims are to follow what Muhammad said. To obey the *sunna* and thus imitate the lifestyle of Muhammad is a duty of all Muslims.

Here are other examples of hadiths.

Muhammad said: "If a fly falls in your drink, dip it, pick it up and throw it away then take your drink. This is because in one wing it has disease and in the other medicine."[4]

Narrated Aysha: "I said, 'O Allah's Apostle! I have two neighbors! To whom shall I send my gifts?' He said, 'To the one whose gate is nearer to you.'"[5]

Narrated Abu-Hurayrah: "I heard Allah's Apostle saying, 'By Allah! I ask for forgiveness from Allah and turn to Him in repentance more than seventy times a day.'"[6]

PART TWO

Keys to Understanding Islam and Muslims

4 | *A page from history*

How did it happen? How did a group of nomads run the Byzantine Empire and the Persian Empire? How did they, with only a few thousand troops, take over Egypt with a population of about two million? And Syria, Iraq, Palestine, North Africa all the way to the Atlantic Ocean, Spain, and all the Eastern nations to the Indus river and the borders of China? How did they conquer these lands?

Today, more than forty-five countries claim a Muslim majority population. A number of these exert tremendous power both politically and economically. They control important energy resources and strategic waterways. When their masses are fired up with religious zeal, they often demonstrate single-minded commitment and fanatical devotion. These nations form a powerful block and occupy a prominent place on the world's stage. How did this happen?

An awareness of Islamic history will help answer that question. At the beginning, the obscure followers of Muhammad were barely able to cling to a foothold in one city in the deserts of Arabia. From there they went on to conquer and dominate tribes, villages, countries and whole regions.

ISLAM'S PHENOMENAL ADVANCES

Early Conquests

Within one hundred years from the time Muhammad escaped from Mecca in 622, Muslim troops had conquered Palestine, Jordan, al-Sham (Syria, Lebanon, and other areas nearby), Iraq, Egypt, Nubia (southern Egypt and northern Sudan), North Africa (today's Libya, Tunisia, Algeria, and Morocco), Persia (Iran), Sind (part of today's Pakistan), and Spain.

These phenomenal territorial gains served to propel Islam forward on several geographical fronts at once. In a short period of time, it had become a powerful political and cultural force on the continents of Europe, Africa, and Asia.

Subsequent Events

Islam's complex history from the time of its initial conquests up to the modern era spans some fourteen centuries. Beginning with the death of Ali, the fourth Caliph (661), until the abolition of the caliphate (1922), there were three major dynasties.

1. *The Umayyad Dynasty, 661–750.* The Umayyads belonged to Muhammad's tribe, the Quraysh, and were mostly merchants. From Damascus, the seat of the Caliph's authority, two branches of the family ruled the dynasty: the Sufyanid (661–684), and the Marwanid (684–750). In addition to the areas dominated by Muslims in the first century, parts of central Asia came under Umayyad control. Arabic became the official state language, and many conquered peoples who began as protected minorities eventually converted to Islam.

Umayyad power was challenged both internally and externally. Tribal wars between the Arabs of southern Arabia and those of northern Arabia reduced the dynasty's military might. Umayyad efforts to advance into Europe were repulsed: in the East at Constantinople by Leo the Isaurian in 717–718, and in the West in 732 by Charles Martel at the Battle of Poitiers in France, better known as the Battle of Tours. The Umayyad dynasty came to an end in 750 when it was defeated by the Abbasids. However, the Umayyads in Spain continued their rule until 1013.

2. *The Abbasid Dynasty, 750–1258.* The Abbasids belonged also to the Quraysh tribe, but they were descendants of al-Abbas, one of Muhammad's uncles. The Abbasid dynasty turned its attention toward the East instead of concentrating on North Africa, the Mediterranean, and southern Europe. The Abbasids established their capital in Baghdad.

Culture flourished greatly under the Abbasids. Islamic law was developed and elaborated; theology and qur'anic studies moved forward. Greek books were translated into Arabic. Tremendous advances were made in the fields of science, medicine, mathematics, natural science, and in the arts of government and administration. Islam as a religion, rather than Arabic ethnicity, became the important unifying factor. As a result, the status of religious minorities deteriorated under the Abbasids.

During this period, Islam entered the West African kingdom of Ghana (1067). It also expanded further into India, where a capital was established in Delhi (1206). Muslim traders carried Islam into the sub-Sahara, Central Asia, and across the sea routes to Indonesia, Malaysia, and the Philippines.

The Abbasid Dynasty witnessed serious clashes between Islam and Christendom. Muslim efforts to advance into Byzantine territory (areas dominated by the Eastern Orthodox Church) provoked the Crusades in which Christians fought Muslims for control of the Holy Land. Beginning in 1095, the Crusades lasted for almost two hundred years. Though they were mainly unsuccessful, they left a bitterness toward Christianity in the minds of Muslims that continues to the present day.

The Abbasids' rule over Muslim lands was by no means uniform. By this time, Islam had grown into a tremendous cultural force, looming much larger than the political authority of the Baghdad caliphate. Powerful Muslim dynasties in Egypt (Cairo), North Africa (Marrakesh), Spain (Cordoba), and other places also claimed caliphal status. The Abbasid Dynasty came to an end in 1258, when

Baghdad fell to the Mongolian armies of Central Asia. Eventually, the Mongol conquerors converted to Islam.

3. *The Ottoman Empire, 1258–1924.* While the Mongols were extending their power over Iran, Russian lands, and China, a new wave of Muslims, the Ottoman Turks, began to rise to power. Advancing from northwestern Anatolia (northern Turkey), the Ottomans challenged the Byzantine Empire. At that time the Byzantine territories had been reduced and included only Romania, Yugoslavia, Bulgaria, Albania, Greece, Turkey, Corsica, Sardinia, Sicily, and Crete. Constantinople fell to the Ottomans in 1453 and its name was changed to Istanbul.

The Ottoman Empire reached the zenith of its power under the reign of Suleiman the Magnificent (1520–1566), who besieged Vienna in 1529. Though Suleiman's siege was unsuccessful, it showed how far into Europe the Ottoman Turks were able to penetrate at that time. The empire eventually included all of Turkey, parts of Persia, Iraq, Syria, Palestine, Egypt, Libya, Tunisia, Algeria, Bulgaria, Rumania, Hungary, Greece, Crete, Cyprus, Albania, and lands bordering the north coast of the Black Sea in Russia.

Spain was an exception to the general pattern, however. There Islam began to lose ground from the 1150s onward as the northern Roman Catholic kingdoms of Leon and Castile expanded southward. In 1212, the Muslims suffered a serious defeat at the battle of Las Navas de Tolosa. The last remaining Muslim ruler was defeated in the southern caliphate of Granada in 1492 by the Spanish monarchs, Ferdinand and Isabel.

With the beginning of the 1500s, European powers began to challenge Ottoman domination. Muslim trade routes in East Africa and India were disrupted, and the empire began to decline. From the late 1700s and onwards, Ottoman lands were lost one by one to France, Britain, Russia, Austria, and Italy, who colonized and occupied them. On the eve of World War I, the empire had shrunk to an area that included only Turkey, parts of Iran, Syria, Palestine, and some of Arabia. In the aftermath of World War I, the caliphate was abolished (1922).

Overall Impact

A look at Islam's history shows that its political power has often reached great heights. At one time, the Mediterranean Sea seemed practically like a lake inside Islamic territory. Allah-u Akbar ("God Is Great") was heard at the very gates of the Vatican, and the Roman Catholic pope paid tribute to the Muslims for two years. As recently as the nineteenth century, the government of the United States of America paid $83,000.00 a year to the Muslim government in Turkey so that American ships would not be attacked and robbed by pirates in the Mediterranean. Many European nations also paid hundreds of thousands of dollars for similar protection.

Although the sun set on the empires of the Umayyads, the Abbasids, and the Ottomans and the caliphate was abolished, Islam was by no means extinguished. In modern times, the oil-rich nations of the Middle East remain firmly Muslim, setting the stage for the powerful economic role Islam plays today.

Over the centuries, Muslims took their culture and religion with them wherever they traveled and settled, spreading their beliefs far and wide. Fiji, for example, has a Muslim population which can be traced to the arrival there of Muslims from India in the late 1870s. Many other nations have been similarly affected. The end of the colonial era also worked to Islam's advantage. As former colonies threw off the yokes of their masters from the "Christian" West, Islam was often identified with nationalism.

Present Status

Islam today exhibits remarkable vitality and has experienced a dramatic resurgence in recent years. What is the picture like now? Consider the following facts.

About 1.3 Billion Strong

Numerically, Islam claims a hold on approximately 1.3 billion people in the world. This means about one person out of every five is a Muslim. Muslims are on every continent, in every country and in every large city in the world. In addition to large populations of Muslims in predominantly Muslim countries such as Indonesia, Bangladesh, Pakistan, Egypt and so forth, there are considerable numbers in countries that are not predominantly Muslim such as India, Nigeria, China and so on.

Strategic Control

Islam's numerical strength is supplemented by the vast, strategic control it wields over some of the world's major shipping routes. Huge areas in Asia, Africa, and Europe are considered Muslim lands. Muslims control all of the southern coasts of the Mediterranean, all of the Red Sea, more than half of the Black Sea, and more than two-thirds of the Caspian Sea.

Muslims also exert control over the most important water passages in the world, the only exception being the Panama Canal. They are in command of the Suez Canal, the southern shores of the Straits of Gibraltar, the Dardanelles, the Bosporus, the straits of Hormuz, and of Bab al-Mandab at the southern entrance to the Red Sea. In addition, three of the world's five greatest rivers are almost entirely in Muslim lands—the Nile, the Euphrates, and the Tigris.

Petro Power

Muslim nations produce more than 25 percent of the world's consumption of oil and own more than 65 percent of the world's oil reserves. Because of this, Muslims carry vast political and economic weight. The industrialized world's dependence upon them for oil has thrown the door wide open for them to begin pulling economic and political strings as never before. As a matter of fact, Islam's sphere of influence goes beyond the industrialized West. It is worldwide.

The fact that Muslims have this power comes as no surprise to them. In the early history of Islam, they considered their sweeping victories and the subjugation of tribes, peoples, and nations to the sword of Islam as a clear evidence and sign of God's approval of the ummah (nation) of Muhammad.

Today, the same conviction prevails with a slight variation. Oil power and the flow of money into Muslim bank accounts is looked on as proof of God's approval. My friend al-Mallakh told me about a party he was invited to. The host was a rich Saudi who threw the party just to have a good time with his friends. A professional musical group and one of the most famous Arab singers helped to liven up the evening. My friend emphasized that the lavishness displayed that night, even down to the tips the singer received, was an important indication that God favored Muslims. "No one gave less than $500 tips," al-Mallakh assured me. "As a matter of fact, most people gave the singer $1000 tips! Isn't that wealth a clear proof that God is pleased with Muslims because they are good people?"

Religious Solidarity

In spite of a vast number of sects and myriads of sub sects, Islam is characterized by religious unity. Staunch enemies within Islam still remember that they are brothers in the faith when that faith is threatened.

SECRETS BEHIND THE SPREAD OF ISLAM

What factors contributed to Islam's global expansion and powerful impact on world economics and politics? What are the secrets behind its phenomenal spread and its vast clout? Here are several of the main reasons.

Answer to National Expectations

The Arabs were in dire need of recognition. True, Muhammad met with fierce opposition from his own tribe and the city of his birth. Yet, in a general sense, Arabs at that time had great expectations. If every great nation, they argued, had its own great prophet and its own religious book, the Arab nation should have the same. The Qur'an says:

> To each people God sends an apostle... We [God] have sent to every nation an apostle... They [the Arabs] swore by God and by all their oaths, that if a preacher came to them they would believe more than any other nation... And they were saying: "If we just had some of the Book the others have, we would become faithful worshipers of God" (Sura 10:47; 16:36; 35:42; 37:167–169).

So Arabs were hoping for a prophet like other nations had. This person would give them leadership, present them with a book and help them become faithful worshipers of God. Hence Muslims claim that Muhammad was sent to a nation which had never had a prophet but was in vigil for one. And this paved the road for him and his message to be accepted.

Gifted Leader

No doubt, without Muhammad there would have been no Islam. Muhammad is essential and central to this religion. It is understandable that some Muslim scholars would want to refute such a statement. But how can a person deny the cardinal role that Muhammad played in forming Islam? His ability and attraction were the driving force behind its birth, and his strong leadership and prophetic conviction gave it reinforcement.

Message Adapted to Audience

Many times Muhammad adapted his message to please his hearers. In order to lessen the impact of jolts of change, Muhammad kept many pre-Islamic pagan Arab religious practices. Sometimes he had to give them new meanings. Many Muslims acknowledge that the Muslim fasting, prayers, almsgiving, and pilgrimage were all known and practiced by Arabs before Muhammad.[1]

In addition, Muhammad molded the requirements of Islam to suit his audience. For example, at first the time of eating during the Ramadan fast was only a short time between sunset and evening. But when followers complained of the immense hardship, Muhammad extended the time of eating to include the hours from sunset until dawn. Also, originally, marital sexual relations were not allowed at all during the whole month of the fast. But some followers complained about that, so Muhammad allowed sexual relations during the time of breaking the fast (from sunset to dawn).

At the beginning of Muhammad's religious career, Muslims turned their faces toward Jerusalem when they prayed (the direction toward which the worshiper prays is called the *qiblah*). By allowing them to do this, Muhammad was trying to please the Jews and rally them behind him and perhaps win them as converts to Islam. When they did not convert but strongly opposed him instead, he changed the *qiblah* to Mecca as his movement grew stronger.

Devoted Followers

It is not difficult to imagine what the fate of Muhammad's career would have been if he had not received help from his key followers (traditionally called "the Companions"). The Companions gave him the greatest support and loyalty a leader could ever dream of. Without their devoted allegiance, it is unlikely that his mission would have ever succeeded.[2]

Concern for Social and Religious Needs

Muhammad championed tremendous reforms in Arabia. In his own tribe, he pioneered worship of one God—Allah—alone. Since he himself was an orphan and his mother was a widow, he defended the cause of orphans and widows. He banned the killing of female babies. He preached the Day of Judgment, reverence for leaders, personal piety, and brotherly and friendly relations.

Use of Power

Muslims have used the power of the sword to both defend and advance Islam. Even prior to the more recent avalanche of wars in which Muslims have been implicated, a historian of renown said that three-quarters of the wars of modern history have taken place because of and under the banner of Islam.[3] These include nomadic wars and jihad (holy wars).

At times, when their power has met with serious checks and victory has been impossible, many Muslims have masochistically welcomed death for the sake of Islam.

The Qur'an reserves ominous punishment for those who fight against Muhammad's religion. They are to be killed or crucified, have their hands and feet on alternate sides cut off, or be banished from the land (Sura 5:33).

Favored by the Law

Muslims have also used the avenue of law to maintain control. Legally, Islam is a one-way street. There is no way out, either for the convert to Islam or for the one born Muslim. The Qur'an provides the penalty for apostasy in such verses as Sura 4:89: "If they turn apostate, take them and kill them wherever you find them. Never take from among them a friend or a helper." Muhammad said: "Whoever leaves Islam, kill him."[4]

Once I was witnessing to Nivine, a Muslim young lady from the Middle East. As I was reasoning with her, I asked her this question: "In your country, who has more religious freedom, the Muslim majority of eighty percent or the Christian minority of twenty percent?" She answered immediately: "Of course Muslims have more religious freedom than Christians!"

How surprised she was when I objected, saying: "As a matter of fact, Nivine, Christians have more freedom in the area of religious conversions. A Christian can convert to Islam, Judaism, or any other religion without harsh treatment from the government or Islamic authorities. But Muslims who convert are punished, imprisoned, or killed!" She thoughtfully agreed. (Nivine has since accepted Jesus Christ as her Lord and Savior.)

Financial laws in some Islamic countries favor Muslims. Non-Muslims are sometimes required to pay religious taxes from which Muslims are exempt. In Muslim countries, Islam is also the protégé of the State. Since the mosque is God's house, the imam, the preacher and other religious workers are to be supported by the State treasury. Islamic missionaries have been sent out, backed, and financially supported by Muslim governments. Vast amounts of money were given by Saudi Arabia, Libya, Qatar, Kuwait, Oman, Bahrain, the United Arab Emirates, Egypt, and Jordan to build the Islamic center in the United States' city of Toledo, Ohio.[5]

Visible Focal Point

Mecca is the visible, magnetic focal point of Islam. There the strong brotherhood of all Muslim believers is emphasized, no matter what their national origin. They are all equal. They have one confession, one common history, one book, one law, and one Prophet. Gathered there, they feel emotional excitement, unity, equality, strong brotherhood and self-respect. Mecca also gives the follower of Islam a powerful sense of security. There, as he finds himself among hundreds of thousands of other Muslims, he sees that he is not alone.

Attractive Religious Features

As a religion, Islam contains many features that appeal to human desires. The doctrine of the absolute oneness of God, for instance, which is Islam's main focus and emphasis, attracts many. It seems to have a powerful appeal even though it encounters some serious problems when subjected to the test of logic. We will say more about that later.

To people with a pagan background, the doctrine of absolute oneness is presented as the only true and the most superior concept of God. All other concepts are declared to be false and are condemned. Simplistic as it is, it is this doctrine that actually draws the line between Islam and most other religions. Islam's additional tenets are presented in a similarly simplified way.

Ease of conversion to Islam also makes it attractive. The convert does not have to sacrifice anything of real importance or endure any particular hardship in order to follow his new religion of Islam. The transition is an easy task, since Islam has adopted many concepts from other religions in its travels and conquests around the world. The keeping of the month-long fast of Ramadan is the only feature that requires the follower to exhibit strong will and determination. But even this requirement is not a serious barrier to conversion because a number of rewards and fairly easy moral rules compensate for the rigidity of the fast.

Sheikh Gad al-Haqq, the Grand Sheikh of al-Azhar, describes Islam as the religion that matches man's nature! He says,

It is similar to the nature of man, his thoughts and his behavior. And because the laws of the religion and the Shari'a are not rigid, and are flexible enough for man to embrace without fanaticism, it is logical that the religion should be spread.[6]

Islam is attractive also because it is a set of beliefs and rules that include the educational, social, and judiciary aspects of life. Here we have a "low religion"—one that addresses the issues of daily living, the immediate folk needs. In Islam there are rules and laws for almost every practice in daily life: eating, washing, praying, working, traveling, sexual relations, interpersonal relations, and so forth. This feature makes Islam appealing because it supplies regulations for everyday problems and crises.

Zeal

Another secret of Islam's spread is its zeal. This is clearly seen in both Islam's spirit of triumphalism and missionary drive.

Spirit of Triumphalism

The sweeping victories of the Arab troops in the early history of the Islamic movement appear to have had a lasting effect. They seem to have planted an irreversible and unbendable sense of triumphalism in the minds, emotions, and wills of the Muslim peoples. The result is seen in their attitude today, for when they decide to do something, they do it, no matter what means they have to use or what the consequences may be. Only total success can keep them from feeling defeated.

The 1979 hostage crisis in Iran provides an important example. More than fifty United States citizens were held by Iranian fanatics for over a year. For the terrorists, any compromise was out of the question. The full achievement of their own objectives was the only outcome they would accept. Such a spirit of triumphalism appeals to many people and attracts them to Islam.

Another illustration of Islamic triumphalism is Iraq's invasion of Kuwait in August 1990. The world community clearly opposed the policy of Saddam Hussein, the President of Iraq, so one would have expected him to withdraw and save his countrymen and others from bloodshed. But that was not the case. Even if the whole world opposed him, Saddam Hussein insisted that he had to win some way somehow. It was immaterial whether his actions seemed reasonable or not and whether his countrymen suffered misery or not. There was no prospect of compromise or giving in. The same scenario repeated itself in the 2003 Iraq War. Saddam Hussein had not learned his lesson. This time, however, he fell into the hands of his enemies.

For Muslims, the equation is simple: Allah rewards those whom He approves with power, riches, and victory, and punishes those who displease Him with sickness, poverty, and weakness. The Christian concept of humility and lowliness or Jesus' teaching to turn the other cheek is, to many Muslims, nothing more than the despicable signs of a weak and inferior religion.

Missionary Drive

Islam is also marked by a religious fervor and a desire to spread the "religion of Allah." The Qur'an contains many commands telling Muslims to carry arms in order to spread Islam and bring the whole world to submission to God. Muslims take these commands seriously. Since they belong to the House of Islam, they are proud and aggressive in their attitude. Over the centuries, they have used force to impose Islam on the people they conquer, believing they have the right to do so. They are not only interested in occupying lands and ruling countries; they want also to convert people to their religion.

It is noteworthy that throughout history when a Muslim Arab has gone to a country and the people there have converted to Islam, that country has become his. The national and cultural differences are not important. He can adopt them and consider himself as belonging to his new country, while still a Muslim. He is able to do this because his identity is tied to Islam, not to his country of origin. His true allegiance belongs to the ummah or nation of Muhammad. The Arabic saying, "Pitch your tent wherever you find your heart"[7] captures this idea. The "tent" is Islam.

The history of Islam in South America provides an example of Islam's missionary zeal. During the days when slaves were brought to the new world, African Muslim slaves were brought to Brazil. They promptly set to work in their new land, laboring to propagate their religion. They succeeded in establishing Muslim kingdoms that persisted for many years in the jungles. It was discovered later on that many of these Africans had been Muslim scholars who had sold themselves as slaves in order to spread Islam. Since its beginning, Islam has been on the march.

The Lure of Gifts

Gifts of all kinds have played an important role in the advance of Islam. Muhammad himself sent spoils, presents, and money to non-Muslims whom he sought to have as friends and allies. Dr. M. A. Khalaf-Allah reports that Muhammad once gave four men one hundred camels each in hopes of converting them to Islam. Khalaf-Allah also says that when some people came to see Muhammad, they would praise Islam if he gave them gifts but criticize Islam if he did not.[8] And, according to Von Julius Wellhausen, the Caliph Omar ibn Abd al-Aziz sent messages to the leaders of Sind (in today's Pakistan) telling them that if they would convert to Islam, he would make them kings. They converted and adopted Arabic names.[9]

Tax exemption has been another enticement. It is an established fact that across the Muslim empire, hundreds of thousands converted to Islam in order to avoid paying the religious taxes that were imposed on non-Muslims.

Favorable World Conditions

World conditions were conducive to the expansion of Islam at the time of Muhammad and his immediate successors.

Political Fragmentation

The sun had set on the Western Roman Empire. For several decades there were series of wars between Byzantium and Persia. The resulting weakness of these two empires allowed the Muslim armies to invade them with very limited opposition. In Europe, there were countless internal divisions and conflicts. In Spain, rival kings and rulers were fighting each other to gain control. The political climate of decline and disunity in the world empires of these regions favored the Arab Muslim conquerors.

Collaboration and Cooperation

In this climate of political fragmentation, some people were willing to collaborate with the armies of Islam. Muslim soldiers often received help from inside the lands they were seeking to conquer. In addition, the presence of large numbers of Arabs in Syria, Palestine and Iraq, according to many historians, was a major factor in preparing the way for the Islamic conquest of those areas. The Islamic sweep through that region was indeed a nationalistic take-over by Arabs on the inside as well as a military victory for Muslim Arabs from the outside.

In some places, Christians gave assistance to the Islamic invaders. Copts in Egypt welcomed the Muslim conquerors and helped them. Egyptian Christians at that time were hard-pressed under the Byzantine rulers who persecuted them for adopting the Monophysite teaching that the incarnate Christ had only a single nature—divine clad in human flesh. The Byzantine persecution of Egyptians caused the Egyptians to look to the Muslim invaders not as conquerors but as deliverers.

Apparently, there were also occasions when Muslims befriended Christians. One Nestorian bishop considered the Arabs who came to Damascus not as enemies of Christianity but as defenders. He reported that they respected the pastors and saints and gave gifts to the churches and monasteries.

Alfred Guillaume has this to say:

The amazing rapidity of the Arab advance east and west to which all writers refer was due to the cooperation of the local Christians disgusted with Byzantine cruelty and oppression. All the Arabs had to do was to defeat a number of disaffected garrison troops; and this was comparatively easy, because in Syria the population welcomed them and joined forces with them, while in Egypt they made a separate peace, stipulating that the power of Byzantium must be irrevocably destroyed. It was not until the Muslim Arabs came up against native opposition farther west that they met with a serious check. In Egypt and the Arab world they were accepted as deliverers.[10]

Muslims and Christians often cooperated with each other. In Persia and Egypt, for example, the Muslims utterly depended upon the Christians to run the government and interpret local documents for them.

In the nations they conquered, Muslims gained access to the ancient classics through Christian scholars. Thus hundreds of years before Western Europe ever heard of Plato, Aristotle, and the rest of the Greek philosophers, these great thinkers were known to Muslims because of help the latter received from local Christians.

Christians also helped the Arab invaders in areas such as education, economics, and science. Will Durant says that the Nestorian Christians in Syria "translated the Bible, Aristotle, and Galen into Syriac, and played a vital part in acquainting the Moslems with Greek Science, Medicine, and Philosophy."[11]

Further, the help that the Jews gave to the Muslim conquerors was indispensable. At the very beginning, it was the Jews who welcomed Muhammad and his persecuted followers to Medina when he fled from Mecca. Muhammad banished the Jews later on when he had established himself in Medina.

The history of Spain gives us another example of Jewish cooperation. It reveals that the Spanish Jews were actually the first to suggest that the Arabs conquer Spain. Under the kings of the late seventh century, the Jews had suffered a great deal. Anti-Jewish feelings had risen high and Jews had been persecuted and mistreated by Catholics. Many had lost their property and had been forced to emigrate. When the Muslims came, the Jews who were still in Spain gladly accepted the followers of Islam and collaborated with them.

The Jews of Damascus, Constantinople, the Balkans, and central Europe helped the attacking Muslim forces to conquer and occupy these lands.

Weak Religious Front

At the time of Muhammad and his followers of that period, the religious situation among both pagans and Christians was marked by weakness. Belief in the traditional Arabian and Persian gods had waned, and Christians were beset by heresies and factions. The Monophysites in Egypt and Syria and the Donatists in North Africa were two such unorthodox groups. Some factions actually hated and fought each other. The majority of Christians in Iraq during the Abbasid rule, for instance, were Nestorians. Their patriarch had the right to live in Baghdad, the capital of the empire. The Jacobite Christian minority also wanted to have their patriarch live in Baghdad, but the Nestorian patriarch prevented them from achieving this honor. These two sects brought accusations against each other at the caliph's council.

Persecution also played a role in weakening the church. Caliph Omar ibn al-Khattab forced the Christians of Najran to leave Arabia and go to Iraq or Syria. He confiscated their property in Arabia and gave them other land in Iraq and Syria instead.[12] Deportation was not Islam's only weapon. Many Christians were forced to convert to Islam, either as individuals or as groups. At one time, Caliph al-Mahdi ordered five thousand Christians to convert.

AND TODAY...

Although we have dealt with the factors that contributed to the spread of Islam at its onset, we see parallel situations today that are causing Islam's resurgence in our generation. In the last few decades, a sleeping giant, Islam, has awakened. He has shaken himself and is sizing up his potential realm: the world!

Backed with money from Islamic governments, corporations, banks, institutions and individuals, Muslim missionaries are spreading out over the entire globe. It is reported that non-Muslims in Egypt are promised a spouse, a job, exemption from military service, and a generous money gift to lure them to convert to Islam. In Africa, food gifts are distributed to induce the locals to convert to Islam. An African-American Christian minister told me that in Chicago, Blacks are given housing and jobs if they become Muslim. Another African-American Christian minister in Memphis, Tennessee reported the same for his area. These financial and material enticements are some of the strongest weapons Islam uses to increase its ranks. Clearly, the lure of gifts is not just a thing of the past!

Besides giving gifts, Islamic missionaries make other offers and claims. However, unlike the financial inducements, these usually prove to be hollow and false. Muslims try to project Islam as one, big brotherhood that is non-racist, color-blind, and indifferent to class or wealth. The solidarity of the ummah is always presented as an object of pride. Divisions are glossed over, and the lack of affinity among the various Muslim groups is concealed under a thick veil. In reality the dream of a one-world State under the banner of Islam has been thwarted by bickering, misunderstanding, hatred, factions, fighting, wars, and bloodshed that continue to divide the brothers of the ummah. Nothing illustrates more the reality of this "house divided" than the fact that for almost a century Muslims have been without a Caliph! They are unable to unite to select one.

Another important weapon Muslims claim to have in their arsenal is, as they would express it, "the high moral standard of Islam versus the decadence of the West." This so-called moral superiority is a mirage. We will explore that in detail later.

Islam's resurgence today presents a complex picture. In some ways, it poses less of a threat, because its false claims can be exposed. In other ways, it is more dangerous than ever. Muslim militancy is not a thing of the past. Stealing money from non-Muslims and shedding their blood is lawful with some extreme groups.[13] And even today a

Muslim leader states that "spilling the blood of heretics is the sacred duty of all Muslims."[14] In the fall of 2005 and the spring of 2006 the world paid little attention to repeated threats from President Ahmadinejad of Iran who vowed to "wipe Israel off the map."[15] Only when world leaders realized that the Iranian president was serious because of his ambitions for nuclear arms did they start half-hearted efforts to contain him!

5 | *The Islamic System, Din*

Islam is a very complex system. Austere living is admired. Strict moral codes are the norm. Adherence to high moral standards is expected from everyone, but more so from women. Yet sexual permissiveness is not unusual. Dishonesty in financial dealings and trading is often praised. Homosexuality, though attributed to different causes from those given in the West, is not uncommon. As long as such acts are done under cover, and as long as participants do not bring shame or scandalize their community, immorality can go unchecked. Using technological advances such as Western business and household machines and the internet is accepted and encouraged, but freedom of thought is resisted.

How do we understand and analyze a culture so full of contradictions and conflicting values? Let's read on...

slam is an Arabic word that means submission, surrender, and yielding. As a religion, Islam teaches complete submission to the will of God in everything. A Muslim is someone who has yielded to God according to the Islamic faith. Even historical characters who lived many centuries before Islam appeared are called Muslims in the Qur'an. These include Abraham (Sura2:128, 133–136), the Jewish prophets (Sura 5:44), and the disciples of Jesus (Sura 3:52).

As a religion, what does Islam teach? What does it require? What does it offer? Within Islam's broader framework, do variations and differences exist? If so, what are they?

The Arabic word *din* (pronounced "deen") basically means "religion." In Islam, however, it has much wider implications. It is religion that encompasses all of life's activities. It means religion in its cultural setting and with its historical background. In this light, Islam is a political, judiciary, educational, religious, and cultural system. Compare that with the popular, yet unbiblical, Western notion that religion is something related only to God or church. It has very little or nothing to do with everyday life and activities. Work, ball games, court cases and so on, are outside the realm of religion. This is not the case in Islam. Let us look at the following characteristics of Islam to understand the wide reaches of the concept of "religion."

God

Muslims worship God and talk about Him. He is the center of their philosophy. He is one—the Sovereign Creator, Almighty Ruler, unquestionable Judge, and Planner of everything—and He is absolute in His will.

Average Muslims mention reverently the name of God several times a day. At the beginning of a day, a meal, a talk, or any other activity, they often say *bismellah* ("in the name of God"). Other expressions such as *insha' Allah* ("God willing"), *subhan Allah* or *al-hamdu lellah* ("praise be to God"), *masha' Allah* ("how nice"), and *Allah-u Akbar* ("God is great") are but a few of the most commonly heard statements throughout the day in a Muslim community. A typical answer to the casual question "How are you?" is not "Fine, thank you," but "Praise be to God." It should be noted, however, that people use such pious expressions more because of tradition and habit than religious fervor. These phrases do not particularly indicate a conscious faith, although faith in God's existence is a norm and is unquestionable.

He Is One

Muslims believe that God is one. His oneness is simple and absolute. He has no equal, no associates. Actually, Muhammad was not the first

Arab to present Allah as the only God to his fellow Arabs. Even before Islam, many Arabs preferred to worship only Allah. They were called *hanifs*. The belief in God's absolute oneness is so important that it is considered the most essential tenet of Islamic theology. We will say more about it later.

He Is Above All

Muslims hold that God is superior and above all. He is the Creator, but He is far above His creation and does not get involved with it. He is everywhere. He sees and watches over people, but He stands aloof from them. He is eternal, while everyone else is mortal. He is perfect in majesty and beauty. He is almighty. He is an abstraction, and people cannot comprehend Him. In fact, they should not even try to explain Him. He is above analogy. For most Muslims, to experience the reality of God or His essence is out of the question. He is remote and inaccessible, but very close in a mysterious way. According to James Freeman Clarke:

> Muhammad teaches a God above us; Moses teaches a God above us, and yet with us; Jesus Christ teaches God above us, God with us, and God in us.[1]

He Is the Sovereign Master

God's will is supreme, and He does what He wants. He forgives whom He wills to forgive and punishes whom He wills to punish. People are not God's children. Rather, they are His slaves or servants and are not to question or protest against His will. No matter how close one may get to God, he still stands in the Almighty's presence as "*abd*" (a slave).

Islam absolutely rejects the Christian concept of a personal Father-God. To them this diminishes God's greatness (Sura 5:18). Further, the concept that "God is love" is lacking in the Qur'an. According to Islam's holy book, God's love is reserved for good people only (Sura 3:76; 9:4; 2:195; 3:146). In addition, even if God is concerned about human suffering, He does not get involved. Islam sees nothing wrong or problematic with such an idea.

The general Muslim understanding of God can be compared to a judge sitting on a throne in the pomp and luxury of paradise. He places humans on earth to run in an obstacle course. He issues laws and rules to people through messengers. Yet, He Himself does not get directly involved by experiencing what they go through or helping them in their struggle. While they run, climb, jump and fall on the obstacle course, the judge passes out rewards or punishment to each person on the basis of his or her achievement.

In the Christian understanding, God gives the rules and is also directly involved by running the same course Himself. In the Bible, God chose the road of suffering. Through the Incarnation He identified Himself with suffering humanity; and that did not belittle Him or diminish His glory and greatness. In Islam God manifests His sovereignty by sending; in Christianity, by coming. In Islamic theology the extent of God's dealing with people is through revelation and the prophets; in Christian theology, God goes so far as to give Himself in love.

The heart of the gospel then is that God Himself took the initiative to seek and save people. He visited humans and interacted with them. Such a concept is totally incomprehensible and unacceptable to Islam, which teaches that God stands aloof from people. They must take the initiative and run the course alone through sheer struggle and perseverance in order to change their situation.

The Bible teaches that God who is the sovereign Lord is deeply compassionate toward helpless, sinful humans. In His love God reached down to rescue people from their destitute and depraved state (I John 4:10). This is the greatest and most comforting truth. The eternal, sovereign King of the universe is also the compassionate, loving Father!

The Muslim mind refuses and rejects such an idea, finding it unthinkable. Islam teaches that people are supposed to love God first and obey His orders. Then God will love them (see Sura 3:31). In the Hadith we read:

Abu Hurayrah said that Muhammad said that Allah said:

"If My servant continues to approach me with sacrifices, he will get closer to me until I love him. And once I love him, I'll become for him the ear with which he hears, the eye with which he sees, the hand with which he strikes, and the foot with which he walks. And if he asks me, I will give to him; and if he needs my help, I will help him."[2]

In the Qur'an God has many names. Muslims have taken ninety-nine of these and call them "the beautiful names of God."[3]

These ninety-nine names speak of God's characteristics and attributes. Although some of the names touch on His compassion and mercy, most of them are concerned with His might, power, and vengeance. So He is great, upright, exalted. He is the Judge, the King of the Day of Judgment, and so forth.

Occasionally one gets the impression that the Islamic God is capricious because, while He guides in the straight path, He also sometimes leads people astray. Moreover, He occasionally brings damage and destruction. He is described also by terms like "the Bringer-down," "the Compeller" or "Tyrant," "the Haughty"—all of which, when used to portray people, have an evil sense.[4]

Even the most devout Muslim is not sure whether God will accept him on the Last Day or not, whether he will go to paradise or hell. Abu Bakr (the first male convert to Islam, the Prophet's closest companion, and the first Muslim caliph after Muhammad) once swore that he would never trust God's cunning even if he already had one foot in paradise.

Ali, the Prophet's son-in-law and the fourth Caliph, said: "I wish God would let me know whether I was created for eternal doom or eternal bliss!"[5]

In reality, the way we think about God shows in our actions. Ishak Ibraham says that

> ...a man's behavior is the most convincing demonstration of his understanding of God; and his concept of God exerts a profound influence on the way he acts.[6]

This is true for Muslims as well as for adherents of other religions.

A. W. Tozer makes these profound comments about our concept of God:

> What comes into our minds when we think about God is the most important thing about us.

The history of mankind will probably show that no people has ever risen above its religion, and man's spiritual history will positively demonstrate that no religion has ever been greater than its idea of God. Worship is pure or base as the worshiper entertains high or low thoughts of God.

For this reason the gravest question before the Church is always God Himself, and the most portentous fact about any man is not what he at a given time may say or do, but what he in his deep heart conceives God to be like. We tend by a secret law of the soul to move toward our mental image of God.[7]

G. Campbell Morgan expresses the same thought in a slightly different way:

Everything in the life of a man or a nation depends on the character of its worship. Whatever is worshiped is served. The service ennobles or degrades according to the character of those worshiped.[8]

And George W. Peters has this to say:

The God concept of a people determines the quality and character of religion and life, the progress or stagnation of culture. It is central, foundational, and directive in all philosophies of religion and world and life views.[9]

The result is that Muslims are impoverished by a concept of God that transforms all relations with Him into rules and regulations. Following such rules cannot give humans access to the living God. Rather it is an attempt to appease Him and keep Him at a distance to avoid His anger and revenge. Muslims believe that people can approach God from afar and that since He is unpredictable, they must perform their duties and wait and see if that will please or displease Him!

Muhammad

Volume upon volume has been published on the life of Muhammad. Millions of his followers have studied and admired his personality. It seems that we can detect in some Muslim thought and daily life that God has somehow retreated and that Muhammad has taken more and more a position of prominence.

Beliefs about Muhammad

God is so awesome, so majestic, so unreachable. But Muhammad is human—he is more available. Muslims tend to be more impressed by Muhammad. He is a legend. He is their hero. They use his name for an oath. They praise his achievements and elaborate on the details of his daily life. As Ray Register explains,

> Muslims have developed an aura of holiness around Muhammad. His every act as a man has set the pattern for the daily life of the devout Muslim.[10]

Consider the following beliefs about Muhammad.

1. *He was created before any other creation or human life.*

2. *He was born pure.* Tor Andrae reports that Muslims believe Muhammad "was born clean and without spot like a lamb is born, circumcised and with the navel cord already cut."[11]

3. *He is the seal of all the prophets.* That is, he is the last and the most important of all of them. He is God's final messenger to the world. Thus his message is the end of all divine messages. It is meant for all people of all races and languages until the Judgment Day (Sura 7:158). All apostles and prophets before Muhammad were regional, and their messages were meant for the people in their area.

4. *His is the perfect religion.* The Qur'an says that Islam is the perfect religion from God. Through it God has completed His favor to man (Sura 5:3).

Veneration of Muhammad

In fact, one can notice indications of veneration, worship, and almost deification of Muhammad, although Muslims claim not to worship him and he himself exhorted them to worship only God. Let us consider the following.

1. *Muhammad is revered above any other human being.* He is exalted and blessed. That is because he "is lord of every servant... [God's] culminating apostle... The light of Muhammad was the first creation of God and the genesis of mankind..."[12] Muhammad is "the lord of all creatures"[13] and "lord of the two worlds, the earth and the heavens and the animated beings, spirits and men of every sort..."[14]

In April 2004 I received an announcement of a celebration in honor of Muhammad's birthday in London. The email described the one to be honored as:

> The mercy of mankind... the closest, the... dearest to the Creator, the cause of creation, the reason of creation, the first to be created, the Light of Allah, the Prophet of Prophets, Leader of Leaders, reviver of revivers, the praised one... his name is Muhammad.[15]

Many Muslims, after doing the pilgrimage in Mecca, travel to Medina to visit the Prophet's tomb. A hadith reports that Muhammad said: "Whoever visits my tomb will be entitled to my intercession."[16]

However, some fundamentalist Muslims know very well that this is a form of idolatry and oppose such a custom. They state that those who visit Muhammad's tomb "...are committing the most flagrant acts of idolatry and thus nullify their Hajj."[17]

2. *He is thought to be sinless.* The Qur'an says that Muhammad was instructed to tell his followers, "I am only a human being like you are" (Sura 18:110). He was to ask God to forgive his sins (Sura 40:55). In spite of that, Muslims in general believe that Muhammad was created sinless to distinguish him as a prophet. They regard him as infallible in judgment. He is

> portrayed in the Qur'an as a person who makes mistakes but who does not sin against God. However, God corrected Muhammad's mistakes or errors in judgment, so that his life serves as an example for future Muslims to follow.[18]

That is why Muslims revere the Hadith and hold it in the highest regard second only to the Qur'an. They cherish the example of the Apostle and seek to follow it as a model. They are fond of memorizing statements of what he did and said and how he behaved in various situations.

3. *His intercession can gain entrance into paradise for people.* Muhammad is the only intermediary between God and humans, so they need his approval. Muslims treasure his link with the divine so much that they would never let go of him, even if they would have to let go of

God! "Muhammad is explicitly acclaimed as the sole intercessor and channel of communication between the Muslim and God..."[19]

4. *He is called upon when praying.* Muslims address Muhammad in some of their calls to prayer. "Addressing the Prophet with blessings and prayers constitutes an important facet of daily religious life for most Muslims."[20] The most conspicuous statement they address to him is part of the call to prayer and says: "O, the most beautiful in the creation of God; O, the one with the handsome [pleasant] face; O, the messenger of God..."[21]

The Book

Since God is so far beyond human understanding, people are unable to define Him. Even if one were to try to describe Him by saying "God is love," as Christians do, that could mean that He is not hatred. If one were to say "God is good," that could mean that He is not evil. Muslims see such descriptions as imposing boundaries on God's nature. The idea that God is limited is unacceptable to them.

Islam does teach, however, that one can know God because He has declared Himself and revealed Himself to the prophets to guide people on the right path. According to Islam, God sent the Qur'an down to the greatest of the prophets, Muhammad. Islam is a religion with a book—the Qur'an. For Muslims, the Qur'an is the final revelation. It is the greatest of all books in language, style, and meaning.

The Qur'an is read, learned, studied, committed to memory, and recited. Its contents are sacred and revered. As a book, it is not to be handled lightly or carelessly. It is the essential and central declaration of religion, which makes it of extreme value to Muslims. It influences them greatly in all of life's aspects and activities.

Five Duties

There are five duties or pillars on which the religion of each Muslim should stand. These are the most essential practices for all Muslims from all walks of life:

The Creed ("Shahada")

The creed is the "witness." It is the confession or statement of faith made by a Muslim: "I confess that there is no god except God and that Muhammad is the apostle of God." The creed is to be repeated several times a day and is included in each call to prayer. The mere recitation of this creedal statement makes one a Muslim.

Prayer ("Salat")

For the most part, Islamic prayer is not free conversation with God. Rather, it is ritual in nature and comprises the recitation of memorized statements. Prayer is observed five times a day at specific hours: dawn, midday, mid-afternoon, sunset, and nightfall.

A muezzin calls the faithful to prayer from a minaret of a mosque or similar place. Muslims prepare for prayer by performing ritual ablutions of the face, hands, arms, head, feet, ankles, and other parts (Sura 5:6). One cannot address God until he is clean. Muhammad said: "God will not accept your prayers unless you do the ablutions."[22]

Once Muhammad was asked about two men who died and were buried. He said: "Both are in hell, but not for anything big! One of them did not clean himself after urinating and the other spread scandalous talk about others."[23]

So, doing the ablutions is an integral part of prayer. According to tradition, Muhammad said that when a Muslim washes his face during ablutions, every sin his face has committed is washed away with the water. When he performs ablutions of the feet, the sins that his feet have committed are washed away.

The worshiper faces toward Mecca and prays only in Arabic, no matter what his mother tongue may be. While he repeatedly recites memorized statements, he alternates a standing posture with kneeling and prostration. During prayer Muslims affirm the existence of God, His oneness, and other attributes. They also call down the blessings of God upon Muhammad and Abraham and their descendants. Then they greet their fellow worshipers.

Fasting ("Sawm")

During the month of the Muslim year called Ramadan, everyone is required to fast from dawn to sunset with exceptions made for the sick, travelers, pregnant women, nursing mothers, and young children. Since ladies are considered unclean during their menstrual period, they do not have to fast at that time. Because the Muslim calendar follows the lunar year, which is shorter than the solar year, Ramadan falls in different months of the Western calendar. Each solar year it comes eleven days earlier than the previous year.

Fasting means complete abstention from eating, drinking, smoking, smelling nice odors, and having marital relations. During Ramadan the pace of life slows down. Productivity is low, and emotions usually run high. Accidents increase and absenteeism on the job is much greater than the rest of the year. Government offices, schools, and businesses have shorter workdays.

Each day after sunset, Muslims break the fast. The first meal usually looks like a feast. An average family spends more on food during Ramadan than at any other time. This creates a tremendous economic burden on households with limited incomes. Although all Muslims celebrate Ramadan, in reality many of them do not strictly observe the fast. Most claim to fast, however, because of respect for community ties and fear of criticism.

Alms ("Zakat")

Almsgiving, as the other duties, is considered a work of merit. People are to give different percentages of their income depending on whether they are merchants, landowners, workers, and so forth. Some have suggested that the zakat system in Muslim societies often creates a class of professional beggars and discourages the establishment of social institutions to care for the needy and physically handicapped. However, in recent times there have been great efforts in several Muslim countries to collect zakat funds to establish mosques, schools and hospitals.

Pilgrimage ("Hajj")

Every adult Muslim who can afford it, whether male or female, is required to visit the Ka'aba in Mecca at least once during his or her life. This pilgrimage is made during the twelfth month of the lunar calendar. Muslims all over the world share the hope that someday they will be able to go to Mecca and tour the Ka'aba.

Each pilgrim wears a white, seamless garb, abstains from marital relations, shaving, haircutting, and nail trimming, and participates in certain specified rites. A Muslim who has completed this pilgrimage acquires the honorific title of hajji. Muhammad promised that paradise is the reward of a pious pilgrim.

It is important to note that there are serious differences between the Islamic meaning of these duties and what the Bible teaches. For example, in Islam, by performing these duties one gains merit with God. He forgives you because you pray, because you give alms, because you fast, and so on. In other words people are saved by their own works, while the Bible teaches that salvation is by faith. Also worship through prayer in Islam is indeed an external performance. God accepts your prayer only when you are physically clean, when you face toward Mecca, pray in Arabic, recite memorized words, do prescribed movements and prostrations, and so forth.[24]

Other Basic Beliefs

In addition to the concept of God and the five religious duties, Islam has teachings on the following subjects.

Prophets

Islam teaches that there are hundreds of thousands of prophets. The Qur'an itself names only twenty-eight. Most of these are biblical characters, while two are simply historical personages: Luqman (probably Aesop), and the Two-Horned (Alexander the Macedonian). The major prophets are those who received revelations. They are: Moses who received the Torah (Pentateuch); David who received the Zabur (Psalms); Jesus who received the Injil (Gospel); and Muhammad who received the Qur'an.

In Islam a prophet's mission included both the spiritual world and the material world. Muhammad's spiritual mission was to be God's messenger. His practice of polygamy is accepted as a part of his earthly, physical mission. So in the account of his life, cruelty goes hand in hand with piety, warring with praying, and fighting with fasting.

Man

According to the Qur'an man is weak (Sura 4:28); erratic and unreliable (Sura 41:49–51); stingy (Sura 17:100); and feels self-sufficient (Sura 96:6–7). This applies to everyone. Islam does not differentiate between a spiritual person and one who is carnal.

It is interesting to note that Muslims believe that people by nature are good enough. Yet in reality and in a general way, a Muslim reacts with suspicion and mistrust toward others, even if they are Muslim. On the other hand, Christians believe that human nature is corrupt. Because of sin people are fallen. Yet, in personal relations, a Christian generally treats the other person with an attitude of trust.

1. *Sin.* Sin is an act of breaking the code of dos and don'ts. The biblical teaching that sin is a condition of the heart, that it grieves God, and that it causes one's relationship with God to be broken is unknown in Islam, which teaches that the Supreme Being is not affected in any way nor is He hurt by the sins people commit.

Accordingly, individuals do not particularly need a sacrifice to atone for their sin. Good works such as prayer, fasting, almsgiving, and so forth, are used to appeal to God to cancel a person's sins and thus obtain forgiveness. However, even if one's good works are many and outweigh his evil deeds, he cannot be sure of salvation. No Muslim can declare that he has already earned or received forgiveness. He will know only on the Last Day. And even then, if his good works are not enough, "God is merciful." If God wants to forgive, He will. So the Muslim continues to hope that God will overlook his failures on the Last Day.

Islam divides sins into two categories—those that are mild and those that are more serious. God forgives the mild sins but not the serious ones (Sura 53:32).

The Bible teaches that sin results from the fallen nature of humankind and leads to alienation from God. The outward symptoms of this condition are wrong actions such as violating divine and human ordinances. In other words, sin (the fallen condition of humanity) is the root of sins (the misdeeds of the person). The Qur'an does not touch on this deeper concept of sin at all. In a sense, it completely overlooks the root of sins. There are sins, to be sure, but in the Qur'an, they are external ailments rather than characteristics of humanity's depraved, fallen nature.

2. *Moral code*. Islam has a strict code of ethics. It forbids adultery, gambling and drinking alcohol (Sura 5:90, 91). It encourages honesty, generosity, and respect. Severe and sometimes brutal punishment is meted out to lawbreakers. Here are examples: a thief's hand should be cut off (Sura 5:38), and an adulterer should be "flogged with a hundred stripes" (Sura 24:2, 3). Other references say an adulterer should be stoned to death. In some countries such as Saudi Arabia, beheadings are a part of the penal code. In July 1977 Princess Misha'il, great niece of the king of Saudi Arabia, was forced to kneel in a public square in the capital city of Riyadh and was shot dead. Close by was her lover who, minutes later, was beheaded. Both were executed for adultery.[25]

These punishments are meant to be deterrents. Yet, in my estimation they are neither humane nor work as deterrents as long as sin comes from the heart and not the eyes or hands.

Islam permits revenge: "A life for a life, an eye for an eye, a nose for a nose, an ear for an ear, a tooth for a tooth..." (Sura 5:45). Further, although circumcision is not required in the Qur'an, it is considered an essential practice in Islam. Muhammad is quoted in the Hadith as saying, "Circumcision is a must for males, and excision is an honor for females."[26] Today, many Muslim reformers strongly oppose female excision and describe it as barbaric since it causes misery, pain and horror.

In most Muslim countries, the moral standard played out in everyday life is much more lax than the ideal stated in the Qur'an. Lying, swearing, and many kinds of violations often pass without people labeling them as immoral acts. Incidents of moral corruption and doctrinal heresies, practiced discreetly or undercover, may be encountered at all levels of society.

Muslims say that their morality puts to shame Western immorality. I would never defend the sins of the West; yet, something needs to be clarified here. Sin is not the monopoly of one culture or certain segments of people. It belongs to all humankind. Ever since Adam fell into disobedience, men and women have been sinners and their cultures have been tarnished and tainted. Muslims say: "Western moral standards are corrupt and they are exporting their decadence to us." But as Moroccan sociologist Fatima Azrouel points out, the spread of prostitution in her country is not a result of the influence of Western society. Rather, she puts the blame on the miserable conditions in which women live, especially the younger ones.[27]

Some of the areas Muslims like to cite as examples of Western corruption are the loose behavior of women, sexual immorality, drunkenness, homosexuality and movies featuring sexual immorality. It is true that the West exhibits a far greater degree of permissiveness in these areas than do Muslim countries. However, sin also manifests itself in less observable forms such as bribery, extortion, stealing, cheating, lying, and hypocrisy. The truth is that these and other sins are the characteristics of humans in their depravity—of people anywhere and in any era of history.

Accounts and writings show these same sins to be rampant throughout the history of Islam. The Abbasid caliphs did not have to wait one thousand years for Europeans to export debauchery to them. Rather, these political and religious leaders led lives marked by an excess of luxury and decadence unheard of in the West.

Islamic writings reveal that Caliph Watheq (ruled A.D. 842 – 847) was a homosexual. Young boys stole his mind and his ability to rule. Caliph al-Amin (ruled A.D. 809 – 813) had no taste for women. He bought eunuchs for his sexual enjoyment. His life prompted a contemporary poet to say:

Caliphate lost!
A cheating ruler
A corrupt prince
An ignorant counsel
The Caliph's sodomy is indeed a wonder![28]

Yazid Ben Mu'awya was called "the wine bibber" because he was always drunk. Al-walid b. Abd al-Malek drank day in and day out. Caliph Hesham drank even on Fridays after prayer. Abu-Nawas, the famous eighth-century Muslim Arab poet, was known as "the wine poet" for his love of drinking. He was a close friend of two caliphs in Baghdad. One of his famous poems expressing his love for wine says:

When I die bury me
Next to a vine
That would water my bones
After my death, with juice
From its roots.[29]

It would appear that the Persian poet Omar Khayyam (A.D. 1048–1122) was not very concerned that wine had robbed him of his robe of honor. He wonders what wine producers could buy that would be half as precious as their product! He says,

And much as wine has played the infidel,
And robb'd me of my robe of honor—well,
I often wonder what the vintners buy
One half so precious as the goods they sell.[30]

He goes on to say,

Let me go to have a drink and enjoy music,
And exchange my good reputation with shame and impurity,
Let me sell my prayer carpet for a glass of wine…
When I come reverently to a mosque,
It is not to do the prayer duty,
But because I stole a carpet from there
And it got old and frayed,
That is why I came to get a replacement for it![31]

Caliph Al-Walid b. Yazid was also given to homosexuality and wine. As a Muslim ruler living in lavish luxury, he had a pool that was filled with wine. He would undress, get into the pool, and remain there drinking the wine until the level of the pool had visibly gone down. Here are a few lines of his poetry.

O Yazid! Give me a drink
Give me a drink
A barrel of drink
I am so enraptured
It is music time
Give me, give me a drink
My sins are so many
And they have no atonement![32]

By the time he was forty-seven years old, Ottoman Caliph Mahmoud was "prematurely old from drink and dissipation."[33] The rulers of Tunisia (called Beys) did not fare any better:

To judge from all that has been written about the later Beys, it would seem that their abilities showed themselves not so much in affairs of State as in bed. Many are depicted as bisexually insatiable; others as contentedly homosexual; and one as combining the two spheres of activity mentioned above by initiating the "Order of Little Ali," a decoration bestowed upon those... mignons capable of "a certain sexual feat."[34]

Late in the nineteenth century, the Arabs taught King Mwanga of Uganda to practice sodomy. The king tried to practice it with young Christian men. When the boys refused to make themselves available to the passions of their master, he was infuriated and ordered their murder. It was unheard of that African subjects would refuse their king's desires.[35]

Men were not the only ones involved in such corruption. Walladah B. al-Mustakfi was a caliph's daughter and a poet of renown. She was severely criticized for her obscene verse and for a questionable relationship with a beautiful young woman named Muhjah. Walladah never married.[36]

Early in the history of Islam, when the capital of the Muslim state was moved to Damascus, the chief of Caliph Yazid's army conquered the city of Medina. During the three days that followed the conquest, his troops slaughtered four thousand Muslims and raped one thousand unmarried girls. Then when the citizens of Medina refused to become the caliph's slaves, the troops beheaded several thousand of them.

Today, the same sins are common. Princess Sultana of Saudi Arabia expresses this fact with great courage:

While inside the country, men socialize with men and women with women. Since we are prevented from engaging in traditional behavior, the sexual tension between those of the same sex is palpable. Any foreigner who has lived in Saudi Arabia for a length of time becomes aware that homosexual relations are rampant within the kingdom.

I have attended many all-female concerts and functions where quivering beauties and suggestive behavior triumphs over heavy veils and black abaayas. An orderly gathering of heavily perfumed and love-starved Saudi women festers into spontaneous exuberance, bursting forth in the form of a wild party with the singing of forbidden love accompanied by lusty dancing. I have watched as shy-faced women danced lewdly with other women, flesh to flesh, face to face. I have heard women whisper of love and plan clandestine meetings, while their drivers wait patiently in the parking lots. They will later deliver them to their husbands who are at that same evening captivated by other men.[37]

The same Princess also admits:

Most Saudi men and women I know drink socially... I have never been in a Saudi home that did not have a large assortment of the finest and most expensive alcoholic beverages to offer to guests.[38]

I am including these examples not because the West is righteous. By no means. Neither are my remarks a defense of the West's sins. What I want to emphasize here is that both Islamic and non-Islamic cultures are tarnished by sin and that Jesus Christ is the Redeemer of people from all cultures. Hence Muslims cannot rightly claim moral superiority.

Woman

The Qur'an enjoins men to treat women with kindness and equity (Sura 4:19; 65:2), protect them and support them (Sura 9:71; 4:34). On the other hand, the Qur'an says that a woman should receive only half her brother's share of the inheritance (Sura 4:11).

Looking at various statements and teachings of the Qur'an and the Hadith regarding women, it is clear that a woman is given a very restricted role in life. Often she is considered an object for man's sexual pleasure, and her job is to reproduce and raise children and be a homemaker. Women do not normally participate in decision making on major issues. Men have the final say.

Fatima Mernissi in one of her books quotes the Hadith which says that

Muhammad once saw a woman, so he went to [his wife] Zaynab and made love to her. When he came out he said, "A woman comes in the form of Satan. So, when one of you sees a woman and likes her, he should go to make love to his wife..."[39]

Professor Mernissi goes on to cite Imam al-Ghazali's position regarding women:

Woman is a dangerous cause for distraction, therefore she should be used to accomplish fixed goals; namely providing the Muslim ummah with offspring and quenching [our] sexual desire. Woman should not become the object of [our] emotion or care. These are to be directed only toward God...[40]

Mernissi also refers to the conviction popular among Muslims that "the most serious two dangers that threaten Islam are 'unbelievers from outside and women from inside the community.'"[41]

Moroccan fundamentalist Sheikh A. Yasin describes women in one of his books as "second class citizens in both life and eternity."[42] This and other similar Muslim convictions about women seem to be in harmony with statements Muhammad made such as: "A women is [twisted] like a rib. If you try to straighten her out, she breaks. If you want to enjoy her, enjoy her as she is—twisted."[43] "O women, give alms because most of you are wood for hell-fire."[44] "I was allowed to look at hell-fire and I saw that most of its inhabitants are women."[45]

Emily Van Dalan says that Islam considers women as

inherently unstable, weak-willed, incompetent and illogical. Their physical attractions are an irresistible and dangerous entrapment for men who have no choice but to respond according to their physical primal urges.[46]

A Muslim husband, in general, understands that sex on demand is sanctioned by the Qur'an: "Your women are for you as land to be tilled. Thus, approach them whenever and however you like" (Sura 2:223).

The courageous Tunisian poet Al-Shabbi regrets that

Arabic literature looks at woman as a means to satisfy man's pleasure and sensuality. In their poems and songs all they talk about is

her mouth, her neck, her breasts, her bosom, her belly, her hips...
it is a low-down, cheap and inconsiderate look that sees woman
only as a body to be lusted after and a pleasure to be had...[47]

Imam Al-Ghazali states that marriage is slavery for woman since
she is forced to absolutely obey her husband in everything he demands of her.[48]

Further, Islam believes that man is superior to woman and even
has the right to beat her. The Qur'an says:

Men have the upper hand over women because God has made
the one superior to the other and because they [men] spend their
money [to support women]. So pious women are obedient and
keep guarded the parts that God has kept in secret. But those you
fear would get rebellious, admonish them and do not go to bed
with them and beat them. Then if they obey, do not look for a
chance against them. God is high and great (Sura 4:34; see also
2:228).

Sometimes women are thought of and treated as commodities.
While visiting Morocco in June 1994, Sara, one of our team members, was priced for marriage to a Muslim man. The college girl from
California had gone with several other college students to do short
term mission work in the Muslim North African nation. A local man
approached Sara's fellow team member who was walking with her,
thinking he was her father. The Moroccan offered Sara's "father"
3000 Dirhams (approximately $350.00 at the time) and four camels
in return for marrying "his daughter!" Everyone in the group had a
good laugh, except for two people: The Moroccan suitor was dead
serious and Sara was very offended and outraged that she would be
priced for sale!

Once, in Saudi Arabia, a drunk driver crashed his car into another
carrying two wives of an elderly Saudi man. The two women died. The
driver, who was a foreigner, was jailed. Under Saudi law based on the
Islamic Shari'a, he was now at the mercy of the bereaved husband. The
husband had the right to demand and be granted the death penalty for
the offender or ask for blood money and thus spare the offender's life.
In court, the guilty foreigner and his lawyer were shocked when the
husband of the two dead women stood before the judge and said,

Your honor, I request that the prisoner be released. I do not call for his death, nor do I want his money. The two women killed were wives that I had taken in my youth, and had grown too old to be of service to me... I am glad to be rid of them, for now I can replace them with two young wives.

Under the law, the Saudi judge had no option but to release the lucky foreigner. It was further reported that the husband actually *thanked* the foreigner, saying that he had wanted to divorce his wives for a long time, but had not wanted to make a financial settlement![49]

The most common qur'anic word for marriage is the one used for sexual intercourse. Every Muslim is expected to marry. Polygamy is permitted in Islam. A man is allowed up to four wives at one time and an unlimited number of concubines. The Qur'an says: "Marry from among the women those that seem good to you—twice and thrice and four times what your right hand possesses" (Sura 4:3). Some fundamentalists interpret the preceding verse as allowing up to nine wives (twice plus thrice plus four times equals nine). They argue that the verse does not say twice or thrice, rather twice and thrice. They further claim that Muhammad himself had up to nine wives at a time.

Fatima Mernissi and some Muslim women like her openly express their extreme frustration with polygamy. For them it is a way for man to demonstrate his sexual prowess and humiliate woman and beat her into submissiveness.[50] Egyptian Muslim writer Nawal Sa'dawi considers polygamy as promiscuity and damaging to the family.[51] Many others see polygamy and divorce as the sure means to destroy the family cell, since they both inhibit and often put a stop to any emotional relationship between husband and wife.

There are some women, however, who do not mind this kind of family structure, and some even request it! The following are two advertisements that appeared in an Arabic magazine on the matchmaking page:

I am 27 years old, female, Saudi, college-educated. I would like to get married to a Saudi man that lives in Mecca. I accept a polygamous situation with no conditions.[52]

I am 27 years old, female, light brown, 175 centimeters tall and weigh 85 kilograms. I live in Saudi Arabia, never married before. I would like to get married to a Saudi or Hadhramautian husband, college-educated, well-to-do. I desire a polygamous situation.[53]

This openness to and even preference for polygamous marriage is not limited to Arab women. Some Western women also seek to be part of such a marriage! The reason they give is that it is better to be part of a legal situation that allows the husband multiple wives rather than oblige him to have secret affairs with other women.

The Qur'an states that women should be veiled when they go out of their home (Sura 24:31). Muhammad's wives were ordered to speak to men from behind a partition. There are various reasons given in support of wearing a veil, all related to modesty. However, it is clear from Sura 24:30 and 60 that a veil is meant to protect weak men from the seduction of women's bodies. Streets and other public places are seen as a man's domain, and when women invade that sphere they have to be covered.

Many educated Muslim women today find ways to reinterpret the qur'anic injunction regarding the veil in order to do away with it. In the 1920s, the Egyptian feminist Huda Sha'rawi removed her veil and other Muslim women followed suit.

A man has the right to divorce his wife for any reason or for no reason. He can remarry her and even divorce her again (Sura 2:236, 237). But if he divorces her three times and then wants to marry her again, he can do so only after she marries another man who then divorces her. She can then be the first man's wife a fourth time (Sura 2:230). A woman, however, cannot sue for divorce for any reason. According to tradition, Muhammad said that of all things permitted to Muslims, divorce is the most hateful. A high-society Muslim Pakistani woman described the dire state of Muslim family life in these words: "In our society, marriage may be purgatory, but divorce is hell."[54]

There are impressive stories, however, of fidelity, love and appreciation toward women. I personally knew Saleh, a humble grammar-school teacher, and his wife Khayriah. The couple could not have children. The husband could have divorced his wife or added another who would have given him children. But, no! Saleh loved Khayriah and respected her. This is not an isolated instance. I have known a few others who considered their wife as a companion and friend for life in spite of the options allowed them by the teachings of the Qur'an and the Hadith.

Professor Bernard Lewis states that under Islamic law, there are three underprivileged groups: unbelievers, slaves and women. Of all these, women are the worst-placed. He explains: "The slave could be freed by his master; the unbeliever could at any time become a believer by his own choice, and thus end his inferiority. Only the woman [is] doomed forever..."[55]

Jan Goodwin relates the following.

In 1985, the president of Pakistan established a commission to investigate the status of women. The report concluded, "The average woman born into near slavery, leads a life of drudgery, and dies invariably in oblivion. This grim condition is the stark reality of half our population simply because they happen to be female." Not surprisingly, the government suppressed the report.[56]

For Muslims closest to the Qur'an and the Hadith, to grant women liberty and a status equal to man is "neither necessary nor useful but noxious, a betrayal of true Islamic values. It must be kept from the body of Islam, and where it has already entered, it must be ruthlessly excised."[57]

In contrast, the Arab thinker Salman Masalha represents a number of liberals when he courageously challenges such reactionary notions:

The Islamic motto of "Islam is the solution" must be replaced by "the woman is the solution." A large part of the backwardness and tragedy of the Arab world lies in its abhorrent treatment of women.[58]

Mut'a marriage is allowed among certain groups of Muslims. The word *mut'a* means "pleasure" or "enjoyment," so these "marriages" are in reality temporary unions for pleasure. A *mut'a* marriage is a contract between a man and a woman to practice sex for a specified period, which can be from one hour to 99 years. A man in this case is not bound by the limit of four wives at a time, and may have as many *mut'a* wives as he pleases. A woman, however, is allowed only one partner at a time in *mut'a* marriage. This proves to be "convenient" for male travelers, giving them the right to contract a *mut'a* wife for the duration of their stay in her town. Some find support for this practice in Sura 4:24. They interpret the qur'anic verse to mean, "Since you draw pleasure from them, give them their wages."

Some Hadiths indicate that Muhammad sanctioned *mut'a* marriage. Here is an example:

R. ibn Sabra reported that his father said: "When we conquered Mecca, I went on an expedition with Allah's Messenger... where we stayed for fifteen days. Allah's Messenger...permitted us to contract temporary marriage with women. So I and another person of my tribe went out... and we came across a [beautiful] young woman... We said: 'Is it possible that one of us may contract temporary marriage with you?' She chose me over my friend because I was more handsome than he..."[59]

While most Muslims look at mut'a marriage as scandalous and even consider it legalized prostitution in some circumstances, currently, these temporary unions are not limited to Shi'as who have practiced them for centuries; they are finding more and more acceptance among Sunnis. Journalist Emad Nassef states that in the late 1990s mut'a marriages started to flourish and spread in the universities of Sunni Egypt.[60] In his book on mut'a marriage, Saleh Wardani states that a Muslim is allowed to enjoy a mut'a liaison with an adulteress (though not preferred), especially if she is a prostitute or notorious for committing adultery. In that case the new husband should forbid her to commit further adultery![61]

Spirit-Beings

Angels exist, and anyone who denies that is considered an infidel. Angels are spiritual beings with wings. They are formed of light and do not sin. They are assigned different responsibilities. The angel Jibril (Gabriel), sometimes confused with the Holy Spirit in Islam, is believed to have carried the inspiration of the Qur'an to Muhammad. Some angels are assigned to keep records of people's works whether good or evil.

Another category of spirit-beings is that of the jinn. There are multitudes of jinn. Some are righteous and some are evil. They are created from blazing fire (Sura 15: 26). They eat, drink, and have sexual relations. Evil jinn occasionally hurt people and help magicians and fortunetellers. They often appear as animals. Frequently they possess people. The Muslim holy book says that a company of jinn listened to the Qur'an and believed in it and became Muslim. Those who did not believe are destined to hellfire (Sura 72:1, 2, 14, 15).

Fazlur Rahman explains the Islamic concept of Satan in his book, *Major Themes of the Qur'an*:

> The Qur'an constantly speaks of Satan not so much as an anti-God principle (although he is undoubtedly a rebel against God, and, indeed, personifies this rebellious nature) but rather as an anti-man force, perpetually trying to seduce man away from his natural "straight" path into deviant behavior.[62]

Fate

Mainstream Islam holds that everything happens because it is maktub or "written"—it is predestined by God. Muslims believe that God has decided everything that will happen and has sent it (Sura 54:51–53, 65:3); nothing happens to man except what God has decreed (Sura 9:51); God causes some to go astray and guides others to the right way (Sura 2:7; 7:178, 179; 14:4; 32:13; 74:31).

The Hadith reinforces this belief and reports that

> Adam and Moses were arguing together. Moses protested to Adam that he caused all of us humans to be cast out of the garden. But Adam replied: "Moses, do you blame me for something that God decreed I would do forty years before He created me?"[63]

Another hadith records Muhammad as saying:

> Maybe one of you will be doing the works of the people of paradise, so that between him and paradise there is only an arm's length; but then what is written for him overtakes him, and he begins to do the works of the people of hell. And to hell he will go.

Or maybe one of you will be doing the works of the people of hell, so that between him and hell there is only an arm's length; but then what is written for him overtakes him, and he begins to do the works of the people of paradise. And to paradise he will go.[64]

This fatalistic view can lead people to have no sense of moral responsibility, because if everything is predetermined through fate and destiny, who are humans to change or challenge what God has written (Sura 36:7–10; 32:13)? A former Muslim puts it this way:

Luck, accident, death, misfortune, and failure are often credited to Allah. Fatalism is deeply entrenched in Islam and slows man down in his activity and responsibility. This means that a Muslim's attitude toward life is fundamentally different from that of a Christian. Intellect and incentives are restrained by the concept of God.[65]

The foundations of Islamic fatalism are not the same as those of chemical determinism (man is a pawn to chemical forces—Marquis de Sad) or psychological determinism (past experiences are the driving basis of present activities—Sigmund Freud). Yet, the end results are similar. That is, "Man is not responsible for what he is or does nor can he be active in making significant history."[66]

An example of this kind of reasoning is the case of a passenger who hires a taxi to take him to a certain place. On the way to his destination, the taxi is involved in a collision. According to this way of thinking, the passenger is the one responsible for the accident. The theory is simple and reflects the fatalism of Islam: if the passenger had not hired the taxi, it would not have been where the accident occurred.[67]

The Last Day

In Islamic belief there is a "Last Day" of reckoning or judgment. No one knows its hour. When it comes, everyone will be raised for judgment. The books kept by the recording angels will be opened and God, the Judge, will weigh each person's deeds in the balances. Those whose good deeds outweigh their evil ones will be ushered into paradise. Those whose evil deeds outweigh their good ones will be sent to suffer torment in hell (Sura 101:6–9). However, all depends on God's will. Punishment or reward will depend on His ultimate decision. In Islam, fear of the Last Day is the believer's strongest motivation to lead a good life and thus receive a place of honor with God in the life to come.

Paradise, according to Islam, is the place of everlasting pleasure and enjoyment, abundant sensual gratification, and eating and drinking. There are gardens filled with plants producing figs, olives, dates, and grapes. There are rivers of fresh water. Believers will be waited on by dark-eyed houris and beautiful young boys, and they will drink wine from golden cups (Sura 44:51–55; 56:15–38; 13:35; 55:46–78). Muslims believe that there are scores of virgins every night for each believer. Even some Muslim preachers claim that men in paradise will have sex with the beautiful boys that serve them food!

The Saudi princess quoted earlier describes man's paradise in these words:

> Seductive beautiful virgins, not yet touched by another man, will attend to his every need, and fulfill his every sexual desire. Each man will possess seventy-two of these lovely virgins.[68]

She goes on to say:

> Pious women will also enter paradise, and it is said that these women will receive the greatest joy from reciting the Qur'an and experiencing the supreme ecstasy of beholding Allah's face. All around these women will be children who never grow old.[69]

If a woman marries two, three, or more husbands during her lifetime, she will be given the freedom to choose which one of them she wants to marry in paradise. Muhammad is reported to have said: "She will choose the one who has the best character and will ask God to let her marry him."[70]

In contrast, hell is scorching, burning fire. It is the place of eternal punishment for unbelievers (Sura 55:42–44; 104:4–7). There, those who are damned

> languish amid pestilential winds and in scalding water, in the shadow of black smoke. Draughts of boiling water will be forced down their throats. They will be dragged by the scalp, flung into the fire, wrapped in garments of flame, and beaten with iron maces. When their skins are well burned, others will grow for fresh torture.[71]

6 | *The Muslim Community — Ummah*

Ummah in Arabic means "nation." All Muslims throughout the world belong to one community called "the nation of the Prophet," or "the nation of Muhammad." It is comprised of people of all colors and cultures and from all walks of life. It has no racial or national barriers. Ideally, geopolitical boundaries should be of no significance. The ultimate allegiance of community members is to Islam.

The ummah has distinctive characteristics.

COMMUNITY TIES

Among the different world societies, Islamic groups can possibly claim to have the strongest sense of community. Consider the basic concept of the House of Islam and the House of War, the two camps into which Islam has divided the world. The House of Islam includes all Muslims. There, Islamic law is the rule. In the House of War all non-Muslims are found. Muslims are to spread Islam among them by the power of the sword.

The House of Islam, the ummah, is bound together by several very strong ties.

The Five Duties

Muslims are proud of their religion and the duties it entails—the creed, the prayers, the fast, the giving of alms, and the pilgrimage. These five requirements, the most noticeable elements of Islam, generate in Muslims a great sense of solidarity and togetherness. They do not hesitate to make it known that they are Muslims, readily praying in public and stating that they are fasting or giving alms and that they have visited Mecca.

One should not think, however, that all of these duties are equal in importance as community ties. The pilgrimage to Mecca which includes marching around the Ka'aba may be the most emotional and thus the strongest of the five requirements. In fact, many Muslims the world over are willing to protect the Ka'aba with their very lives.

History and Calendar

Muslims, although of many nationalities and races, consider the history of Islam their history. Even a Filipino or an Indian Muslim looks at the early days of Islam as his own history.

Further, all Muslims adhere to the Islamic lunar calendar. Its use is important for at least two reasons. First, the calendar dates back to the *hijra* of Muhammad from Mecca to Medina when the Islamic ummah indeed became a reality. It thus serves as a reminder of success and new identity. Second, the calendar dictates when Muslim observances are celebrated. For example, the dates for events such as the fast of Ramadan, the feast of breaking that fast, the feast of sacrifice, and the birth of Muhammad are all set by using that calendar.

Islamic Law (Shari'a)

Another unifying factor of the Muslim community is Islamic law, or the Shari'a. The Shari'a contains the divine commands which regulate the whole of life. God reportedly gave these regulations to serve as the basis for Muslims' relationship with the Almighty, with each other, with people in general, with the environment, and with the universe. Thus the Shari'a encompasses the entire scope of human existence in all of its aspects: material and spiritual, worship and religious practices, political activities, social manners, relationships between people, eating and drinking, and so forth. Islam is legalistic. To comply with the law and obey it is to do God's will.

Even small Islamic communities in non-Muslims societies require adherence to this law. A case in point is the meal served by the airlines of some countries where Muslims have political power. That meal now usually comes with a notice that the meat is *halal*—that is, the animal was killed according to Islamic law codes, and no pork is included. Where did the Shari'a come from? Four sources can be traced:

1. The Qur'an. Commands and rules found in the Qur'an are part of the law.

2. The *sunna*. That is the example of the Prophet as stated in the Hadith. When the Qur'an gives no directives regarding a particular issue of everyday life, Muslims follow the example of their prophet.

3. The ijma'. The *ijma'* is the consensus of knowledgeable people in forming a judgment relative to a specific issue.

4. The *qiyas*. The word qiyas means analogy. If no rule exists to cover a particular kind of circumstance or case, Muslims apply analogy to the Qur'an and the Hadith to come up with a law that is binding for the Islamic community.

So in effect, the Qur'an and the sunna are the preliminary sources of Islamic law. Other rules have been adopted through consensus by analogical reasoning.

SENSE OF SUPERIORITY

A sense of superiority is another characteristic of the ummah. Muslims consider Islam the most perfect religion and Muhammad the last and greatest of all prophets. They believe that the Qur'an is the final revelation from God to man. In fact, the Qur'an makes statements that instill this lofty attitude. For example:

> You [Muslims] are the most virtuous community of all mankind. You command what is good and forbid what is evil, and you believe in God (Sura 3:110).
>
> Do not lose heart; do not be sad, you have the upper hand if you are believers (Sura 3:139; see also Sura 5:3).

INTOLERANCE OF OTHER RELIGIONS

Islam is definitely intolerant of other religions. The Qur'an stamps non-Muslims as enemies of God and Muhammad and exhorts Muslims to wage war against such people (Sura 5:33). Large numbers of Muhammad's followers, incited by their religious leaders, take that literally. The following quotation serves as an example to illustrate the sentiment of many a Muslim toward Christians:

> Tolerating Christians, using their help, and more still, giving them the right to worship according to their religion... is considered breaching Islamic law and contrary to our religion...[1]

There is a hadith that says:

> Muhammad said: "Do not greet the people of the book, and do not answer their greetings, and if they meet you on the road force them to the narrowest part of it."[2]

In general, wherever a Muslim community faces a neighboring community of non-Muslims, their negative attitude is clearly seen. It is one of intolerance or at best a grudging tolerance that manifests itself in a latent antagonism and an irreconcilable spirit of suspicion and distrust. Even minor incidents can fan the smoldering animosity against non-Muslims into flames of overt persecution.

Islam cannot accept a situation in which its adherents are subjects under the rule of non-Muslims. Let me illustrate. When Catholics reconquered Spain and especially Andalusia, some Muslims stayed in the reconquered parts. Many Islamic religious leaders and legislators accused those people of heresy and unfaithfulness to Islam because they had agreed to let themselves be ruled by non-Muslims. The accusers claimed that the Muslims in question had accepted to be in the House of War with its infidelity rather than cling to the House of Islam and advised them to emigrate from the reconquered lands immediately.

That is why today Muslim fundamentalists in the Philippines, Thailand, Kashmir and many other places do not accept to be under the rule of non-Muslims. They fight to control of the government of their land or have an independent Muslim state.

The Muslim fundamentalist thinker A. A. Mawdudi (1903–1979) was a prolific Pakistani author who did not see how Muslims could preserve their identity under the Hindu rule in India. He maintained that a Muslim's real nationality is Islam. Mawdudi strongly opposed the involvement of Indian Muslims in India's struggle for independence from the British. As a Muslim, he feared that Hindu rule would bring evil and danger as he believed the British rule had.

The situations that have existed in Spain and India are not isolated examples. In general, Muslims contend that when an Islamic community is ruled politically, economically, or culturally by a non-Muslims power, it becomes part of the House of War. Therefore a Muslim should not give obedience to non-Muslims authorities.

PARANOIA

There is an attitude of fear that permeates Islam. In the past, when Muslims conquered different peoples, in most cases they gave their subjects two options: either convert to Islam or be killed by the sword. People converted to Islam out of fear of death. With this historical background, Muslims fear that if they ever come under the authority of non-Muslims, their subjugators will somehow force them to relinquish Islam.

One incident after another illustrates this paranoia. Al-Madina, a respected Saudi Arabian newspaper states: "There is now a modern revival of the ancient Christian crusades against Islam, this time under the aegis of the United States in an unholy alliance with Zionism..."[3]

Some decades ago, Muhammad A. Samman stated that Zionism, Christianity, and Marxism were plotting against Islam. In his view, all three had one common goal—to abolish the Muslim faith. So Muslims should forget about their ideological and political differences and unite to ward off the dangers that threaten their existence.[4]

Muslim populations often respond readily to agitation. They need only to be told that the question is a religious one and that their religion is imperiled. Soon they are ready to flock together and move in masses, demonstrating and shouting that "Allah is great."

For Muslims, the mere existence of Christianity and the Christian Church is an implied criticism of Islam. Why? Christianity teaches that Jesus Christ is God's final revelation to people, that the Bible is God's complete and perfect Word and guide for humanity, that Christ is God become man, that God is three Persons in one Godhead, and that Jesus died on the cross to redeem sinful humans. Islam denies all of these doctrines because they contradict the Qur'an and are therefore considered a serious threat. The fact that Christians continue to hold to these beliefs signifies to Muslims that Christians are outright dissatisfied with Islam and reject it entirely.

One can detect roots of such paranoia in the Qur'an itself. Muslims, for example, are instructed to beware of non-Muslims and not to make friends with them: "You who believe! Take not intimates from those who are not your own people. They desire to ruin you. Their hatred is clear from what they say, but what their hearts conceal is much worse" (Sura 3:118). The Qur'an also specifically instructs Muslims to shun friendship with Jews and Christians: "You who believe! Take not Jews and Christians for friends. They are but friends to each other. Anyone of you who takes them for friends is one of them" (Sura 5:51).

GROUPS AND SECTS

From information already presented, we can see that Islam does not differentiate between civil and religious authorities or civil and religious law. Rather, religion and the state are one. After the death of Muhammad, many people who had been forced to convert to Islam reverted. Further, there was a lot of strife, and power struggles were common among the leaders of the Islamic nation. Polarization and divisions occurred. People attempted to vindicate their divisions on the basis of religious reasons. In other words, political differences took on religious appearances. As a result, Islamic sects began to appear at an amazing speed. Today, there are many, many sects, sub-sects, branches of sub-sects, schools of theology and of jurisprudence, mystic groups, secret associations, and so forth. We will look briefly at the largest main groupings of these: the Sunnis and the Shi'as. We will also survey some of the smaller groups.

Two Major Groups

The differences between Sunnis and Shi'as basically concern who should have been caliph after Muhammad! Thus, the quarrel between them does not involve serious doctrinal issues. Both believe in Muhammad, both believe in the Qur'an and so forth. Yet, for political ends, some people try to make much of the differences. A Muslim convert stated: "Although I came from a Shi'a family, I was unaware of much difference between Shi'as and Sunnis... Those differences are not serious at all."[5]

	Sunnis	**Shi'as**
Their number in the world today	1.1 billion	200 million
Their percentage of all Muslims	85%	15%
Where they are today	They are the majority in most Muslim countries.	They are the majority in Iran, Iraq, Bahrain, and Azerbaijan. There are significant numbers of them in Pakistan, Afghanistan, India, Saudi Arabia, Turkey, Yemen, Lebanon and Syria.
The meaning of the name	From sunna which means "method or example." They are the followers of the traditions, example, and method of Muhammad.	Shi'a means "party." They are the followers of the party of Ali, Muhammad's cousin and son-in-law.
Who should have been caliph after Muhammad	Abu Bakr (as it happened)	Ali

	Sunnis	Shi'as
Which hadiths are authentic	Those compiled by qualified persons	Only those compiled by members of Muhammad's family
Mut'a marriage	Not practiced by most Sunnis	Practiced by Shi'as
The spiritual and political head of the community	The caliph	The imam (considered infallible)

Other Minor Sects

1. The *Kharidjites*. Their name means "rebels." Originally these were the twelve thousand men who fought under Ali to secure the caliphate for him. Later when Ali decided to submit the matter of his caliphate to the arbitration of men, they rebelled against him. They insisted that God should be the arbitrator. In Kharidjite belief, the imam is fallible and the group's decisions are infallible, which is just the opposite of the Shi'as.

2. The *Murdji'a*. Their name means "those who postpone or delay something." They believe that it is not for man to pass judgment on a grave sinner or an oppressive leader, for example. Fate is in God's hand, and one ought to postpone judgment on people until the Last Day.

3. The *Djabriya*. Their name indicates that they believe people are compelled to do what they do. They have no freedom of choice. God compels them to act the way they do.

4. The *Kadariya*. Their name indicates that they believe man has a certain power over his actions (the opposite of *Djabriya*). Therefore people are free moral agents and thus have a free will.

5. The *Mu'tazilah*. Their name means "separatists." They hold that any Muslim who commits grave sins should be considered neither Muslim nor non-Muslims. They also reject any anthropomorphic descriptions of God. Further, they believe that the Qur'an is not eternal but was created.

6. The *Ash'aris*. They believe that God has speech, sight, and other anthropomorphic characteristics. They teach that the Qur'an is eternal and not created.

7. The *Sufis*. These are the mystics of Islam. They believe that God alone is perfect love and beauty, and one's goal should be to be absorbed into that love. We will explore Sufism in a later chapter.

8. The *Ahmadiyyas* (called also Kadianis). Founded by Mirzah Ghulam Ahmad Kadiani (hence the two names). The Ahmadiyyas are a small group that came into existence in India in the 19th century. They are considered heretical by orthodox Islam and are banned in many Muslim countries. They believe that Jesus was crucified, but that He only fainted on the cross. They also say that when He was put in the grave, the spices revived Him. He then got up and walked to Kashmir, India, and lived a long life there. The Ahmadiyyas are zealous missionaries who endeavor to convert others, especially Christians, to their fold.

7 | *Jihad*

"In time, all mankind must accept Islam or submit to Muslim rule... it is the duty of the Muslims to struggle until this is accomplished. The name of this duty is jihad... The word occurs in the Qur'an a number of times in the military sense of making war against the unbelievers... It is a collective duty of the community as a whole... an individual duty of every Muslim... also a perpetual duty, which will lapse only when all the world is won for Islam.

"Between the Muslims and the rest of the world there [is] a... state of war, which could only end with the conversion or subjugation of all mankind. A treaty of peace between the Muslim state and a non-Muslim state [is]... impossible. The war could not be terminated; it could only be interrupted, for reasons of necessity or expediency, by a truce."

(Joseph Schacht and C. E. Bosworth, Eds. *The Legacy of Islam.* London: Oxford University Press, 1979, p. 175.)

The Muslim theological basis for jihad is found in Islam's holy book. The Qur'an commands Muslims to

...kill the infidels wherever you find them, and capture them and besiege them and lay in ambush for them (Sura 9:5).

It also says:

God has purchased from Muslims their lives and their possessions in exchange for paradise. Thus, they fight in God's cause
and they kill and get killed (Sura 9:111).

It is clear then that the purpose of such war is to subdue non-Muslims in the hope that they will convert to Islam: "Fight them until there
is no dissention and God's religion [Islam] prevails" (Sura 2:193). Jews
and Christians are mentioned explicitly as its targets (see Sura 9:29).

Nevertheless, throughout the history of Islam, Muslims have
fought other Muslims for one reason or another, and usually each side
has declared the others to be infidels. Leaders, desiring to instill courage and sacrifice in their troops, have applied the name and principles
of jihad to such wars. When Iran and Iraq fought each other during
the 1980s, this inter-Muslim war was called jihad by both of the warring governments.

In his scholarly work, *Jihad in the West*, Paul Fregosi defines jihad
as the attempt to

expand and extend Islam until the whole world is under Muslim
rule. The jihad is essentially a permanent state of hostility that
Islam maintains against the rest of the world, with or without
fighting for more sovereignty over more territory.[1]

JIHAD IS A RELIGIOUS DUTY

Jihad is a religious duty. It is an obligation. The jihad verses quoted
above and others like them are orders, commands. This is not an option. Just as the followers of Islam are required to fast, so they are also
required to make war (compare Sura 2:183 and 216, "You are to fast..."
and "You are to fight...").

The Arabic word jihad initially means "struggle." Some moder-
ate Muslims, in an attempt to maintain peace, adopt a much milder
meaning than what is taught in the Qur'an and Hadith. For them,
jihad means moral struggle to achieve higher spirituality. Nevertheless, people who follow the teachings of Muhammad closely refuse
this interpretation.[2]

Jihad, in its classical meaning, is holy war against non-Muslim
infidels and seeks to eradicate them by any means. The primary and

more important qur'anic meaning of jihad is to war against people and shed their blood. Journalist Serge Trifcovic says:

Islamic terrorism, far from being an aberration, became inseparable from modern-day jihad. It is legitimized by it, and it is its defining feature. The late medieval redefinition of jihad as spiritual battling with the evil impulses of the soul—a rendering endlessly repeated by Islam's apologists in the Western world—is quite properly rejected by today's Islamic activists not only as theologically incorrect (which it is) but also as a dangerous and harmful distraction from the path of divinely ordained struggle.[3]

To kill for the cause of Islam is considered a good deed.[4] The Prophet said, "The believers who kill are the most wholesome of all people."[5]

All qur'anic verses that instruct Muslims to wage jihad come from the time Muhammad was in Medina rather than in Mecca. This is logical, because in Mecca Muslims were few and weak, while later in Medina, Islam became strong as Muhammad made more and more converts. Gone are the Meccan instructions to convert people to Islam with "wisdom and good preaching" because "there should be no use of force in religion" (Sura 2:256, 16:125). In Medina, with the growing number of followers and dramatic military victories, qur'anic verses began to declare jihad a religious obligation: "O Prophet! Rouse the believers to make war" (Sura 8:65).

From the Medinan period on, the use of force was not only condoned, but commanded, as the following statements from the Qur'an further demonstrate:

O Prophet! Fight the unbelievers and hypocrites and be harsh with them (Sura 9:73).

Fight those who do not believe in God nor in the Last Day, nor abstain from what is forbidden by God and his apostle, nor acknowledge the true religion, [even if they are of] the People of the Book [Jews and Christians], until they submissively give the religious tax and feel themselves humiliated (Sura 9:29).

Wherever you find unbelievers, strike their necks until you have made a lot of slaughter, and then bind them firmly. From then on, it is either by grace or ransom [that you deal with them] (Sura 47:4).

In a jihad war, Muslims are instructed to shed lots of blood first. After that they are to take prisoners of war.

It is not correct that a prophet would take captives until he has first bloodied the earth [heavy loss of life on the side of the enemy] (Sura 8:67).

In A.D. 627 the Jewish tribe of Quraiza was subjected to the Prophet's fury and rage. They pleaded with him to allow them to leave Medina. But he refused, and so they surrendered to him without any resistance. Yet, he ordered trenches to be dug in the market place in Medina. About 600–900 Jewish men were beheaded and dumped in the trenches. The women and children were sold as slaves.[6] Commenting on this incident Adolph L. Wismar says:

Muhammad made himself guilty of a hideous atrocity, and that without much provocation that might be alleged in palliation [as an excuse] of this execrable [repulsive] deed. Let it not be overlooked that the Quraiza would have been safe, had they… become Muslims.[7]

Such qur'anic verses and stories from the life of Muhammad have fired the militaristic zeal of tens of thousands of Muslims to rally together to fight non-Muslims. Jihad actually enhances Islamic solidarity as Muslim scholar Caesar Farah indicates:

The idea of jihad in a military context with its emphasis on the notion of continuous struggle against non-believers in God as the sole deity tended to keep alive the spirit of solidarity in the community over and against outsiders.[8]

Small wonder that the violent death of 3,000 Americans and the destruction of the World Trade Center along with many other buildings on September 11, 2001 caused thousands of Muslims in several cities around the world to dance with joy! Alan Dershowitz quotes an Egyptian newspaper columnist who describes his exhilaration when he saw the World Trade Center towers fall. The journalist said:

[Those moments of] exquisite, incandescent hell were the most beautiful and precious moments of my life… The generations of the past, and with Allah's help, the generations to come, will envy us for having witnessed [these images].[9]

Commenting on the terrorist acts of that day two former Muslims say:

> Were the men who flew planes into the towers and into the Pentagon acting out the wild ranting of a cultic leader who has bastardized the peaceful religion of Islam? Or did they offer their lives because they believed orthodox Islamic doctrine? ....The terrorists were not some fringe group that changed the Qur'an to suit political ends. They understood the Qur'an quite well and followed the teachings of jihad to the letter.[10]

The overwhelming number of Muslims worldwide with their passionate conviction that they are right and all others are wrong is comparable to owning nuclear weapons! Dr. Ramadan Shalah, Secretary-General of the Palestinian Islamic Jihad, says:

> The weapon of martyrdom... is easy and costs us only our lives... human bombs cannot be defeated, not even by nuclear bombs.[11]

A French periodical has called jihad "the hydrogen bomb of Islam".[12]

Historian John Laffin, who authored more than 100 books, reports the following statements by two prominent Muslim leaders:

> Jihad is legislated in order to be one of the means of propagating Islam. Consequently non-Muslims ought to embrace Islam either willingly through wisdom and good advice or unwillingly through fight and jihad.
>
> It is unlawful to give up jihad and adopt peace and weakness, unless the purpose of giving up is for preparation...
>
> War is the basis of the relationship between Muslims and their opponents...
>
> Allah, the Almighty, loves the Muslim to be arrogant when he is fighting... [this] manifests that he is indifferent to his enemy and that he determines to vanquish him.
>
> Jihad is not confined to the summoning of troops and the establishment of huge forces. It takes various forms. From all the territories of Islam there should arise a group of people reinforced with faith, well equipped with means and methods; and then let

them set out to attack the usurpers, harassing them incessantly until their abode is one of everlasting torment ...Jihad will never end ...it will last to the Day of Judgment...[13]

PARADISE IS THE REWARD

According to Islam, to die in jihad is to secure entry into paradise. This teaching has fired Muslims with fanatical patriotism and produced militants who have gone about defeating enemies and gaining victory after victory. Muslims who are killed during jihad are not to be considered dead, but rather alive in the presence of their Lord where they are provided for and rejoice in His bounty (Sura 3:169–170); where their sins are forgiven (Sura 3:195); and where their reward is great (Sura 4:74).

> Muhammad taught that a martyr would have his sins forgiven, be shown his abode in paradise, avoid purgatory, and receive the crown of honor.[14]

Caesar Farah confirms this belief:

> The incentive for jihad lies in its two-fold benefits: booty for this life and martyrdom with its immediate promise for a blissful eternal hereafter for those killed in battle...[15]

For a Muslim who takes part in jihad, he is a winner no matter what happens: either he kills the enemies of Islam and rids the world of them, or he gets killed and thus goes to paradise as a reward!

Some experts on Islam, both Muslim and non-Muslim, dream of a "peaceful Islam," an Islam that would "live and let live." Bishop Cragg says:

> ...world Islam today can be, and needs to be, seen primarily in its Meccan orientation... the vocation to be only and essentially a religious witness that neither enjoys power to impose itself, nor covets it...[16]

How can that be? How would Islam accept to return to a stage that it calls "the stage of weakness?"[17] How can Islam become docile? This is an impossible dream—a "pie in the sky!" If the Qur'an tells Muslims that God loves war and those who make war (Sura 61:4), how can they be Muslims without implementing that?

A leading Muslim journalist and author dismisses the dream of a peaceful Islam and speaks very frankly for the rest of his co-religionists when he says:

> Jihad is the signature tune of Islamic history. If today's Muslim rulers are reluctant to sound that note, it is often because they are concerned about the consequences of failure. As in every bargain, there are two sides. Allah promised victory to the Muslim, but only if the believer kept faith with him. Defeat becomes an indictment of the ruler, and is therefore risky, particularly as Muslims have a long tradition of holding their rulers accountable...[18]

Sir Hamilton Gibb (1895–1971), the Scottish orientalist, author and professor of Arabic, states that the

> view of Islam as a conquering religion was universally held by its adherents; the theologians found justification for it in the Qur'an, the jurists made it the basis of their expositions of Moslem law, and the mass of the people accepted it as self-evident fact. Its expansion by this means was regarded as having been divinely ordained, and as the supreme proof of its divine origin.[19]

The famous Muslim general Okba b. Nafea, after conquering Morocco in A.D. 681, reportedly exclaimed and as he arrived at the western coasts of Africa:

> O Allah, I attest that I did my best, and were it not for this ocean, I would have gone farther, killing all who do not believe in Thee, so that all might worship only Thee![20]

In recent years people have sometimes read or heard about a "wedding celebration" called by the family of a suicide bomber. The family members are certain that their son who killed himself and others during jihad was ushered into paradise where he married the promised black-eyed virgin brides!

A Palestinian Muslim young man who blew himself up along with 23 Israeli teenagers in Tell Aviv on 1 June 2001, wrote in his will:

> Call out in joy, oh my mother; distribute sweets, oh my father and brothers; a wedding with the black-eyed awaits your son in paradise.[21]

8 | *Folk Islam*

"Habiba, a 50-year old female Moroccan, is handicapped. Yet, she has transformed her disadvantage into a means of livelihood...She decided to become a clairvoyant. For her initiation, she, along with many others, went barefoot in a procession...hens and roosters were sacrificed. Then they started dancing. While they were doing the dance of the possessed, if they saw someone passing by with an animal, they would take it from him, put it in the middle of the crowd, hack it to pieces, and eat it raw.

"Some did the cries of joy, others called out the name of the Prophet Muhammad. Most of them were in a trance. Some of them cut open their head with an axe; others broke earthen pots over their heads. You see their blood spurt out and run down their faces. They were all covered with blood, front and back. Other people ate mud, while others swallowed cactus covered with thorns...Then they gave me bread and told me it was from God, and that was the gift of becoming a clairvoyant."

(Fatima Mernissi: "An Interview With Habiba The Clairvoyant." In *Le Maroc Raconté Par Ses Femmes*. Rabat, Morocco: Societe Marocaine des Editeurs Reunis, 1986; pp. 153–174.)

There is another world of Islam behind the facade of the Qur'an, the Hadith, the sunna, and the imam's sermons at the mosque. Missionaries to Muslims will understand the people among whom they are working only as they become familiar with these real, down-to-earth beliefs and practices.

Samuel Zwemer correctly suggests that: "The student of Islam will never understand the common people unless he knows their curious beliefs and half-heathen practices."[1] Donald McGavran voices the same wisdom when he says:

> The witness to Christ must have a knowledge of the other man's actual religion, not "according to the book," but to the "haphazard bundle" of what is actually believed and practiced. This bundle does have a certain undefined relationship to the accepted religious systems. In a general way it stems from it, but it has also departed a long way from it.[2]

A closer look at Islam worldwide reveals that Muslims at every level of society observe and live out folk beliefs and practices. In fact, folk religion occupies a more important place in people's lives than do high religious traditions. This is true for Muslims of various social levels, diverse educational backgrounds, and in most societies.

Many Muslims are willing to go to great lengths to receive healing or appease spirits, even if it means abandoning orthodox Islam and resorting to unorthodox folk practices.

What do Muslims believe about spirit-beings and other-worldly powers? How do they live out those beliefs during times of transition and crisis? How do these beliefs and practices hinder or enhance Muslims' exodus into the freedom of Christ? This chapter attempts to find answers to these questions.

FOLK ISLAM WORLDVIEW

All over the Muslim world there are myriads of folk practices and beliefs related to invisible entities, transempirical powers, taboos and so forth. These practices employ and deal with spirits, magic, witchcraft, sorcery, divination, sand reading, numerology, mediums, clairvoyants, talismans, amulets, fetishes, dreams, trances, dancing, curses, blood sacrifices, the evil eye, jealousy, and ceremonies that mark an event or transition in a person's life. Examples of such events are: birth, marriage, festivals, disease, death, and personal or family loss. These practices and beliefs hold sway over the majority of Muslims. Their presence reveals the powerful grip that folk religion has on people's lives.

One may think of many features of Islam in an attempt to discover the secret of its grip on its adherents. But in my estimation, the single most important factor of all is not Islam's creed or dogma, the Qur'an or the five duties. Rather, it is folk religion and the spiritual forces behind it. In effect, folk beliefs and practices are attempts by humans to change events by appealing to spirits and invisible forces.

In Marrakech, Morocco, there is a regular display of folk practices in a big square of the downtown area. Participants perform black magic, cast spells, tell fortunes, read palms, and practice divination, necromancy, and sorcery. People of different ages and social levels and from all walks of life seek help and guidance there. Spirit forces are at work in an obvious way in those gatherings.

Like other humans, the average Muslim is concerned about the immediate problems he faces, the issues of the here and now. He does not mind resorting to unorthodox practices that are not "according to the book" as long as they bring him help and relief. He often considers the tenets of his orthodox religion too idealistic and impractical.

The folk Muslim is a practitioner. To him, nothing can be so barren as cognitive religion. Existence takes on meaning as it is experienced on the stage of life where the actors are permitted the freedom to improvise their contribution to the drama of humanness. Little does it matter if he is misunderstood or maligned. Actually, he is convinced that it is the world—not himself—that is out of synchronization with life.[3]

Although orthodox Islam occasionally rises to attack folk practices and beliefs, it is difficult to imagine that such confrontations will ever lessen the tight grip of down-to-earth religion. Some purist, educated Muslims, determined to confine themselves solely to the teachings of the Qur'an and the Hadith, voice their anger and dismay at unorthodox practices. But folk Islam, undisturbed by such attacks, remains undeniably stronger than orthodox beliefs. Understandably, the Secretary General of Missions at al-Azhar University in Cairo vehemently attacks many popular practices, calling them heresies that plague Islam. He exposes such practices, threatening that those who participate in them will be eternally damned.[4] But in spite of the opposition, folk Islam flourishes all over the Muslim world—in the East and West, among the illiterate, the educated, the poor, and the wealthy.

Here is a brief table that outlines the difference between orthodox Islam and folk Islam:

Orthodox Islam	Folk Islam
Official Islam	Popular Islam
Islam according to the book	Islam according to life
Islam presented to the outside world	Islam practiced by its own people
Ideal Islam	Real Islam
Follows codes of belief and conduct	Finds solutions to life's problems
Publicized Islam	Hidden Islam

FOLK BELIEFS AND PRACTICES

The many and varied components of folk Islam defy most attempts at classification or categorizing. But the following represent five major groups:

1. Unseen powers
2. Magic and spells
3. Sufism
4. Reincarnation and transmigration
5. Taboos

Please note that this classification does not mean that there are five clear-cut areas of folk beliefs and practices in Islam. Usually two or more of these categories overlap and intertwine. For example, in magic transactions the medium often appeals to spirit-beings and transempirical force. In a *zar* ritual, magic formulas and taboos are used, and so forth. Now let us look at the five individual areas.

Unseen Powers

Like animists, many followers of Islam believe they are surrounded by spirits and invisible forces that animate beings and objects and live and operate in mountains, rocks, lakes, rivers, trees, animals and so forth. They believe people can control these spirits and powers to their advantage and they try to avoid handling them improperly, for fear the spirits may hurt them.

Spirit-Beings

The belief in an invisible realm of spirit-beings—angels, spirits, demons, jinn, and others—is rooted in the Qur'an and is an important part of the Islamic folk worldview. Angels are created spirit-beings. Jinn are spirit-creatures also, but they occupy an intermediate position between people and angels. Whereas people are created of brittle clay, according to the Qur'an, jinn are made of fire. The jinn eat, drink, marry, have sexual relations, and die,[5] while angels do not.

Jinn are either believers or unbelievers, while all angels are believers. Evil jinn help sorcerers and magicians. Sometimes they appear as animals, and they often possess people. The Arabic word *majnun*, translated "lunatic" or "mad," literally means someone possessed by jinn.

Ibn Taimiya, the famous Muslim theologian (A.D. 1263–1328), rejected many folk practices of his time such as miracle working and saint worship. Yet he believed strongly in jinn. Once he stated that if a person is able to subdue jinn, they can carry him on their back to faraway places. He also said that he had once encountered jinn masquerading as disciples in his class. But when they were beaten severely, they took to flight and never came back!

Al-Ahram, the largest Egyptian newspaper, reported on 29 April 1983 the exciting news that Astronaut Neil Armstrong, while walking on the moon, heard strange calls in a language he did not understand. He soon forgot the incident. But when he was visiting Cairo, he reportedly heard the same calls again. When he asked what they were, he was told that they were the Muslim call to prayer. Immediately Armstrong converted to Islam.

You can imagine the excitement such news brought to Muslim readers. Ahmad Bahgat, a Muslim columnist in *al-Ahram*, commented on the incident. He said that even if there were no life on the moon, Muslim jinn could sound the call to prayer there. Bahgat wanted to confirm the story for his readers and asked the American Embassy in Cairo if they could locate Armstrong. When the columnist was finally able to interview the astronaut by telephone, Armstrong denied the story, saying that he had heard no calls on the moon, and neither had he converted to Islam. Bahgat reported the results of his interview in *al-Ahram* of 26 May 1983.

A famous Muslim preacher reported that once when the prophet Muhammad saw a [jinn], he tried to tie it to a pole by the mosque so that the children of the town could see it [and be amused].[6]

A man once went to the legendary Sheikh Abd al-Qader, pleading for help to locate his daughter who had disappeared. The sheikh told the bereaved father that when a jinn, flying over the city of Baghdad, saw the girl, he fell in love with her and kidnapped her. The sheikh sent the father as his own emissary to the king of jinn to say: "One of your subjects has stolen my daughter, and I do not know where she is or what he has done to her. Can you find her for me?"

On hearing the name of [Sheikh] Abd al-Qadir, the king immediately summoned his captains to go and find out which of the jinn had captured a human girl. After some time they came back with a big male jinn and the man's daughter. The king spoke to the man: "Here is your daughter back. We do not want to harm any of Abd al-Qadir's friends, for he could bring down the wrath of the Almighty upon our heads!"[7]

In several places the Qur'an speaks about the *qarin*, which in Arabic means a companion, mate, comrade, or intimate. This is a familiar spirit which is born with each individual and accompanies him or her throughout life. It is believed to be a female spirit mate for males and a male spirit mate for females. On the Last Day, a *qarin* could testify against a person and cause him to be cast into hell fire (Sura 50:21–31). The *qarin* can mislead people and cause their eternal doom (Sura 4:38; 43:36–38 verify this ref.). Thomas P. Hughes' *A Dictionary of Islam* defines *qarin* as a demon.[8] Yet the prophet

Muhammad thought of it as a personal spirit that could be converted to Islam.[9]

Another spirit-being is the *ghoul,* a very dangerous female demon that is said to be fond of eating people. Belief in the *ghoul* is widely accepted among Muslims in the Arab world.

Betjalal is a female spirit well known in Algeria. The Arabic word means "daughter of glory." Many men are married to her and testify to having sexual relations with her.

Lalla Aicha Kandisha is one of the most important and most feared spirits in Morocco. She has characteristics similar to those of Betjalal. She is a beautiful, provocative female. She invites men to have sexual relations with her. Those who succumb to her seduction enter into a lasting link with her and become her slaves.

Zwemer points out that according to Islam even "…the prophets, especially Solomon and Muhammad, had intercourse with demons and jinn."[10]

It is possible that Muhammad also believed that meteors (or meteorites) were part of the spirit world. He evidently thought they were other-worldly beings that could sit and listen and also dart out to pursue an evil spirit. The Qur'an states:

> We have touched into heaven and found it full of terrible guards and meteors. We used to sit there on seats to listen. Anyone that listens now will find a meteor in ambush for him (Sura 72:8–9).
>
> We have set the Zodiac signs in the heavens and adorned them for onlookers. We have kept them from every accursed evil spirit. But any that eavesdrop; a bright meteor will pursue him (Sura 15:16–18).

In folk Islam, there are many ways to ward off demons and evil spirits. They include wearing amulets, burning incense, giving alms, offering animal sacrifices, breaking pottery outside the house, and performing *zar* rituals.

I consider the *zar* rituals, common in villages in many Islamic countries, the Muslims' most conspicuous means of negotiating with the spirit world. *Zar* involves group dancing, rhythms, drumming, singing, swaying, praying, reciting incantations and feasting on special foods. A *zar* party is a visible demonstration of Muslims' strong belief in unseen spirits and their aspirations to influence these spirits.

At some point during a *zar* ceremony, people often experience loss of consciousness, trances, and hypnosis. Sometimes they are subject to convulsions and violent behavior. At times extramarital sex is also practiced! Such sexual activity, normally tabooed by Muslim society, is condoned on the premise that it is an act of the "master spirit" rather than that of the possessed woman. These activities are all signs of entering into communication with the spirit world.

While people resort to *zar* rituals to try to meet the pressing needs of everyday life, it seems that such rituals also provide an alternative to the strict norms of traditional Islamic societies that consider open displays of affection to be inappropriate and unacceptable. Such lack of expression leads to the suppression of emotions, which subjects people, especially women, to tensions brought on by the need for emotional security and assurance. That is why it is often women who resort to a *zar* ceremony to receive support and assistance from spirits. Participating in the ritual also confers on them power and recognition when otherwise they are considered of marginal worth.

A friend who came to Christ from Islam told me that when he was a little boy, he was often gripped by fear. So his mother, wanting to help him, took him to a *zar* ritual. She took a pigeon along. The leader was a medium who sat in the center of the room. The pigeon was killed, its blood was sprinkled on the little boy, and the dead bird along with some salt was buried in front of the door of the family's home. During the ritual, the medium started dancing until he went into a trance and fell to the floor while people continually shouted "Allah-u Akbar" in the boy's ears.

To have access to invisible spirits is an indication of authority, power, leadership, and religious achievement. A person with such ability and access is sought out to give guidance and cast spells or counter spells. I knew of a sheikh who was reputed to have a spirit wife who gave birth to several spirit children—all spirits in the underworld. A close friend of mine, an eye doctor, went to see firsthand what was happening. The man with the spirit wife asked the doctor what he wanted to drink. A few minutes later, a glass of a cold drink on a tray came toward my friend. It was carried by a spirit that the eye doctor could not see! People thronged to the sheikh's house daily to seek guidance and help with their personal problems and hardships.

Transempirical Force

In addition to spirit-beings, Muslims believe that there are forces that operate in and animate certain objects. The word "empirical" means that which can be experienced through natural human senses, that which can be observed and measured by scientific methods. The term "transempirical" means that which is beyond experience through natural human senses, that which cannot be observed and measured by scientific methods.

For example, a tree or a rock is an empirical object that can be seen and touched. But some people think that certain trees, rocks, rivers, tombs, other objects and people have a special force residing in them. This force cannot be scientifically tested or observed; it is transempirical.

Barakah. The concept of *barakah* is important in folk Islam. The word *barakah* in Arabic generally means blessing or goodness. But in folk Islam, it has other usages. Here it refers to an impersonal, transempirical force, a supernatural influence of blessedness, holiness, and spiritual power. It is important to distinguish between the notion of *barakah* as a conventional blessing and the concept of *barakah* as a blessing obtained through transempirical powers. The two are quite different. Our main concern here is with the belief in *barakah* as a transempirical power.

Barakah is a power that is cherished and pursued. It manifests itself in the ability to do miracles or show special wisdom or insight concerning life. Muslims consider *barakah* a means of healing, protection, and blessing.

Ordinary people do not have *barakah*. It resides only in holy people or objects, such as the Qur'an, religious books, shrines, places or objects related to holy people such as their tombs, mosques, wayside prayer enclaves, and prayer beads (rosary). It can be transmitted to other people if they touch a holy person or feel an object where it resides.

Idiots, harmless madmen, and some beggars are also venerated as reservoirs of *barakah*. The belief is that such people's minds are with God. Their reasoning faculties are in heaven while their bodies are on earth!

Sharifs, Muslims who claim to be descendants of the Prophet, are regarded as holy people or saints. *Sharif* literally means "honorable." It is a title usually attached to one's name and commands added respect and veneration. People generally consider a *sharif* a source of *barakah* and go to him to acquire blessings and power.

Muslims seek after saints, whether living or dead, to do miracles for them, give them *barakah*, intercede for them or other people, and give religious instruction and guidance.

Sheikh A. Hebeish, whom I knew personally, lived in a small town in the Middle East and was reputed to have *barakah*. He himself believed strongly that he possessed *barakah* and that he was in a position to dispense it to others. On several occasions, while we were sitting together and talking, Muslims—men, women, and children—came, bowed low to the sheikh, kissed his hand and touched his string of prayer beads in order to receive a blessing. People, including his son-in-law who was well-educated and held a high government position, called him *sidi* ("my master").

Often, after a holy person dies, he becomes the patron saint and protector of a certain place or group of people. His tomb or a shrine dedicated to him becomes a place of pilgrimage which people visit to plead a cause and seek help. A Muslim saint may be given one of many titles, depending on the location of his tomb or shrine. Some of the titles used are sheikh, *wali, marabout, mulay, sidi, pir,* and so forth.

A woman unable to conceive or someone who is sick or in need of a job, promotion, favor, or spouse, may go to the shrine. There, seekers offer food and money to the guardians of the site and to the poor. Then they express their request and absorb some of the *barakah* of the shrine.

Barakah has been an important factor in the spread of Islam in some parts of the world such as West Africa. There, it continues to have a great impact on people's lives.[11]

Curse. A curse, the opposite of *barakah*, is also a transempirical force. When Muhammad fought in the battle of Uhud, his face was injured. Tradition says that he cursed those who hurt him and hoped for their destruction. Before a year had passed, they were all dead![12]

Evil eye. The evil eye, similar to a curse, is the eye of a jealous person. In Arabic, the words jealous and evil in "evil eye" are the same. Muslims fear and dread the evil eye. While people obtain something good through *barakah*, through the evil eye something good is taken away from them or some evil befalls them, such as loss of property or job, sickness, calamity or even death.

According to the Hadith, Muhammad said, "The evil eye is a reality."[13]

The Qur'an instructs people to:

Say, I take refuge with the Lord of the Dawn,

From the evil He created [or from the evil of what He created],

From the evil of darkness as it spreads,

From the evil of female witches [literally, women who blow in knots],

From the evil of a jealous person, when he is jealous (Sura 113:1–5).

Once a woman, greatly enamored with Muhammad, looked at him intently. He, fearing her evil eye, stretched his hand toward her and repeated the above verses. According to the story, her covetous glance passed between two of Muhammad's fingers, struck a nail in a nearby tree, and split it into pieces.[14] Tradition says that Muhammad claimed that the powers of an evil eye are even stronger than those of fate.

Magic and Spells

Magic, an integral part of folk Islam practices, appeals to and uses unnatural and supernatural means in an effort to change the natural course of events. Petitioners may wish to obtain a job for an unemployed person, increase one's business profits, acquire a husband for an unmarried girl, help a woman conceive, insure the survival of a newborn baby, gain the attention and love of a disinterested husband, cause a man to hate and divorce his wife, bring a curse on a new co-wife that the husband has brought home, inflict misfortune on an enemy, ward off the evil eye, and so forth.

An ordinary Muslim believes strongly in the casting and countering of magic spells. Nothing is more expressive of this fact than an article that appeared sometime ago in an Islamic international weekly. The article stated that magic is like sickness. Then the author went on to explain that if prophets fell sick, it was because of magic spells cast on them. Aysha, Muhammad's youngest wife, said that Ibn al-A'sam, a Jewish man, cast a spell on Muhammad that made him unable to have sexual relations with his wives. She reported that "he imagined he was having marital relations, but in reality he wasn't... He was imagining things that were not actually happening..."[15]

Missionary author and educator Phil Parshall relates a story about Shah Dawla. This man had supernatural power. At his command babies were born with

> minute heads, large ears, and rat-like faces, and were without understanding or power of speech. Although they were repulsive, no contempt of them was to be shown. If anyone violated this prohibition, his next child would be born in a similar state.[16]

In spite of the misfortune he unleashed on others, he was called "saint."

To cast a magic spell on someone or to counter a spell, Muslims turn to sheikhs, mediums and spirits to dispense incantations and occult paraphernalia such as amulets, charms, omens, talismans, and so forth.

An amulet is often made of a qur'anic verse written on a piece of paper. It is then wrapped carefully in cloth and secured with stitches. People keep it under their pillow or wear it around their neck.

One of the talismans most used to counter the evil eye is the number five. It is reputed to have a mystic virtue. That is why the five-fingered hand of Fatima, also called the hand of Maryam, is such a popular amulet or charm. People wear it as jewelry and paint it on doorposts, car fenders, and other places.

As a young pharmacist, I worked for a Muslim who had a prosperous pharmaceutical business. In an effort to ward off the evil eye and bring his business good luck, each evening he would leave a sandal in the cash register. For him, a pharmacist, there was no clash between education, position, wealth, and superstition.

The Prophet of Islam himself believed in such omens. The Hadith says:

> Narrated Abu Hurayrah that Muhammad said: "When you listen to the crowing of the cock, ask Allah for His favor as it sees Angels and when you listen to the braying of the donkey, seek refuge in Allah from the Satan for it sees Satan."[17]

Sufism

Sufis believe that man's spirit is an emanation of the Divine Spirit to which it ultimately returns. They also hold that the Spirit of God is in everything He made. God alone is perfect love and beauty, and one's goal should be to be absorbed into that love. A Sufi desires to be near God. He goes through a process of penitence, purification, and renunciation of the world.

Some Sufis such as the Andalusian Muslim mystic and philosopher Ibn Arabi (A.D. 1165–1240) believe that there are gradual transitions or partitionings (*barzakh*) between God and man. One of these is "The Absolute Divine Imagination" which is also called "The Muhammedan Reality." God's throne and the cherubim are also such divine entities. One can easily see in such beliefs a blend of polytheism [the belief in many gods], pantheism [the belief that the material universe and human beings are part of God] and pluralism [the belief that all religions lead to God].[18]

Islamic Sufism is greatly influenced by Indian philosophies. A Sufi is an ascetic Muslim who abandons the world and its pleasures to find God. He has mystical tendencies. He seeks to be in servitude to God and to be assimilated and absorbed into Him. He worships, prays, and fasts.

Originally, Sufis in their abandonment of the world, dressed in harsh, cheap wool. The Arabic word for wool is *suf.* So a Muslim dressed in wool was called a Sufi.

Sufis are ecstatic and enraptured with love for God and for Muhammad. They depend more on feelings than on knowledge. They claim to worship God because He deserves to be worshipped, while others worship Him out of fear and in hope of paradise.[19]

Rabi'a al-'Adawiyya who lived in Basra (in today's Iraq) in the eighth century and is considered one of Islam's most famous Sufis, voices this kind of mysticism in one of her prayers:

O God, if I worship You for fear of hell fire,
Cast me in it.
And if I worship You for hope of paradise,
Exclude me from it.
But if I worship You for Your own sake,
Then withhold not from me Your eternal beauty.[20]

This prayer, although it appears very "spiritual" and to some even "biblical," has serious flaws. Measured by the standard of the Word of God, it proves to be deficient! Rabi'a asks God to admit her to or exclude her from paradise on the basis of her attitude in worship, a concept that is foreign to the Bible, which teaches that identification with Christ's death on the cross is the only means of being acceptable to God.

In order to better understand Sufism, let us look at some statements of its famous, historic leaders.

A Sufi is someone whose heart God has cleansed and who has been filled with light. He takes pleasure in mentioning God (Kharraz, ninth century).

A Sufi dies to self by the truth and is raised to life by the truth (Junaid, ninth century).

Sufism is purity and vision (Kattani, tenth century).

Sufism is casting oneself into servitude, exiting from humanness, and looking into the truth (Jaafar, tenth century).

A Sufi is a person who is completely lost to himself, exists only in God, is freed from the hold of his lower self and is conjoined to the Reality of all realities (Sharafuddin Maneri, fourteenth century).

When one's heart is directed towards God, mercy abounds to that heart, light shines in it, and the secrets of the kingdom are open to it (Al-Ghazali, eleventh century).[21]

Sufism also seeks to find an answer to the question of creation and the relationship between God, universe and man. It often wanders into a maze of wordy philosophical formulations that neither answer the question nor satisfy man's heart.[22]

Through ecstasy and assimilation into God, a Sufi becomes one with God. This belief is in reality pantheism, which asserts that all is God. The following statements made by Muslim mystics show their belief in their own divinity.

I am the Truth …I am He whom I love, and He whom I love is I; we are two souls dwelling in one body …if you see me, you see Him; and if you see Him, you see me (Al-Hallaj, ninth century).

I am without beginning and without end …I am Abraham, Moses, Jesus …I am greater than Muhammad… I am the true God, praise Me, praise Me… (Abu Yazid al-Bastami, ninth century).

It is I who set the Rose in motion and move the hearts of lovers (Fariduddin al-Attar, twelfth century).[23]

I was an unknown hidden treasure and wanted to be known. So, I created people. Hence by Me they knew Me (Ibn Arabi, twelfth century).[24]

The mystic, obscure character of Sufism and its ability to override the Qur'an and the Hadith are two important factors that place this Islamic mysticism in the realm of folk religion. By their techniques and beliefs, Sufis are clearly protesting orthodox Islam. The Muslim mystic Ibn Arabi said:

My heart has become accepting,
Of every image.
It is a pasture for deer,
And a monastery for monks.
It is a temple for idols,
And a ka'aba for pilgrims.
It is for plates of the Torah,
And the scroll of the Qur'an.
Wherever my heart goes,

I believe in the religion of love.
Thus, love is my religion,
And my faith.[25]

In another prayer the Sufi Rabi'a al-'Adawiyya says:

O God, take away the words of the devil
That mix with my prayer.
If not, then take my prayer as it is, devil and all.[26]

Here, this prominent Muslim mystic accepts various sources of impression and impulses. She does not mind offering God a prayer that is a mixture of her own words and the devil's.

To achieve a rapturous, ecstatic state, Sufis use a variety of techniques and movements, swinging, music, drums, recitations and repetitive words.[27] Some depend on drugs to attain this euphoric state. Khalil Abdel-Karim says that some forms of Sufism

get off course into singing, dancing, and the use of marijuana. People become very corrupt... Many engage in pedophilia and homosexuality... their leaders and sheikhs become very rich and live like princes. They ride in the most luxurious cars, live in expensive homes, and marry two or three wives—young wives, the age of their granddaughters![28]

Tehmina Durrani in her book *My Feudal Lord*, describes a Sufi party in a village in Pakistan:

The village was abuzz with activity, and the festival was unlike anything I had ever seen. All norms were abandoned, all standards put on hold. We strolled amid crowds... past fortune-tellers and dismissed the spiels of opium sellers. Many... contend that opium enhances their religious ecstasy. We peeked into sleazy cafes where eunuchs, clad in golden, skin-tight body suits, danced lewdly and made seedy assignations.[29]

Members of the howling dervishes in Turkey, Kurdistan and other areas express their strong faith by cutting themselves without suffering the usual consequences of being cut. Through rhythmical exercises and mental control, they do not bleed (at least no blood appears!). They drive spears into their bodies, eat glass and put lances through their cheeks and tongues. Through pain, they say, they achieve ecstasy and gratification. Some whirling dervishes in their ceremonies can make more than fifty turns a minute and go on for more than twenty minutes!

Miracles have been attributed to some Sufis. Phil Parshall gives this account of two Sufis in India—a saint who lived in the upper story and his disciple who lived on the ground level of a two-story house. One night the disciple did not find his master in his room, so he spent the entire night waiting in front of his master's door. In the morning, however, he heard his master calling out for water from inside the room. The disciple,

> curious to know where his master had been during the night and how he had managed to get inside the room, naturally asked for an explanation. The saint, when pressed, replied, "I generally spend my night on Mount Hira, in the vicinity of Mecca, where Prophet Muhammad used to meditate in his early life."[30]

It is important to note that Sufis are not the only Muslims that have such miraculous powers. In some cases a saint, believed to have influence with God, is thought to have

> the gift of miracles. He can transform himself, transport himself to a distance, speak several tongues, revive the dead; he can produce various phenomena: …thought-reading, telepathy, prophecy …levitation …summon objects from a distance. He can make a dry stick put forth leaves, check a flood, control rains and springs etc."[31]

There are many differences between Islamic Sufism and biblical Christian mysticism. Foremost among these differences is the fact that Christian mysticism is Christ-centered and the cross is foundational while Sufism rejects these notions. There are, however, two other remarkable differences that deserve our attention.

First, in biblical Christian mysticism, God comes down to open the way for humans to have communion with Him. The Holy Spirit draws people into close fellowship with God. In Islamic Sufism humans struggle, sway, and swing to come close to God.

Second, in biblical Christian mysticism, one enters into communion with God, but is not absorbed into God. People do not lose their humanness. A person is still a human, and God is still God; each retains his own identity. In God's presence, people remain human and continue to be transformed into the likeness of Christ (2 Corinthians 3:18). As the bonds of believers' union with the Lord grow and their love for Him becomes deeper, the Bible says that the Holy Spirit witnesses to their spirit (Romans 8:16), meaning that there is still a distinction between God's Spirit and our spirit. Richard J. Foster's book *Prayer* states that in Christian mysticism there is

> no loss of identity, no merging with the cosmic consciousness, no fanciful astral travel. Rather, we are called to life-transforming obedience because we have encountered the living God of Abraham, Isaac and Jacob.[32]

In Sufi mysticism, however, a person is absorbed and assimilated into God. He is lost in God. A merger takes place. There is no distinction between the human and God. They are no longer separate entities.

Certainly Sufism has serious problems. Although it sounds romantically spiritual, it is incompatible with the Bible. I see in Sufism the following three theological perils:

1. It is mystic pantheism. This is the notion that all is God. The soul of the universe is God. But since the soul is not to be separated from the body, man who is part of the universe becomes part of God. Consequently the finite man becomes infinite with God, and the infinite God becomes finite with man!

2. It is self-aggrandizement. How can man, a sinner, become one with God? The Sufi notion of achieving union with God is an attempt to usurp what belongs solely to the Supreme Being!

3. It offers deceptive contentment. There is false, perilous satisfaction in Sufism. Man is no longer in desperate need of redemption and reconciliation.

Reincarnation and Transmigration

Reincarnation and transmigration are two other areas of folk beliefs and practices in Islam. Reincarnation means that the soul, after leaving the body at death, comes back to earth in the form of another human or even an animal. Transmigration means that a being can pass from one place to another without being seen by others.

Omar Khayyam, the Persian Sufi poet and author of the famous Ruba'iyat quatrains was one day

> about to pass an old college in Nishapur, accompanied by a group of his students. A string of donkeys, carrying bricks for the repair of the building, entered. One, however, refused to pass through the gates. Omar looked at the scene, smiled and went up to the donkey, reciting an extempore poem [one he thought of on the spur of the moment]:
>
> "O one who has gone and returned,
>
> Your name has been lost from among names:
>
> Your nails are combined into hooves:
>
> Your beard, a tail, now on the other end."
>
> The ass now readily entered the college grounds. The disciples, puzzled, asked their teacher, "Wise one, what does this mean?"
>
> Khayyam explained: "The spirit which is now within that ass was once inside the body of a teacher in this college. It was reluctant to go in as a donkey. Then, finding that it had been recognized by a fellow teacher, it had to enter the precincts."[33]

The Qur'an reports that Mohammed was transported bodily to Jerusalem and then lifted up into heaven. Islam's holy book calls this the "Night Journey" and gives it a whole Sura. It starts like this:

> Praise be to Him Who carried His servant by night from the most sacred mosque to the farthest mosque which We have encircled with blessings, that We might show him of Our signs! He is the One who hears and sees (Sura 17:1).

The details of this "Night Journey" are recorded in one Islamic book after another and mentioned in countless articles. Briefly, one night the angel Jibril woke Muhammad up from his sleep and in-structed him to mount a winged animal "smaller than a mule but larger than an ass." They traveled all the way to Solomon's Temple in Jerusalem, where Muhammad led all the prophets including Moses and Jesus in prayer. Then the angel carried him to paradise and hell and into the very presence of God. There God told him that he and his followers should pray 50 times a day. But Muhammad talked with Moses to have God reduce that to only five times a day. God accepted. Later Muhammad returned to Mecca carried by the beast. The entire journey lasted a short part of the night.[34]

Taboos

Taboos are restrictions and sanctions imposed upon people in order to protect them from harm. These can be related to foods, objects or certain activities.

There is a story about the king of Cambodia which, although not related to Muslim beliefs and practices, helps us understand the concept of taboos. In July of 1874 the king was thrown from his carriage and lay unconscious. His courtiers stood there not daring to help him because of a taboo against touching the king without his command.

The king might well have died there on the ground if a passing European had not been willing to carry the injured monarch to his palace and care for him until he regained consciousness and gave permission for the local doctors to treat him.[35]

Here are other examples of taboos.

In Islam there is a specific way of slaughtering animals and birds so that they can be sold and eaten. This method consists of a simple ceremony performed to make the meat *halal*, that is, ceremonially clean and religiously legal. Meat that is not *halal* is *haram*, taboo or prohibited.

The Arabic name for the praying mantis is the Prophet's horse, and for Muslims in some parts of the Arab world it is a taboo to kill a praying mantis.

Muslims often consider it a taboo to compliment a baby. Rather, in order to protect the infant from the evil eye, people are to describe a baby as "ugly," which is quite acceptable. A young Muslim lady, whom I shall refer to as M., accepted Jesus as her Lord and Savior. She has suffered a lot of persecution because of her commitment to Christ. She works for a Christian organization. Yet, at the time of this writing, M. was still fairly troubled when someone complimented her baby!

WHAT DOES THE BIBLE SAY ABOUT THESE ACTIVITIES?

God's Word is forthright in warning us against these practices and describes both these activities and those who practice them as detestable to the Lord. Why? In the first place such rituals put God aside and seek the help of counterfeit lords and false gods. Further, in a sense, these are attempts to coerce God to reveal that which is hidden or manipulate present or future situations in order to solve people's problems.

Bible verses that talk specifically about these practices include: Exodus 22:18; Leviticus 17:7; 20:6, 27; Deuteronomy 18:10–5; II Chronicles 33:6; Isaiah 8:19–22; 47:12–13; Jeremiah 10:2; Ezekiel 13:18–23; Galatians 5:19–20.

SIGNIFICANCE OF FOLK ISLAM

Islam boasts that its goal is submission to God, His decrees and His will. People are to resign themselves to their prescribed fate (*maktub*). They are controlled by what has been predetermined for them in life. What God has decreed will not be altered. What is written, humans cannot change. Every single event of life, from birth to death, is predestined for an individual. People must accept what comes to them. It is not up to them to entreat God to make changes.

Yet, the "unspoken" goal of folk Islam is to change God's decrees and will! Here Muslims try to reshape their destiny, alter their predetermined lot. They seek help from quarters outside of God and orthodox religion to meet the needs they feel. In folk Islam there is an obvious attempt to manipulate fate!

What do the folk beliefs and practices of popular Islam reveal? The fact that they are so widespread and deeply entrenched in people's lives indicates three major things: a) Ideal (orthodox) Islam fails to answer people's felt needs, and so they resort to the alternative of folk religion to try to turn events in their favor; b) syncretism is rampant in Islam; and c) there are cracks in the walls of Islam.

Ideal Islam Fails to Answer Felt Needs

The term "felt needs" refers to the everyday, practical problems and questions of life—the needs people feel they must have met immediately. Hunger causes a felt need for food. If one does not have a place to live, his or her felt need is for a shelter. On the other hand there are spiritual needs which have more serious implications. People need God's forgiveness, salvation from sin, eternal life and so forth. A person may not realize he or she has these needs. Or the felt needs may be so strong that they displace the spiritual needs. If people are starving, how can they listen to a sermon? The needs of the "here and now" take humans' attention and energy away from spiritual needs.

Muslims resort to magic, fortune-telling, saint veneration, and so forth in an effort to cope with the situations they face in life here and now. They do not see the realm of high religion, that is, Islam according to its holy book, as answering their immediate needs. They know that God is; they believe in Muhammad and the Qur'an, angels, prophets, and paradise. But all these are cosmic concepts of the hereafter. People turn to folk Islam because they want something that gives them an answer to the problems they face today. Myrtle S. Langley analyses why women in Kelantan, Malaysia resort to folk practices. That society discourages direct confrontation and open hostility, particularly inside the family.

> As a result, there is undoubtedly much emotional repression in the society, especially within marriage. Moreover, a wife's role is restricted both in the home and in the mosque. Her role within marriage is unstable. Kelantan has one of the highest divorce rates in the world, and although Islamic law recognizes the right of alimony this is rarely given. And as it is not considered proper to initiate a direct confrontation, all the repressed anger, jealousy and indignation concomitant with an imminent divorce is transferred to the spirit world. In this neutral and socially acceptable realm, latent hostility can be acted out...[36]

People are looking for an outlet for their emotional stress, a solution to their relational upheavals and financial pressures and a cure for their physical sufferings. In desperation, they seek answers from those people and practices which have or grant access to other-worldly powers. Bill Musk states that

> in the experience of the masses, the official faith by and large fails to address everyday needs. Such a sense of failure may not be

expressed aloud so much as by commitment to alternative meanings and functions of the formal religion. The God of Islamic theology would appear to be so far removed from human's lives that substitute focuses of power are sought in the accessible practitioners of popular Islam.[37]

Syncretism is Rampant in Islam

Folk religion practices are widespread in Islam. Rich and poor, educated and uneducated, at one time or another resort to magic, fortune-telling, and the like. (You may recall here the story of the pharmacist who took steps to ward off the evil eye and the educated newspaper columnist who believed that jinn sounded the call to prayer on the moon.) This phenomenon points to the syncretistic character of Islam. It does not require a change of life or a spiritual rebirth at conversion, but rather adapts to the local population's beliefs and practices.

There are Cracks in the Walls of Islam

The mere fact that folk Islam thrives attests to a widespread sense of lostness, restlessness of the mind, and apathy of the soul. People, thirsty, hungry and helpless, are reaching out for help.

The Muslims' search for answers and help through folk Islam signals an opportunity for the ministry of the Holy Spirit. This opportunity exists because those who practice folk Islam are usually more inclined to be open to Christ than others. As we mentioned earlier, the fact that they resort to magic and the like indicates clearly that they are not satisfied with orthodox Islam. They realize they have to reach outside the formal boundaries of their religion in order to meet their needs and solve their dilemmas. If we present Christ in His mighty power and loving compassion to seekers like these, they will be disposed to accept Him.

The term "power encounter" is used by Christians to mean a confrontation in which the power of Satan is directly challenged and the power of God is displayed. This is a showdown between opposing forces. To initiate such an encounter in a context where people are seeking help through folk Islam is most appropriate. More will be said about that later.

9 | *Direction and Trends*

Past generations did not have the advanced communications systems we have now. Today's world is inter-connected, and for the most part it is impossible to avoid the influence people and cultures have on each other. Even closed societies are subject to outside influence through travel, radio, television and the internet.

Islam is a system founded on and energized by a great deal of tradition (remember the Hadith). So how does it react to the ever-quickening pace of global changes? Does it go along with the shifts and development, or does it resist transformation? How is it coping with the uncontrollable tide of technological advances and cultural exchanges?

This chapter will attempt to answer these questions.

Transformation is not natural or easy in Islam. Yet, at its beginning and particularly during Muhammad's life, Islam made many adjustments and changes. Time and again the Prophet changed some rule or altered some rite.

At first, Muhammad followed the Jewish custom of blowing a horn to call his followers to prayer. Then he considered ringing a bell, as Christian churches did. Finally, he decided to sound the call to prayer, using a man to simply shout it from the mosque or prayer place. Today, in many cities and towns the call is delivered through a loudspeaker and frequently a recording is used.

Muhammad also altered the *qiblah* (the direction people must face when they pray). During his early months in Medina and in keeping with his good relations with the Jews, Muhammad instructed his followers to face toward Jerusalem when they prayed. However, as his relations with the Jews soured, he changed the *qiblah* toward Mecca.

We have already discussed what Islam knows as abrogation. This is the cancellation of a qur'anic teaching or doctrine because Muhammad later received a different and opposing inspiration. The teaching of the newer verse or passage abolishes and cancels that of the previous one. This type of major doctrinal change and modification came to a close with the death of Muhammad.

Yet, dramatic shifts of other kinds are taking place in the House of Islam today, in spite of Muhammad's warnings such as "All innovations are the work of the devil,"[1] and "Beware of innovation; every novelty is a heresy."[2] Muslims, like all other people, live in a rapidly changing world, and Islamic societies have to deal with change on a daily basis.

The advent of modern systems of communication is a major factor of cultural change. Think of the advances in this field that have been made in the past few decades. Consider television, for example. There is no way to fathom the change brought about by such an invention. As you sit in your house watching the news on television, events taking place thousands of miles away are brought right into your home for you to see, watch, hear and almost feel. You see what other people have, how they live, and what their homes, streets, factories, and offices look like. You have a great, intercultural exposure.

Then there are computers, email and the Internet! Muslims in the remotest areas of the world can and do talk with others. They are exposed to other peoples' customs and cultures, their beliefs and practices and their achievements and successes! Invariably there is envy and the desire to imitate and achieve.

Simply, the Islamic system is not able to stand against the torrential currents of change, nor can it impose upon its children a curfew against the incredible technological advances that today's world offers. It cannot command its adherents to withdraw from the world they live in and the forces that affect their generation. In other words, the system is unable to successfully enforce intellectual censorship. At the same time it cannot stop or even slow down the pace of world change.

In the past, Muslims often lived under the rule of the Shari'a within their close-knit societies. But now they are exposed to other philosophies and ways of life. As they mix more and more with people of other religions and cultures, how are they reacting and what is their response?

Certainly, the House of Islam is in the throes of intense change. Some changes are progressive or innovative, others are not. The resurgence of Islamic fundamentalism is an example of transformation which is taking Muslims back centuries at a time! On the progressive side, the news media has reported that for the first time in the history of Islam, a female, Amina A. Wadud, served as an imam to lead a group of men and women in Friday prayer![3]

Changes are taking place also in the economic systems of all the Muslim nations. Both in form and operation, they are simply not what they used to be in the middle of the twentieth century. Even Saudi Arabia, one of the Islamic nations most resistant to change, has seen vast shifts in its economy.

While some Muslim nations have taken an abrupt "economic leap" into the modern world, this does not mean they have resolved their social issues. Youssef M. Ibrahim courageously asserts:

> We say of countries where women are not allowed to vote, choose their life partners, drive, travel or run for office that they are preserving "Arab and Islamic tradition," when in fact they are committing flagrant violations of human rights for half their population...Our governments, our schools, our social systems, our economies and our very sense of ethical conduct are all failed models whose shelf-life is over.[4]

In recent years, various new Islamic movements have appeared with startling suddenness. Some of these are social; others are religious, purist, or militant. All indicate that a giant has awakened, and no one can ignore it. Today Muslims are no longer on the periphery of world history and geopolitics. Instead, they are at the very center. This position of prominence puts great stress on the Muslim ummah, for Islam is Islam and it has a certain brittleness and rigidity about it. When it faces a tide of change that is too strong for it, spectacular jolts, disruption, and confusion unfailingly ensue.

IMPACT OF WORLD CHANGES ON ISLAM

As a student and observer of Islam for many years, I have always tried to understand which directions Islam is going. But attempting to pin down a pattern of such developments can admittedly be elusive and frustrating. Nevertheless, I would like to suggest a few directions that Muslims today, from various walks of life, are taking.

Urbanization

Urbanization is the process of shifting from the village to the city. It occurs when masses of rural dwellers move from their homes on the farm or in the village to urban areas that promise to offer jobs, better housing, better living conditions, and modern lifestyles. As more and more people move, huge cities grow with hundreds of thousands and even millions of inhabitants.

Urbanization often leads to the weakening of family ties. Away from the village, the individual loses close family contact. No longer subject to the social group in which he had lived for years, he is less accountable to them. He becomes independent. He has to make major decisions on his own. Such behavior is unfamiliar in most Muslim societies where decisions are made by the group which is the immediate family, the extended family, the tribe, or any other recognizable body of people. Urbanization poses hard questions for Islamic societies: What will urbanized Muslims believe and how will they behave a few years down the road? And what will Islam be like in a generation or two?

Migration

As in urbanization, here also there is mass movement of people from one place to another. But in migration, people leave their country to settle in another. They migrate to study or to find better jobs and lead better lives. Today, most Muslims who leave their homeland go to the West. Such a move gives average Muslims shocks and jolts because the new society they move to usually has traits, characteristics, beliefs and practices that are rather foreign and strange to the followers of Muhammad.

It would be worth noting here that some Muslims migrate with the clear goal of populating and gradually taking over "infidel" (non-Muslim) societies.

When Muslims relocate to the West and become citizens of their adopted country, how do they see themselves? As French, British or American? Or, as Muslim? In other words, where is their allegiance, to the ummah or to their new country? Mark Gabriel, a former Muslim, answers very clearly:

> Muslims who have any sense of loyalty to Islam will have a hard time justifying loyalty to their country if that country is not Islamic. The true Muslim believes that the whole world is his home and that he is commanded to submit the world to the authority of Islam.[5]

Gabriel goes on to say that a good Muslim will not die for a patch of dirt of his new country. On the other hand he would be willing to die for Islam and Muslim holy places.

Islam sees the world as divided into two camps: the House of Islam and the House of War. The "faithful" belong to the House of Islam. Secular societies and non-Muslims belong to the House of War. Sayyed Qutb emphasizes this worldview in these words: "Islam knows only two societies [in the world], a Muslim society and a pagan non-Muslim society."[6]

The Islamic system demands an allegiance that overrides any other. A true Muslim cannot be faithful to a non-Muslim system. This would be outright treason. So, in general, Muslims' true identity is tied to Islam, not to the country where they live. Their first loyalty is to the community of Islam.

The violent civil unrest in some Islamic areas of French cities in the fall of 2005 illustrates such allegiance. Muslim youths burned hundreds of cars and vandalized shops and buildings. The authorities asked some of them why they were causing all that destruction in France since they themselves were French! They agreed that they were French, but not that French! Muslims in the United Kingdom also mirror this sentiment. According to reports, 85% of them state that their first allegiance is to Islam, not to their adopted country.[7]

Modernization

Today it is easy to go to a bakery or a grocery store in the Middle East and buy bread. But it was not always like that. In the past in Middle Eastern societies, people made their own bread. They bought wheat from the farmer. It had chaff, small sticks, and dirt, and it needed to be cleaned. Women would invite some neighborhood ladies to their home to help them as they sat together, spread quantities of the wheat on a small, low table, and worked for hours to clean it. All the while they visited with each other, sharing personal news. They talked about what their families were doing, how their husbands were treating them, the state of their intimate life, and so on. This is how they would socialize. The cleaned wheat would then be taken to the village mill to be ground, and there more socializing would take place, but this time among the men. Later, women would gather again to knead the flour into dough and bake it in clay ovens located behind the houses or on the roofs. Again the women would have a great time of visiting and socializing.

Now, all this is past. People usually just go to a shop and buy bread. Such dramatic change results in less social contact and therefore the weakening of group ties.

Another illustration of modernization is a high-tech divorce! A Muslim in Malaysia decided he had had enough of his wife's visit to her parents' home. He sent her a text message on her cell phone saying, "If you don't leave your parents' house, you will be divorced." She chose not to leave, and the court granted him the divorce he wanted! Later the judge stated that under the Shari'a law, a husband can end a marriage by text-messaging "I divorce you" to his wife three times![8]

In 2006 the President of Tunisia declared that "the growing practice of women wearing headscarves does not fit with Tunisia's cultural heritage."[9] This certainly does not mirror the convictions of traditional Islam.

Secularization

Secularization is the process of adopting a worldly and temporal value system to the neglect of that which is religious and spiritual. In Muslim countries, as in the West, secularization brings drastic social and economic changes such as depersonalization and overemphasis on achievements, success, and possessions. All this is detestable and repulsive to orthodox Muslims for whom there is no separation between state and religion and no dividing line between secular and religious. In 2001, Recep Tayyib Erdogan declared that it was impossible to be a secularist and a Muslim at the same time. But after he became Turkey's Prime Minister, Erdogan changed his view. Now he argues that secularism is good for Islam!

In Islamic societies, secularization distances Muslims from the religious norms that are familiar to them. During the twentieth century a few Muslim countries took courageous strides toward secularization. Throughout the 1920s and 1930s, Turkey underwent a number of changes: the caliphate was abolished; Islam was no longer taught in schools; the Christian calendar was officially adopted; polygamy was prohibited by law; the script in which Turkish is written was changed from Arabic to Latin; and European codes relating to civil, criminal, contract, and commerce law were adopted. Around the same time, a few voices were heard in Egypt calling for separation of state and religion. But the movement was not as strong as in Turkey, and the results were not as significant.

Tunisia, under the 30-year presidency of Habib Bourguiba (1957–1987), became one of the most secularized Arab countries of its time. Friday became a work day; polygamy and the veiling of women became illegal; women were allowed to vote; the Ramadan fast was officially discouraged; night clubs, movie houses, and the consumption of alcohol were all permitted.

M. Jamil Hanifi, a dissenting Muslim voice, protests that "In Muslim systems, motivation is frozen... the value system and the structure of Islam must change... to a secular type."[10]

A further area of significance in today's Islam is the role of women. In many Islamic societies women are assuming roles that are not prescribed for them in the Qur'an or the Hadith. Women hold jobs and work next to men in many areas of the Muslim world. They drive their own cars in Amman and Ankara. They ride motorcycles in Casablanca and Cairo. They direct the traffic in Tunis and Tangiers. They smoke publicly in Ibadan and Istanbul. They walk out on the street without veiling themselves in Baghdad and Bandung. They are doctors and lawyers, engineers and architects. They are university professors and cabinet ministers. Just a few years ago, who would have ever thought that Muslim women would become Prime Ministers or presidents in one Muslim country after the other, as has been the case in Pakistan, Bangladesh, Turkey and Indonesia? These are the first Muslim women to rule in modern history.

Liberalization

Those who advocate liberalization are willing to reinterpret hard-line beliefs and adjust traditional practices to the spirit of the age. Many Muslims who have been educated in the West belong to this category. They have been exposed to analytical and critical methods of investigation and study. Surprisingly, the areas they are willing to adjust would include the Qur'an, Muhammad, the Hadith, and traditional Muslim practices.

1. *The Qur'an.* Viewpoints on the translation, the content and the criticism of the Qur'an are changing.

In the past, Islam did not endeavor to offer any understandable version of the Qur'an to people who did not speak Arabic. That is because translating the Arabic Qur'an into other languages was forbidden. Now, the situation has changed. Today we see scores of translations of the Qur'an into several languages. It is true that most of them use the precautionary titles of "Interpretation" or "The Meaning" of the Qur'an rather than "Translation" of the Qur'an or simply "The Qur'an."

What does this mean? It may indicate a weakening of the staunch belief that Arabic, and only Arabic, is the vehicle of divine revelation. This conviction has been supported by the fact that Muhammad was an Arab, that the Qur'an is in Arabic, and by the notion that Arabic is the language spoken in paradise. Does this mean that Muslims on the road to liberalization are willing to move away from such long-held views? We do not know yet, but time will tell.

This new willingness to translate the Qur'an into other languages has brought some benefits to the ummah. These translations are being used as tools to spread the teachings of Islam and help convert non-Muslims. Some years ago a parallel Arabic/English copy of the Qur'an was published, and millions of copies were distributed to English-speaking people as a gift from the King of Saudi Arabia. One printing press in the city of Medina produces ten million copies of the Qur'an in fourteen languages every year.[11]

The Muslim world is also facing new challenges regarding the text of the Qur'an. In the early twentieth century, Dr. Taha Hussein, a renowned Egyptian author, university professor and government minister, encouraged his students to criticize the Qur'an as a literary work. He once stated that he too could author a Qur'an. In his book, Pre-Islamic Poetry, he suggests that the qur'anic persons of Abraham and Ishmael never existed and that Ishmael's move to Mecca was a kind of scam invented by early Muslims to make the Arabs and Jews look like they are related![12]

Former President Bourguiba of Tunisia also engaged in criticism of the Muslim holy book. In one of his speeches he stated that the Qur'an contained contradictions and statements contrary to reason.[13]

Some decades ago, Egyptian intellectual Dr M. A. Khalaf-Allah dared to question the accuracy of the qur'anic narrative. He suggested that the stories in the Qur'an were only for the purpose of exhortation, not for providing historical information. His intent was to defend the Qur'an against non-Muslims who questioned its divine source on the grounds of historical inaccuracies. However, Muslim religious leaders took Khalaf-Allah's statements as a daring attack on the Qur'an. He was branded as a traitor, an ignoramus, and a liar.[14] Consequently, Khalaf-Allah lost his position as a university professor.

Another Muslim author, N. A. Muhei-Dinoff, claimed that several writers had composed the Qur'an after the death of Muhammad.

In his view, this was the reason for the great number of contradictions in it. Muhei-Dinoff's writings were distributed widely in Muslim Somalia.[15]

Some modern Muslim interpreters hold that Muhammad's Night Journey was only a vision or a dream. This certainly contradicts the Islamic tradition and folk religion belief that Muhammad's voyage and bodily ascension to heaven were real, not a mere vision.

In the summer of 1994, tens of thousands of fundamentalists marched in the streets of Bangladeshi cities, demanding that their fellow Muslim compatriot, Taslima Nasrin, be hanged. Nasrin, a feminist author, had said that "the Qur'an should be thoroughly revised" and "Islam treats women like slaves."[16]

In the midst of Algeria's struggle between fundamentalists and non-fundamentalists where bloodshed became almost commonplace, a doctor in Algiers made this courageous statement: "By teaching children qur'anic verses from the age of six, we have created a mental structure with which we can't reason."[17]

In recent years hundreds of manuscripts of a Hijazi Qur'an were found in a mosque in San'a, Yemen. According to experts, these manuscripts are the oldest existing text of the Qur'an. Yet this text differs substantially from the Qur'an we know which has been the standard edition for generations.[18]

In 2000 Christoph Luxenberg, an expert on qur'anic manuscripts, published a book in German about the text of the Qur'an. The author uses a pseudonym to protect himself from Islamic rage. In his work he discredits some of the most important pillars of the Qur'an. He claims that the original language of the Muslim holy book was not Arabic and that there were mistranslations and mistakes in transcribing some of the material. He also asserts that the Qur'an, as we know it, has wrongly promised the faithful beautiful virgins in paradise, since the correct translation of the original word is "white raisins"—not "virgins!"[19]

Professor Andrew Rippin of the University of Victoria has this to say regarding the ancient qur'anic manuscripts recently discovered in Yemen:

The impact of the Yemeni manuscripts is still to be felt. Their variant readings and verse orders are all very significant. Everybody agrees on that. These manuscripts say that the early history of the qur'anic texts is much more of an open question than many have suspected: the text was less stable, and therefore had less authority, than has always been claimed.[20]

Though a harsh critic of biblical Christianity, Robert M. Price, says that the discovery of these manuscripts

means that all we thought we knew of the Prophet Muhammad is really a mass of fictive legal precedents meant to anchor this or that Islamic practice once Muhammad had been recast as an Arab Moses. And the question of the origin of the Qur'an is no longer "from Allah?" or "from Muhammad?" but rather "from Muhammad?" or "from countless unnamed Hagarene jurists?"... And it becomes equally evident that the line between the Qur'an and the hadith must be erased, for both alike are now seen to be repositories of sayings fictively attributed to the Prophet and transmitted by word of mouth before being codified in canonical written form.[21]

True, we do not know yet the full implications of such discoveries and suppositions. But I am certain that if they prove to be true, Islam will not continue to be the same. Of course, its conservative defenders will fight to discredit such ideas and attempt to liquidate their proponents.

2. *Muhammad.* Along with the Qur'an, some beliefs about the Prophet have also been shaken and adjusted. Colonel Kadafi of Libya in one of his speeches said:

The prophet had only the role of bringing us the Qur'an... Therefore the Qur'an rule is what we are bound to... but as for Muhammad's hadiths, these were his personal sayings and ideas, and we are under no obligation to follow them... Muhammad was not a genius.[22]

Some Muslim scholars today claim that Muhammad's own pure soul and imagination were the source of the Qur'an. This is unacceptable to traditional Islam which claims that God is the source of the Qur'an, not the Prophet. Other Muslim scholars say that Muhammad was merely an example for Muslims. Such an assertion is unacceptable to Muslim orthodoxy which maintains that Muhammad occupies the exalted place of final Prophet and recipient of God's final revelation to man.

3. *The Hadith*. From various liberal Islamic quarters today, Muslims hear a call to dismiss the Hadith and stick only to the Qur'an. While such ideas may sound reactionary or even fundamentalist, the opposite is true. If adopted, they would lead to unimaginable consequences. One illustration will explain what I mean. Muslim prayer, one of the five pillars of Islam, is, in its format, content, and details, drawn from the Hadith, not the Qur'an. So, Muslim conservatives see any proposal to dismiss the Hadith as a very serious attack on Islam itself.

4. *Traditional Muslim Practices*. In recent years, some traditional practices and systems that have been observed and exercised by Muslims for many generations have become the target of liberal criticism.

An example of one such target is the fast of Ramadan. World conditions are not the same as when Islam began. Muslims now live in places all over the globe. How can a Muslim keep the Ramadan fast from sunrise to sunset, say in the Arctic Circle? That is, how can he or she keep the fast according to the letter of the rite itself? Islam demands abstention from food, drink and other pleasures during Ramadan from the time of day when a person can distinguish a white thread from a black one until the time when he cannot distinguish these (that is, from dawn to sunset). And in the Arctic Circle, in the summer the sun never sets and in the winter the sun never rises.

Ramadan is under attack for other reasons as well. Habib Bourguiba, former President of Tunisia, encouraged his country of 100% Muslims not to fast Ramadan for economic reasons. In an attempt to reinforce that idea, he invited some friends for a noon meal during Ramadan. When some people wondered why their President would do such a thing, he answered that Muhammad himself invited his friends to eat and drink during Ramadan![23]

At the University I attended in a Muslim country, one of my Muslim professors was head of the Medical School's Department of Physiology. During Ramadan, he had the habit of asking a staff member to bring him a cup of coffee and a glass of water during the daytime lecture. Since the majority of the students and all of his staff were Muslims, it seemed to me that he was challenging the traditional practices of his Muslim society.

Other Muslim practices are being questioned. Qasem Amin (1863–1908) strongly advocated the emancipation of women, proclaimed their right to education, jobs, and a voice in politics, was also an unusual advocate of freedom of expression. He said:

Real freedom consists in the individual's being able to express any opinion, preach any creed, to propagate any doctrine… In a truly free country no one should be afraid to renounce his fatherland, to repudiate belief in God and his prophets, or to impugn the laws and customs of his people.[24]

The head of a department at a North African university expressed the following opinion: "If our women want to have any hope, they have to get away from Islam."[25]

A few years ago in a hotel cafeteria in a European city, I heard a man speaking Arabic to his two little children. I introduced myself to him. After we shook hands, I noticed that he was having an alcoholic drink. Although I did not make any comments about that, he became visibly disturbed and immediately started to apologize for drinking. His excuse was: "It is the only chance I have. I drink only when I am away from home. You know I cannot drink in my town in Kuwait."

We have already referred to Omar Khayyam, the Persian Muslim scholar, poet and mathematician who lived in the eleventh century. His rebellion against some of the strongly held Muslim moral principles was legendary! One of his verses serves to illustrate that rebellion:

I have one hand on a wine cup,
And the other on a Qur'an.
One time I am reprobate,
Another time I am innocent.
I live, and in this world,
I have no principle.

I am neither a wholesome Muslim,
Nor a straightforward infidel![26]

Although beheading is a means of punishment for some crimes in
Saudi Arabia, a Saudi royal princess courageously speaks out against
its use in her society: "I have always found the idea of beheadings utterly horrifying! Actually, many people find our entire Muslim system
of justice primitive and shocking."[27]

It is true that many Muslim thinkers today lament the anti-pro-
gressive attitudes that are part of Islam. One Muslim writer expresses
it this way:

Man under such a system is a quantity without quality. His life
is planned in advance for him politically, and philosophically. He
does one thing because he is ordered to do it and abstains from
another because he is warned not to do it. So his life is between
two poles, dos and don'ts![28]

Salman Masalha, an Arab intellectual and poet from Israel, courageously states in an interview:

There's something in the Islamic perception that drives you crazy,
and that is the looking only backwards, not to the future. If the gold-
en age was in the past, your entire vision is rearwards. This causes
deterioration. In our mentality as Arabs, there is a poisonous formula
that can lead to nothing good at all. There is a need for change in
this programming. There is a disk in the Arab mind that must be
replaced with another disk, and only this way can change come.[29]

Irshad Manji is a Muslim author whose book, *The Trouble with
Islam*, is in print in several languages. On her web site she lists three
areas that she would like to straighten out in Islam. They are:

1. The inferior treatment of women in Islam

2. The Jew-bashing that so many Muslims persistently engage in

3. The continuing scourge of slavery in countries ruled by Islamic
regimes.[30]

Egyptian author Dr. Nawal Sa'dawi considers polygamy to be
immoral![31]

And the list goes on. Practices that are integral to Islam are being
challenged and re-evaluated by one Muslim party or another.

Material prosperity

Many people today have more and want more—more money, more possessions and more luxuries. Goods and gadgets invented in the West, attractively displayed in shops and presented in television commercials, are invading the markets in Muslim countries. Material prosperity promises comfort and speaks of success, power and self-confidence, all of which are very attractive to any group, including Muslims.

The pursuit of prosperity and material possessions often demands certain disciplines, sacrifices and liberties such as higher education, longer work hours, freedom of expression, and liberal thinking—features not always widespread in many Muslim societies today. Also the outward signs of prosperity and high living standards include luxury, gold, silk, delicacies, alcohol—all of which the Qur'an forbids. Consequently there are strong outcries from conservatives against material prosperity.

Syncretism

We have already discussed syncretism in folk Islam, the blending of animistic beliefs and practices with the Islamic system. Now let us look at the synthesis that is taking place between Islam and other social and philosophical worldviews. Islam displays an ability to absorb certain ideologies and practices that are foreign to it, all the while continuing to call itself Islam. Some Muslims reason that such assimilation affects only the outer form and not the heart of Islam. They claim that the spirit of Islam persists without alteration, and so is by no means endangered.

> Islam assimilates and its spirit will persist while its form may alter. If the imams were free to use their judgment and boldly discard 500,000 [hadiths] and retain only 8,000... we must reserve for ourselves a similar liberty of action.[32]

Here are a few instances where the Islamic system has blended with other worldviews. In the sixteenth century, the Muslim Emperor Akbar of India built a house of worship and

> forced orthodox Muslim preachers to share their pulpits with Zoroastrians, Hindus, Jains, Buddhists and even Jesuits, many of

whom were more than willing to excoriate the Prophet... Muslim conservatives accused the Emperor of developing his own religion... but Abul Fazl [his Muslim historian, praised that act] for not losing what is good in one religion while gaining whatever is better in another.[33]

In China during the Manchu Dynasty, Muslims, though staunchly monotheistic, did not mind putting in their mosques paintings of the Emperor with the inscription: Long live the Eternal Emperor![34]

When Communism was in control in the central Asian republics of the former Soviet Union, Somalia, Afghanistan, and South Yemen, a similar synthesis took place. For purposes of survival, both Islam and communism managed to come together and create a kind of "patch-up work" where there was no open disagreement between the two opposing ideologies. Thus Marxist-Leninist philosophy coexisted with qur'anic and Islamic principles!

This seeming fusion, however, was not to last. After the Taliban take-over in Afghanistan, the pendulum swung to the other extreme in that country, and fundamentalist Islam was reimposed through ruthless violence. When North and South Yemen were reunified into one country, fundamentalist Islam began gaining ground in that land. And at this writing, after years of chaos and fighting among warlords in Somalia, it seems that a fundamentalist regime is trying to take control of that nation.

Another kind of syncretism is that of Islam with some forms of Christianity. Of great interest to me are the Isawas of Nigeria, who have clearly adopted Christian ideas and added them to their Islam. They emphasize the greatness of Jesus (*Isa*, hence their name) and His second coming. Yet, in recent years, that group has experienced persecution and murder and only a small number of them have survived.

On the road of synthesis, is it possible that somewhere, sometime, Islam will reject its own creed and pillars of belief and assimilate a sizeable body of evangelical biblical doctrine? I am talking here about evangelical biblical convictions, unlike the document I received a few years ago that contained a proposal from a "Christian" missionary. He wanted to start a movement where Muslims could continue to say the creed in its two parts (asserting that Muhammad is God's apostle), practice their Islamic rites, hold the Islamic view of the Qur'an and so forth, and be viewed as practicing a form of Christianity!

Democracy

There is a lot of talk today about democracy and Islam. Various media venues discuss the pros and cons of democratization in Muslim societies. Books have been written about the subject. Perhaps we have the idea that some Muslim governments will not be able to stand against the worldwide march of democracy. Yet, the idea of democracy is considered foreign to conservative Islam. A. A. Mawdudi, one of the most influential Muslim fundamentalists of the twentieth century, says:

> In Western democracy, if a particular piece of legislation is desired by the masses, howsoever ill-conceived it may be from a religious and moral viewpoint, steps have to be taken to place it on the statute book; if the people dislike any law and demand its abrogation, howsoever just and rightful it may be, it has to be expunged forthwith. This is not the case in Islam. On this count, Islam has no trace of Western democracy. Islam... repudiates the philosophy of popular sovereignty and rears its polity on the foundations of the sovereignty of God and the vice-regency of man.[35]

The same writer says:

> God is the real law-giver and absolute legislator. The believers cannot resort to totally independent legislation nor can they modify any law which God has laid down, even if the desire to effect such legislation or change in Divine Law is unanimous... The Islamic state seeks to mould every aspect of life and activity in consonance with its moral norms and program of social reform. In such a state no one can regard any field of his affairs as personal and private. Considered from this aspect the Islamic state bears a kind of resemblance to the Fascist and communist states.[36]

Fundamentalist Muslim Hassan al-Turabi is a Sudanese graduate of the Sorbonne in Paris. He states that "The majority/minority pattern in politics is not an ideal one in Islam."[37] He is right. The ideal Islamic state cannot be a democracy. The Qur'an and Hadith are considered documents of rules and laws in addition to religious precepts. Yet, there is no mention in either nor is there precedent in Islamic history of representative democracy, multiparty systems, or majority/minority concepts—the essentials of democracy. Some suggest that an advisory council (*majles shura*) could be formed. However, the same people go on to explain that the ruler would not be bound to this council's advice. Fundamentalist Muslims denounced Iraqi elections in 2005 and 2006 and claimed that such elections are un-Islamic because democracy means the people, not God, are in charge of the country.

In Malaysia Prime Minister Dr. Mahathir Muhammad remained in office for twenty years. In Egypt, since the 1952 revolution, the presidency has become an office to be grabbed and occupied for life. In Tunisia, since its independence in 1956, there have been only two Presidents. It looks like the office of the President of Syria is a family inheritance. And the list goes on. Looking at the situation in these Muslim countries and many others like them one cannot avoid noticing their weak democratic institutions, pathetic electoral systems, and "puppet" parliaments, judiciary, and media!

There are, however, many voices for democracy. Some even come from the quarters of fundamentalist Islam! This is not surprising. They cherish democracy until they are in power, and once that dream comes true, they apply the Islamic Shari'a. In other words, when a Muslim country becomes a real democracy, at that very instant its democracy is doomed! Why? Because Islam will use the democratic process to take over the government. Then, because the rulers are of necessity good Muslims, applying the Shari'a will be their duty. And the Shari'a objects to and annuls democratic institutions!

This is not conjecture; it is a historical truth. In every situation where fundamentalists demanded and received democracy, that was the end of the democratic road. One needs only to look at Iran and Sudan to see that.

Yet, there are some Muslims who honestly believe in the rule of law and in democracy. They cherish the experience of genuinely elected governments. For now, this is only a dream.

Rejection of Religion

In recent decades, many Muslims have experienced tremendous confusion and bitter disappointments with their religious symbols, institutions, and leaders.

Challenged by the pressures on Islam, some disappointed Muslims have responded by rejecting their religion completely. This option seems attractive because it provides the Muslims in question with a scapegoat to blame for their shattered hopes and aspirations. What causes them to go in this direction? Disappointment with Islam!

The Iranian Revolution serves as a vivid example. Many Iranians under the harsh rule of the Shah were looking forward to the Islamic revolution to rid them of the king's oppression and tyranny. They were hoping for a breath of fresh air. Millions of them rallied behind the revolution. They took to the streets in demonstrations, defying the Shah and his forces. The Shah fell, the Muslim religious leaders took over, and the Islamic republic was established amid jubilation and joyous manifestations of happy crowds.

But soon afterwards, Iran went through a period of near anarchy. There was a rampage of killing; and the evils done by the agents of the Shah were dwarfed by the crimes of the agents of Khomeini. Many Iranians were shocked and became discouraged and disappointed with Islam. They were ashamed to be called Muslim. Some claimed they should never have been Muslim anyway and thought of adopting Zoroastrianism, Iran's pre-Islamic religion. Consequently, today many Iranians readily admit that the Islamic revolution they had put their hopes in actually turned into a monster.

The suppressive machine of the Islamic Revolution in Iran was made to protect the "divine political system." That machine outdid the Shah's oppression in severity, torture and mass murder... Many people now stand against Islam itself. Everywhere signs indicate that religious schools are drawing fewer students [than before] and parents are choosing for their children pre-Islamic Persian names![38]

Some years ago, an Iranian Muslim lady told my wife and me that she believed that Islam was a false religion that was started by a false prophet. In all my experience with Muslims, only a few times have I heard such comments from a Muslim.

Jan Goodwin tells this story of her visit to Khomeini's tomb:

A young woman nearby who had only her eyes uncovered, and who had apparently overheard me talking English to Sima, leaned over shyly to ask me in stumbling English where I was from and why I had come today. "I am here only because our school bused us here. It was required," she told me. "The government pays for buses to bring people from the schools, colleges, factories. They even go to the villages. The factory workers get double salary to make sure they come." Dropping her voice, she added, "Otherwise no one would be here...well, many fewer than today."

Not sure if she had convinced me, she added, still whispering, "Do you think I dress like this at home? No, of course, I don't." And to prove it she flashed open her chador to show me her jeans and lavender T-shirt underneath. "I hate it, hate all this. I am sixteen, this is my time, my youth, I should be having fun. Instead, I am here, dressed like a peasant grandmother, to mourn a dead old man who hated beauty, hated happiness. If God meant us to dress black, if He meant us to have no color in our lives, why did He give us flowers? That's what I would like to have asked that dead Imam," she said, jerking her head in the direction of the shrine.[39]

The following conversation took place between a Saudi businessman and his Egyptian partner, who later reported it to me in an Islamic capital. I will refer to the Saudi by the letter S and to the Egyptian by E.

S: Do you know that one of the reasons I go to Switzerland for vacations is to be away from the nagging call to prayer?

E: You're really opening your heart to me by making such a statement. Does the call to prayer bother you that much?

S: I just do not understand how we Muslims want to live like people did so far back in history! Centuries ago when they initiated the call to prayer there were no alarm clocks to wake them up. No watches, no radios and no other means to tell them to get up! Why don't they use their alarms to wake them up early in the morning to do their prayers?

E: I certainly agree with you. How bothersome is that to you?

S: I put in a hard day of work. I take good care of my family. So when I go to sleep I want to sleep well without being disturbed at dawn by a call to prayer that I am not going to respond to. It makes it hard for me to work efficiently that day. Our neighborhood has several mosques, and at dawn I wake up to the sound of competing calls to prayer coming from all those mosques.

E: Have you thought of calling the police to stop them from making that noise?

S: Are you kidding! If I did, the police would arrest me rather than the people who are making the noise!

In the Arabic novel *Heart of the Night* by a Nobel laureate Muslim author, a character named Ja'afar says about Huda: "She has such a strong faith that she has never bothered about prayer or fasting."[40] This statement seems to imply that if your faith is strong enough, you don't have to go to the trouble of keeping the pillars of the Muslim faith!

BACKLASH AGAINST WORLD CHANGE—RETURN TO "TRUE" ISLAM

Such mushrooming changes certainly produce hostile reactions and repercussions. Let us look at some of those reactions.

Fundamentalism

At one time, societies far from each other had little contact and so they had little impact on each other. No more! The world has become one connected, computerized, global village. Now influence travels thousands of miles in a matter of seconds. In the past, people felt culturally secure in their own societies. No intruder would dare come and impose new traits upon them or change their dearly held traditions.

As a matter of fact most people did not know much of what was going on in other parts of the world. Now, they do know. They no longer live in isolation. What happens in one part of the world appears on the television screen in homes half way round the world. For Muslims, a lot of what they hear or see on radio, television, the internet and in the marketplace is perceived as a malicious threat to the fabric of their society, the dignity of their culture and the solidarity of their religion.

How do they protect their culture and their religion? For many, the rise of fundamentalism is the answer. It is a protective mechanism against the possible dissolution of their traditions and legacies.

Fundamentalism is the insistence on strict and literal adherence to the early principles and practices of Islam. It decrees the rigorous application of the Qur'an and Hadith. Fundamentalists believe that Islamic ideology will solve all human problems: social, racial, economic, and otherwise. "Islam is the solution" is one of their maxims.

Fundamentalists take aim at all other groups, Muslim and non-Muslims, and accuse them of being corrupt. The world should be rid of such groups, they say. The two basic goals of Islamic fundamentalism are: a) to impose rigorous Islamic ideas and practices on people inside the House of Islam; and b) to impose Islam, by all means possible, on people in the House of War.

According to Egypt's former Superior Court Chief Justice:

Islamic fundamentalism that follows political lines works toward making religion into politics, perverting the Shari'a into a party, and pushing Islam into war... It looks to the past not to the future... and it freezes its position... it is an enemy of all progress; it refuses to move.[41]

Fundamentalist Muslims refuse to be called by that name. They say they are just Muslims, true Muslims. They consider themselves to be true and faithful to their religion and claim other Muslims have strayed away from the teachings of the Qur'an and from following the example of Muhammad. I do agree that they are the ones who live closest to the teachings of the Qur'an and the Hadith.

Here is a brief idea about their beliefs, practices and goals:

1. They must be in control of government at any price. They work hard to remove all infidels (non-Muslims) from authority.

2. In order to take over a country, they work to penetrate the army, various government departments and agencies, the media, profes-

sional groups, labor unions, financial and banking establishments and schools and universities.

3. That which is necessary allows for what is illegal, (or, if I am in dire need of something, I can use unlawful means to get it.)[42]

4. Terrorism, violence, liquidation of the enemy and destruction of his property are all acceptable and even preferred means to reach one's goal, settle scores with infidels and be in control of government.

5. Parliamentary structures are an invention of infidels. Parliaments are anti-Islamic because they issue civil laws while there should be no law other than the Islamic Law. So, non-Islamic laws are against Islam and antagonistic to God.

6. Voting and elections are unacceptable heresies introduced by Christians. Likewise, the notion of having multiple political parties is a demonic invention. Majority rule is not acceptable unless that majority is fundamentalist Muslim.

7. God is on the side of fundamentalists and they are on God's side. All others are on Satan's side.

When one considers these points, it becomes clear that the major difference between fundamentalists and other average Muslims is that fundamentalists are closer to the Qur'an![43]

Islamic fundamentalism makes itself visible through the increase and intensification of religious observances. People wear traditional Muslim clothes. The mosque is taken out to the streets, and the faithful spread mats to pray out in the open. More emphasis is placed on the Ramadan fast, and activists struggle to impose the Shari'a as the law of the land.

Hussein A. Amin, Egyptian diplomat and author, analyzes the reasons fundamentalist men revert to wearing Muslim long robes (*gallabiyya* or *jalabah*), growing beards, and sitting on the floor to eat. He cites two factors: their inability to carve out a place for themselves in today's mainline society; and Islam's inability to connect with the modern age or to build psychological bridges with non-Muslim societies that are more resilient and more liberal. Hence, "we have rebellion against modernization and sickly venting of feelings of sterility and defeatism."[44]

In July 1993 Dr. Nasser Abu Ziad, a university professor in Cairo, was stamped a heretic by fundamentalists because of his writings concerning reinterpretation of the Qur'an. He had called for an allegorical reading of the Muslim holy book.

Fundamentalists demanded that his marriage be annulled. They reasoned that since his wife was a Muslim and his writings contained anti-Muslim interpretation, she should not be married to him! The case was taken to the Islamic University of al-Azhar for a decision. The couple appeared on television saying they loved each other and that no one had the power to dissolve their marriage. They ultimately fled to the Netherlands.[45]

Violence

What causes some Muslims to kill and commit incredible atrocities in the name of religion? First, it is part of the duty of jihad. But there are other reasons as well, such as unemployment, poverty, social backwardness, repressive governments, the defeat of Arabs and Muslims in various wars, the existence of Israel, lack of people's participation in the kinds of success and achievements pictured on television and communicated on cell phones and computer screens—just to name a few.

Many Muslims think that if they fall behind other nations in the race for prosperity and development or if they are defeated by infidels, especially by America and Israel, it must be because God is punishing them. They reason that they no longer closely adhere to the Qur'an and the sunna and that they have failed to adopt the Shari'a as the law of their land. So, if God is punishing them, what can they do to escape His punishment? Their solution is to get closer to the teachings of the Qur'an and the Hadith.[46]

In reality this translates into fundamentalism and its by-products such as a narrow worldview, fanaticism and violence. Fundamentalist Muslims think it is their duty to correct society's wrongs and faults from the top down and impose strict codes of belief and practice on all. They try to apply the Shari'a law and use force to impose Islam on non-Muslims or collect religion taxes from them. If non-Muslims convert to Islam they become exempt from paying religion taxes.

When Muslims see their plans for an Islamic state stymied and their hopes dashed and defeated by their own institutions as well as by other factors, they turn to terrorism. Iranian dissident Amir al-Taheri makes this observation:

> Frustrations caused by the inability to build an Islamic state sometimes lead to what is called by some "Islamic Terrorism" or "Holy Terrorism."[47]

Islamic terrorism is an integral accompaniment to Muslim fundamentalism, and it has strong sanctions within Islam. Al-Taheri says:

> Although Muslim fundamentalists have dogmatic differences pertaining to essential matters, all their movements make us believe that they generally agree that "liquidating" others is part of their holy war."[48]

In reality the Islamic system has its foundations in violence as encouraged by both the Qur'an and Hadith. Phil Parshall comments:

> My friend, Phil Skotte... wrote an incisive article supporting his thesis that violence is in the DNA of Islam as a religion. Regretfully, I have to agree. Look at its inception—violence; its Scriptures—violence; its spread—violence.[49]

Another factor that spawns terrorism is the belief that when people are killed while fighting for Islam, they are transported directly to paradise. Their many rewards will include food, drink, luxury, comfort and virgins. We referred earlier to the discovery of ancient qur'anic manuscripts which, scientists tell us, state that the faithful will get raisins rather than beautiful virgins. That may seem comical, but one internet article says, "If this doesn't stop Islamist terrorism, nothing will."[50]

Also, fundamentalists who choose the terrorist route have a superiority complex. They are very conscious of being Muslims. They are extremely proud of their identity. They believe that Islam is the only religion that has a right to exist. They strive to take over whatever stands in their way—civil authorities, religious establishments, political powers, or military forces. For decades the Jama'at (Arabic for "groups") and various other Muslim fighters have used terrorism to achieve their political and religious goals. But by far the most ruthless and deadly of Islamic terrorists is al-Qaeda.

The sweeping victories of Arab troops in the early history of Islam have planted an irreversible and unbendable sense of triumphalism in the minds, emotions, and wills of Muslim peoples. One sees the result in their attitude today. When they decide to do something, they do it, no matter what means they have to use or what the outcome may be. Allah has favored them and made them superior to all others, so how can they accept to be the underdog? That would be inconceivable!

What manifestations does Islamic terrorism take? Multiple! Liquidating the "enemies of Islam" is a very common tactic. Mark Gabriel reports a harrowing story that reveals the real face of Islamic fundamentalism. In January 2000 Islamists attacked a village in southern Egypt.

> Twenty-one men, women and children were set on fire with torches, and burned to death... Their bodies were split open vertically from the throat down so their attackers could watch their organs pulsate; others were set on fire while still alive. The perpetrators cut opposite arms and legs off to send back to their village to spread fear.[51]

Sadly, this is not an extreme or isolated case of violence. History is replete with such cruel incidents from the time of Muhammad up to the present.

Even rulers do not escape the death sentence passed on them by fundamentalists. Two of the Rightly Guided Caliphs were slaughtered by followers of Islam who thought that those rulers were not good enough Muslims. President Anwar Sadat of Egypt was assassinated by fundamentalist Muslims because he was considered "a blemish on the face of Islam!"

From the time of the first caliphs until Sadat, a considerable number of Muslim rulers were killed under the same pretext. Of course such assassinations are conspicuous and glaring acts in defiance of authority. But people of all classes and from all walks of life can find themselves facing the sharp sword of Islamic terrorism.

Hijacking is another tactic of fundamentalist Muslim menace and liquidation. In recent times, Islamic terrorists have hijacked airplanes, buses and even a cruise ship at gunpoint. Their goals can be political and/or religious and sometimes include freedom for imprisoned colleagues. They have used this brutal and scary method to negotiate with their enemies and draw attention to themselves and their cause. In the process, they have subjected innocent people to extortion and threatened their very lives.

Another terrorist act is mass killing, which inevitably includes innocent victims. September 11, 2001 has gone down as a horrendous day in American history. A group of fundamentalist Muslims hijacked four airplanes inside the United States and crashed them into the two towers of the World Trade Center and the Pentagon. Three thousand innocent men, women and children died as a result.

What makes a suicide terrorist? Suicide terrorists are those who kill themselves in order to kill others and destroy their properties. Far from being the "scum" of society, as some might imagine, suicide terrorists are often highly educated and come from well-to-do families. They are driven by the strong conviction that their cause is right, be it religious or political. When they cannot reach a desired goal through negotiations, they choose to bring destruction on themselves and others.

The following are samples of news headlines about Islamic terrorism:
• Suicide Bombers Destroy the Barracks of the U.S. and French Military in Lebanon, Killing 241 Americans and 58 French.
• A Suicide Bomber Blows Himself Up in Jerusalem, Killing 20 People.
• A Suicide Car Bomb Kills at Least 17 and Injures 122 at an Upscale Compound for Foreign Workers in Western Riyadh, Saudi Arabia.
• A Woman Suicide Bomber Kills Herself and 10 Others.
• Second- and Third-Generation Palestinian Americans Cheering Suicide Bombers!

Although the tool of suicide terrorism has been used throughout history and by various groups, in recent years it has reached a colossal scale. When a battle is declared a jihad, invariably people are willing to go to that war to die, thus securing for themselves a place in heaven. One Muslim leader stated that "the weapon of martyrdom... is easy and costs us only our lives... Human bombs cannot be defeated, not even by nuclear bombs."[52]

Terrorist acts are revolting. Nevertheless, we must see Muslims as very needy people. They need Christ. They, as any other people away from the expression of God's love at Calvary, have no true peace of mind, joy, or fulfillment. They are driven by sets of strict rules and laws that are based on dos and don'ts. Only God's grace can bring them to the Kingdom of Christ to receive forgiveness, freedom and life. It is my strong conviction that, to achieve that goal, we need to love Muslims deeply and then open our mouth at every possible occasion to share Christ with them.[53]

The Islamic State

Muslim fundamentalists advocate the formation of an "Islamic state." They are convinced that an Islamic state is a fully legitimate, indeed necessary, fulfillment of Islam. Traditionally, the ummah believes that there should be no separation or even distinction between state and religion (such as the West has).

In Medina, Muhammad gathered to himself all known branches of government and authority. He was the arbitrator and the statesman, the religious leader and the ruler, the general and the commander-in-chief, the legislator and the judge. Although the four caliphs who followed him tried to claim the same authority for themselves, none was able to maintain the overarching and massive powers that Muhammad had.

Fundamentalists resort to the writings of people such as Ibn Taimiya, Sayyed Qutb, and Al-Mawdudi as a charter for the Islamic state. Ahmad ibn Taimiya, a Muslim fundamentalist theologian, taught that if religion is separated from power, the state will be plagued with confusion and disorder. His view was that innovations are unacceptable. He stressed that the ummah should return to the principles and practices of the forefathers of Islam (the salaf).

American educated Sayyed Qutb states that to live as Muslims, people need to be in an environment that is totally Muslim and controlled by Islam. Otherwise, they will be abused by pagans.[54] He also asserts that only Islam can rid humanity of its misery and save it from the "barbarism of the industrial civilization." Only those who belong to Islam are capable of such a great leap![55]

A. A. Mawdudi, important proponent of the Islamic state, tells Muslims to do what Muhammad did. When their community is small, weak, and unable to control its affairs, as Muhammad's was in Mecca, they should temporarily submit to those in power in order to prepare themselves for the next move. Then, when their community has more members and is stronger, as Muhammad's was in Medina, they should come out of isolation to do jihad, overthrow their oppressors, and take charge of their own destiny. Ultimately, the Islamic state is to be God's vice-regency on earth.

Nevertheless, some Muslims consider the concept of an Islamic state unwarranted and alien, without any basis in either the Qur'an or the Hadith. Others maintain that the real Islamic state ceased to exist after the first four caliphs. As proof they point out that after those first "Rightly Guided Caliphs," most of the rulers were corrupt; the ummah was allowed to adopt secular laws and non-Muslim practices; and the vast expansion of the ummah made it impossible to administer such a large empire from one center of power.

Is an Islamic state a realistic option for Muslims today? To answer this question, let us look briefly at some of the characteristics of such a state.

1. The government is Islamic, not secular.

2. There are no national or racial distinctions. All citizens have one race and nationality, Muslim.

3. The Shari'a is the law of the land. No further legislation is needed and therefore no legislative body exists.

Hassan al-Turabi, the Sudanese fundamentalist leader, described himself as "directly involved in a political process that seeks to establish an Islamic state." He points out that the ancient caliphate somehow went astray:

> The Caliphate began as an elected consultative institution. Later, it degenerated into a hereditary or usurpatory, authoritarian government. This pseudo-Caliphate was universally condemned by jurists...[56]

The twentieth century has presented us with an array of slogans and themes used by Islamic communities. Terms such as self-rule, independence, democracy, socialism, popular rule, parliament, *Jamahiriyyah* (state of the masses), and so forth have emerged. Such concepts are completely foreign to the ideals of the Islamic state as it existed under Muhammad and his first four successors.

Hence, it appears that the ideologies of the Islamic state are beyond any practical reach today. Consider the following:

1. Not even Saudi Arabia has legislative codes that precisely match the Shari'a.

2. No explicit or implicit provision exists in either the Qur'an or the sunna about how Muslims are to choose their ruler. Open strife and power struggle marked the early history of the ummah. As we mentioned before, all the Rightly Guided Caliphs were assassinated in office, and many of the caliphs who followed them met the same fate.

3. Political opportunities for modern Islamic women are usually nonexistent. Women played an important role in the political life of early Islam. Today, there is no place for women in public life in Saudi Arabia or Libya, two countries that claim closest resemblance to an ideal Islamic state.

4. Islam is given mere lip service in several Muslim countries. The head of state and the government officials in liberal Islamic countries may talk about Islam, but in fact the religious structures are separate from politics. This Western style phenomenon of separation of religion and state is unknown to the ideology of the Islamic state.

RELIGIOUS STAGNATION—MAINTAINING THE STATUS QUO

Another route that some members of the ummah take today is what I call religious stagnation. An example would be the way a group of conservative Muslims react to the changes happening in their world. They become wary of any kind of change, whether good or bad. They see any transformation as unwarranted departure from the known traditional ways. At the same time they do not want to get involved in any religious, social, or political activism. In other words the people in question, tenaciously aligned with the status quo, are at a standstill. The majority of rural Muslims as well as members of the traditional religious hierarchy and structure, such as village sheiks and imams, would be part of this group.

TURNING TO CHRIST

Another direction some Muslims are taking today is turning to Christ. That is what this writer is hoping and praying for, and what this book is about!

There is a new openness to the Christian gospel in many Islamic lands. Many Muslims have not found satisfaction in the religion and traditions of their forefathers. They have felt a vacuum in their hearts, and there is an unprecedented search on their part for the truth. They are finding out that only Christ can fill the vacuum they sense. What an opportunity this represents for the gospel!

The political, social, economic, and scientific changes of the last several decades have become a force too strong for Muslims to resist. Islam is being forced to join in the current world trends. As the waves of change come against Islam, basic shifts and turbulent transformations are taking place on every level.

Many Muslims are looking at things in new ways. People who once clung to long-held traditions now have different attitudes. As they become more receptive to new ideologies and practices, they are more open to reconstruction and compromise. Islam's adjustment is not happening without tension and strain. At the same time, new opportunities are emerging. The face of Islam is indeed changing.

Lea, Jacob's wife, called her fifth son Issachar. The word in Hebrew means reward or wages. Later, the children of Issachar were described as men "who understood the times and knew what Israel should do" (I Chronicles 12:32).[57] Today Christians need that kind of wisdom to be aware of the trends and directions Islam is taking. We also need to understand the implications of these trends and shifts as they relate to our work of spreading the Good News. God has put us here. This is our generation. We are engaged in the divine task of proclaiming the Kingdom of God. If we insist on "doing business as usual," we will be left out and fail to carry out the Great Commission.

May God help us not to be prisoners of our old ways of thinking and doing things! Richard Kriegbaum said: "What I think I know keeps me from knowing what I cannot yet think."[58] King Solomon said: "The wise heart will know the proper time and procedure. For there is a proper time and procedure for every matter" (Ecclesiastes 8:5–6).

As Christian witnesses we need to continue to enlarge our vision, "widen our tents," and think big! God is giving the Church new and powerful tools to evangelize Muslims and bring them into the Kingdom of Christ. There are several new Bible translations available for Muslims. One of these is the Arabic Sharif Bible which, for the first time in history, has broken the Middle Eastern ethnic Christian taboos and used Islamic terms, names and words to bring to the hearts of more than 300 million Arab Muslims God's Word in a language they understand!

Some years ago, it was not uncommon for missionaries among Muslims to hear discouraging statements such as: "You're wasting the best years of your life!" As a matter of fact, those exact words were addressed to me!

Today that has changed. We are seeing missionary mobilization from all parts of the world to take the message of God's love to Muslims around the globe. God has poured into the Church an evangelistic fervor. Let us rekindle that fervor to bring Muslims to Christ.

PART THREE

Islam and the Church

10 | *Christianity*

Muslims believe that Jesus Christ...
- is a prophet
- was born of a virgin
- is sinless
- did great miracles
- is alive in heaven today
- will come again into this world

Muslims do NOT believe that Jesus Christ...
- is God become man
- died on the cross
- is Redeemer or Savior from sin

Now we are going to examine the major theological controversies between Islam and Christianity. Our purpose in exploring these issues is not to give you ammunition for a war of words against Muslims. It is to help you understand what they believe about these matters so you can discuss them in a tactful and sensitive way.

When Islam appeared in the seventh century A.D., the Christian church had already existed for almost six hundred years. A number of Christianity's heretical sects also were at work. Some of their teachings had reached even as far as Arabia and had been adopted there. Thus, some of the "Christian" ideas known to the Arabs of those days were neither biblical nor orthodox.

A similar situation exists today. As we seek to know what Islam thinks about Christianity, we will discover not only that Muslims have misconceptions about Christianity but also that they object to several fundamental biblical doctrines.

We will also look at how Muslims and Christians relate to each other in communities where both live. Our observations will give us a clearer understanding of some of the obstacles Christians must overcome when trying to lead Muslims to Christ.

ISLAM'S VIEW OF CHRISTIANITY

The Islamic view of Christianity comes from several sources. It can be traced in part to the nature of the Christian sects which existed at the time Islam appeared. In addition to the heretical sects that denied or misconstrued the deity of Christ, some suggest that a "Nazarene" sect (called Nasara in Arabic) attracted adherents in Arabia and Mecca. The members of this sect were reportedly a Christian group that occupied a position midway between Jews and Christians. Muhammad had dealings with them. Thus, some of the ideas Islam formed about Christianity are based on possible variants like the Nazarene sect, not on its orthodox form.

Just reading the qur'anic verses related to the Bible, the cross, and the Trinity, one sees that there is a serious chasm between Islam and Christianity. However it is important to notice that the majority of today's Islamic thought about Christianity is not drawn from the Qur'an. It stems rather from the Hadith and the interpretations that came after Muhammad. A study of the Hadith and the traditions shows that Muslims take a view of Christianity which departs even more from the truth than that which is found in the Qur'an.

With this in mind, we will explore Islam's concept of Christianity, using four major headings: Christianity as a religion, the Bible, Jesus Christ, and Paul.

The Christian Religion

Average Muslims have no interest in Christianity. In their view, its day is past, or maybe it is for Western countries, not for them.

Furthermore, Muslims see Christianity as inferior to Islam. It is too theoretical and presents an unrealistic spirituality that cannot be attained. Besides this, it is impractical and has too many restrictions. It does not permit revenge or polygamy, for example. Then divorce is allowed only under special circumstances. The Christian rule that a man must be bound to his wife throughout life is considered a lack of personal freedom.

According to some Muslim thinkers, Christianity was never meant for the whole world. It was meant only for the Jews. Paul, moving to destroy this "original" Christianity through cunning ways, started preaching to other nations that Jesus had been crucified. He succeeded in his "satanic" idea, Muslims believe, and Christianity was distorted. Incidentally, such ideas can also be found in the writings of some liberal German and other Western theologians.

Finally, everyday Christianity is considered dissolute and immoral. Look at Western societies, the Muslim says. Immorality prevails, corruption is called democracy, and the churches are empty. Here is an excerpt that illustrates this fact. The author, a Saudi princess, talks about her brother who was in the United States for a period of time.

> Ali returned from the United States for the summer holiday... He made a great point telling us of his escapades with American women and announced that, yes, it was true, just as he had been told, they were all whores!... [My husband] advised Ali to attend church or cultural events, where he would be surprised at the [decent] conduct of women. Ali was adamant. He said that he had tested the morals of women from all walks of life in America; they were all definitely whores.[1]

Unfortunately, thanks to Hollywood and the films it produces, Ali's view is not uncommon among Muslims.

The Bible

Islam's view of the Bible reveals certain significant misconceptions. Consider the following:

1. *The Bible that exists now has been corrupted.* Several verses in the Qur'an accuse Jews and Christians of tampering with their own Scriptures. See for example Sura 2:40–44, 75, 140, 146, 159, 174–176; 3:69–71, 187; 4:46.

Most Muslim commentators interpret these verses and others like them to mean that both Jews and Christians twisted, changed or concealed the meaning of their Holy Books to suit their own purposes. The supposed result is that the revelation they have now is only a fragment of what they used to have. Therefore, Muslims say, the present Bible has been distorted and forged.

2. *The Bible contains prophecies about Muhammad.* According to Deuteronomy 18:18–19, Moses told the Israelites that they would be destroyed if they served other gods. Sura 46:10 mentions the coming of a message similar to what Moses gave the Israelites. That is, the message that would come would announce destruction upon those who would not accept it. Many Muslim interpreters identify the predicted messenger as Muhammad and believe that this new, but similar message was the one brought by their prophet.

Some Muslims also believe that Jesus prophesied the coming of Muhammad in John 14:16, 15:26, and 16:7. In those passages, the Greek word translated "counselor" or "comforter" is parakletos. However, some Islamic scholars contend that this word should read *periklytos*, which means "illustrious one" or "praised one." In Arabic, *periklytos* is rendered *Ahmad* or *Mahmood*, which Muslims say are other forms of the name Muhammad. Thus, Islam claims that Jesus prophesied the coming of Muhammad by name. The prophecy Jesus supposedly made is found in Sura 61:6. We shall refute such claims in a later chapter.

Jesus Christ

We will begin by examining what the Qur'an says about Jesus' life and person. Three suras in the Qur'an speak in detail about Jesus. These are: "The family of Imran" (Sura 3); "The Table" (Sura 5); and "Mary" (Sura 19). But there are more than ninety references in the Qur'an to Jesus in fifteen different suras. Isa, the qur'anic name for Jesus, is mentioned twenty-five times. In sixteen of these, His name is connected with the epithet, "Son of Mary."

Essential Facts About His Life

The most essential biblical teachings about Christ concern how He came to the world and how He left it.

How He came to the world	Incarnation
	Virgin birth
How He left the world	Atonement*
	Ascension

* Atonement here refers to Christ's death on the cross and His resurrection.

These events are crucial for people's redemption and salvation; and on them, all of Christian doctrine hinges. However, Islam has chosen to accept some of these and reject the others. The following chart illustrates what I mean.

So, traditional Islam disagrees with the Bible on the following major doctrines about Christ:

	Doctrine	**Rejected or accepted by Islam**
How He came into the world	Incarnation	Rejected
	Virgin birth	Accepted
How He left the world	Atonement	Rejected
	Ascension	Accepted

The cross. In Muslim thought, God the Just would never have delivered Jesus the Righteous Prophet to be crucified. In addition, to them the cross is a sign of weakness and cowardice. Christ would have fought His enemies (like Muhammad did). Given the Muslim view of God, the cross is impossible and unthinkable (Sura 4:155–159).

Muslims believe that when the Jews rejected the message of Jesus and tried to crucify Him, God rescued Him and cast His likeness on another man who was crucified. So Jesus never died. This is the basic belief Muslims hold, although some other interpretations have appeared throughout the history of Islam. We will study Islam's view of the cross in more detail later.

The divine nature of Christ. In Christian teaching, this doctrine includes three aspects, all of which Muslims reject.

First, Christians teach the divine Sonship of Christ. In Muslim thought, if Jesus is considered God's Son, it indicates that God must have had physical relations with a woman. For God to have had such a relationship is impossible. Therefore the idea of Sonship is totally unacceptable. According to the Qur'an, "God is but one God. Far be it from Him that He should have a son" (Sura 4:171). "Say: He is God alone; God the eternal! He never gives birth, and He is not born; and there is none like unto Him!" (Sura 112:1–4).

Second, Christians teach the deity of Christ. This doctrine is unacceptable to Muslims because to them it implies polytheism (Sura 5:17, 72, 73). Further Muslims do not accept that Jesus is man and God at the same time. To them, He has to be one or the other. If He is God, as the Christians teach, that means there is more than one God. To associate any other being with God is to commit the sin of *shirk*.

Third, Christians teach the doctrine of the Trinity. The Qur'an rejects this doctrine (Sura 4:171). Muhammad understood the Trinity to include God, Jesus, and Mary (Sura 5:116). Could it be that the doctrine was misrepresented to him? Very possibly! Who could have done such a thing? Maybe anti-Christian Jews defaming Christianity were responsible, or even an unorthodox Christian sect. As a result of this misunderstanding, Islam considers a belief in the Trinity to be polytheism (Sura 5:17, 73; 9:30; 112:3).

Other Teachings About Christ

1. *His names.* In the Qur'an, Jesus is called *Isa*. This name is not too far from the Greek form (*Isous*). He is also called *Al-Masih*, which means Christ, and Son of Mary, in reference to the fact that He had no earthly father.

2. *His titles.* These indicate His attributes and mission. In the Qur'an, Jesus is given a great number of honorable titles, more than any other figure including Muhammad. He is called:

   a) A sign, that is a miracle (Sura 19:21; 21:91; 23:50)

   b) Mercy (Sura 19:21)

   c) A witness (Sura 4:159, 5:117)

   d) An example (Sura 43:57, 59)

   e) Illustrious (or prominent) (Sura 3:45)

f) A Messenger (Sura 3:49; 5:75)

g) A Prophet (Sura 19:30; 33:7)

h) God's servant (Sura 4:172; 19:30)

i) Blessed (Sura 19:31)

j) One close to God (Sura 3:45)

k) Word of Truth (Sura 19:34)

l) Word of God (Sura 3:45; 4:171)

m) Spirit of God (Sura 4:171)

n) One confirmed with the Spirit of God (Sura 2:87; 2:253; 5:110)

o) Righteous (Sura 6:85)

p) One like Adam (Sura 3:59)

q) Mortal (Sura 19:33)

r) Sinless or holy (Sura 19:19)

3. *His miracles*. According to the Qur'an, Jesus did the following:

a) He spoke while still a baby in the cradle (Sura 3:46; 5:110; 19:29 – 33).

b) He made small clay models of birds, breathed life into them, and they became live, real birds (Sura 3:49, 5:110).

c) He cured the blind and the leper (Sura 5:110).

d) He raised the dead (Sura 5:110).

e) He caused a "table prepared" to come down from the sky (Sura 5:112 –115).

f) He knew people's secrets (Sura 3:49).

g) He ascended alive to heaven (Sura 19:33).

4. *His book*. The Islamic concept of inspiration is that God sends a literal message to a prophet. This then is recorded in writing. To the Muslim, the "gospel" means the book that God sent down to Jesus. Thus, Muslims are extremely bewildered when Christians refer to the gospel "of Mark" or "of John." They think this means that the "original" gospel of Jesus has been corrupted and replaced with several other gospels. When talking with Muslims one can avoid a lot of confusion by saying: "The Good News of Jesus Reported by Matthew;" "The Story of Jesus According to Mark;" "The Book of Luke;" or "The Book of John."

The gospel is mentioned in the Qur'an in the following places: Sura 3:3, 48, 65; 5:46, 47, 66, 68, 110; 7:157; 9:111; 48:29 and 57:27.

5. *His disciples.* The Qur'an states that the disciples of Jesus were Muslim (Sura 3:52).

Paul

Why do many Muslim scholars consider Paul to be Islam's staunchest enemy in Christianity? There are two basic reasons.

First, Paul is Christianity's greatest defender of the doctrine of justification by faith. He is the one who talked the most about it, explained it, and defended it. His position on the subject is in direct opposition to the view of Islam, which teaches that people gain a right standing with God by doing good deeds. In Islam, works are the thing that counts. They enable the believer to gain entry into paradise. What Islam teaches is actually legalism—that people are saved by works, by human efforts, by observing rituals and ceremonies.

Second, Paul was the apostle to the Gentiles, the one who pushed for Christianity to invade the rest of the world. He succeeded in carrying the gospel of Christ across the borders of Palestine into Roman territory. From there it spread throughout Europe and eventually to the world. Muslims contend that what Paul did was wrong. He became an intruder when he took the Christian faith beyond Jewish borders. Christianity, in Muslim belief, was meant only to correct and guide the Jews. By acting on his own initiative and taking the gospel to the Gentiles, Paul corrupted and destroyed the "real" Christianity. He was the one who made it into a world religion. This makes Muslims strongly oppose him.

Any student of the Bible would agree that Paul had a major role in bringing out the global nature of the Christian message. In commenting on the book of Colossians, John B. Nielson says that "Paul's is a universal religion. We see here [in Colossians 1:6] his worldwide outlook and ministry. Christianity is basically an evangelistic religion, equally applicable to every man..."[2] Christians would deny, however, that Paul acted simply on his own initiative. They would point to God as the source of Paul's missionary drive. The truth is that Islam hates to think of Christianity as a world religion, and they blame Paul for the fact that Christians believe it is. According to Muslims, Islam is the world religion.

Another aspect of Islam's relationship with Christianity is the way Muslims and Christians interact. In the next part of this chapter, we will consider the two major contexts in which these groups find themselves living together as neighbors. The first is when Christians are in the minority among Muslims, and the second is when Muslims are in the minority among Christians.

CHRISTIAN MINORITIES IN MUSLIM COMMUNITIES

In certain areas of the world, a Christian minority exists in a region where the majority of the population is Muslim. Examples are the Copts in Egypt, the Assyrians and Armenians in Iran, the Armenians in Turkey, and the Chinese Christians in Malaysia.

How do Christians react when they are a minority in a Muslim-majority society? When we say "Christians" in this section, we mean all those who call themselves Christians, whether nominal or born-again. Distinctions between the two groups will be made when necessary.

Their Situation

In the geographic areas mentioned above and other similar ones, there is usually great unease, suspicion and mistrust between the Christian minority and the Muslim majority. A Muslim author has said: "To ignore this situation is like ignoring mines that have been planted in the Arabic and Islamic existence... they will explode... and only God knows where and how... unless we remove and diffuse them."[3]

The Muslim conquerors of lands inhabited by Christians (and Jews) started using the name *dhimmis* for these conquered peoples. A *dhimmi* (pronounced almost like zimmi) is a person that is under protection because he is defeated. The name infers a status of inferiority and disadvantage. Originally *dhimmis* constituted the great majority of the conquered areas. But gradually, with Islamic laws favoring Muslims, *dhimmis* became minorities.

What is the state of the Christian *dhimmis*? What conditions do they live under? When we analyze their situations, we find the following features.

Subjugation. When Muslims conquered Christian nations, they subjugated the people. In the seventh century, Caliph Omar issued a "pact" with the defeated Christians. Briefly, it states that Christians:

> Shall not build, in our cities or in their neighborhood, new monasteries, churches, convents, or monks' cells, nor shall [they] repair, by day or by night, such of them as fall in ruins or are situated in the quarters of the Muslims… Shall not manifest religion publicly nor convert anyone to it… [Christians] shall not prevent any of [their] kin from entering Islam if they wish it… Shall show respect toward the Muslims, and shall rise from seats when [Muslims] wish to sit… Shall not display crosses or books in the roads or markets of the Muslims… [They] shall use clappers in churches very softly.[4]

Thus under the power and legal system of the majority, Christian minorities are suppressed. Their growth is restrained and they have limited freedoms.

Mistreatment. In some situations, discrimination against the Christian minority has caused the Christians to try even harder to achieve success. Here is an example. I was told in Kuala Lumpur that at the university it is a known fact that Muslims are given extra help by their professors and they are favored in the grades they make on examinations. When the university education is completed, the Chinese (non-Muslims) graduate is much better off academically than his Muslim peer for the simple reason that he actually had to study hard in order to graduate. Many people there prefer to go to a Chinese doctor rather than to one who is Malay (Muslim). The first achieved his degree on his own and by his diligent work while the latter was helped to obtain his diploma.

Muslim Malays are called the "children of the soil," the privileged race. However, the Chinese (about 20 percent of whom are Christian) are the achievers—the businessmen, the successful traders, and the company owners and managers. They are the more prosperous group.

Whatever implications these double standards may have, we must be aware that they exist. There is discrimination; there is oppression; there is persecution; and the Christian minority strives to survive.

The same could be said about other Christian minorities, though from different perspectives. For example, in the past several years, we have had reports of churches being burned down by fundamentalist Muslims in Egypt, pastors being murdered in Iran and Nigeria, and Christian believers being harassed and jailed in Turkey.

Their Response

The reaction of the Christian minority has been characterized by fear, mistrust, and lack of love.

Fear and mistrust. Three basic patterns reveal the fact that Christians are afraid of Muslims and mistrust them.

First, Christians are on the defensive. Their efforts are mainly directed at trying to ward off their aggressive Muslim neighbors by defending what they have. The main interest of the Christians is to maintain and protect their fold—their camp!

Second, Christians are against converting Muslims. Many are usually strongly opposed to any endeavor to win Muslims to Christ. They are afraid to evangelize them. They do not want the bother or risk that such efforts bring. A friend told me about a package of Christian literature that was received at the Amman airport in Jordan on a certain occasion. The inspector who opened it was a "Christian." However, he condemned it and refused to release it because he was afraid that Muslims might accuse him of taking part in trying to convert them.

Third, Christians do not accept Muslim converts. Many Christians do not want to associate with them. They do not trust them. They are afraid they could be spies. In many cases, pastors are unwilling to baptize Muslim converts or perform marriage ceremonies for them—"too dangerous," they say. In most cases, Christians are not willing to marry Muslim converts.

Lack of love. In addition to fear and mistrust, the reaction of Christian minorities towards Muslims is marked by a lack of love. This lack of love is shown in the following ways.

Often the persecuted Christian minority has little or no vision to reach out and help Muslims. No passion... no desire to win them to Christ. Some are not even sure that Muslims should be converted. "Is it necessary?" they ask. Maybe one can sympathize with them because they are persecuted and abused, but such apathy and lack of love are certainly not what the Bible teaches. Jesus died for all, and the good news of salvation is for the whole world.

In addition, Christians are not prepared for ministering to their Muslim compatriots. For example, Muslims continually challenge the veracity and authenticity of the Bible. The overwhelming majority of Christians are not trained to respond to these attacks in a learned and loving way. They lack a definite, successful, and productive plan to win Muslims to Christ. This makes it even harder to minister to Muslims. A further problem is the existence of nominal Christianity alongside true Christianity. Since Muslims do not differentiate between nominal and born-again Christians, they see nothing attractive in the lives of "Christians" that would draw them to Christ.

Finally, Christians impose non-biblical demands on Muslims who come to Christ. In some countries, Muslim converts are expected to change their names from typically Islamic names to "Christian" names (such as from "Muhammad" to "Mark"). Some Christian communities, for example, require that a Muslim convert have his name officially changed into a "Christian" name before he can be baptized or accepted as a church member. This requirement causes tremendous difficulty for the convert. If he changes his name, he can find himself facing serious complications, even life-threatening situations as a result. He will be harassed by the authorities, marked, possibly persecuted, even imprisoned.

I do not see names as being "Christian" or "heathen." The real question is this: if Christians are going to require converts to change their names, which names must be changed? For instance, should a convert from Islam whose name is Muhammad or Mustapha or Ali be asked to change his name, while a convert from nominal Catholicism who is called Jesus Maria be allowed to keep his? There are Christians who impose such demands on Muslim converts or boast that they do not give their children Muslim names. Some are either unaware of or intentionally ignorant of the fact that many Muslim names come directly from the Bible, where they appear in the same, exact forms. Examples are the names Hagar (Genesis 16:1), Ishmael (Genesis 16:11), Alvan or Alwan (Genesis 36:23), Hemdan (Genesis 36:26), Galal or Jalal (1 Chronicles 9:15–16; Nehemiah 11:17), Heled or Kheled (1 Chronicles 11:30) and Hashem (1 Chronicles 11:34).

Baptism in water is another issue. Some Christians do not allow a Muslim convert to be baptized until he has been tested or has passed through a period of teaching. Evidently, they want the convert to "prove" his conversion to their satisfaction before he can be baptized. Such requirements seem unbiblical in the light of Scriptures like Acts 2:41, 8:30–38, and 10:44–48, which tell of converts being baptized immediately. Baptism should come at the very beginning of the spiritual life of a believer. It is not a graduation ceremony. Rather, it is an initiation step!

These are some of the problems and issues that arise when Christians live as minorities in Muslim communities. What happens when the situation is the opposite?

MUSLIM MINORITIES IN CHRISTIAN COMMUNITIES

We need to understand the circumstances and feelings of Muslims living in communities where the majority is Christian. Let us remember the important fact that Muslims usually do not make a distinction between born-again Christians and nominal Christians. To Muslims, all are the same.

Settings where Muslims are in the minority can differ drastically from one situation to another. However, there are certain common features that should be noted. These relate to the way they see themselves and the way others see them.

Here are several examples of Muslim minorities: Muslims in the Philippines, North Africans in France, Southeast Asians in the United Kingdom, Black and Middle Eastern Muslims in the United States, Indian Muslims in South Africa, Turks in Germany.

Emotional Insecurity

One would probably expect minority Muslims in one place to be different from minority Muslims in another place. Yet, it is striking that in most if not all situations, Muslims have a lot of fear. They are afraid of secularism, of Western customs, of democratic ways of life, and of the dissolution of their Islamic identity in the overwhelmingly non-Islamic society. They are unhappy about their inability to apply Islamic law. They feel restricted because they are not allowed to marry more than one wife. They are concerned about the upbringing of their children in a non-Muslims community.

New Prosperity

With a few exceptions, Muslims in such communities have been the poor, the unskilled workers, and the uneducated. However, with diligent hard work and with petro-dollars pouring into many Muslim pockets, that image is changing. As a matter of fact, in many areas of the world the current stereotype of a Muslim is a sheikh with a mansion, a Rolls-Royce in the garage, and a yacht in the dock!

Social Mobility

In the midst of a community that is non-Muslim, Muslims find themselves changing as they face different crisis situations.

Numerically, they feel overwhelmed. The number of Muslims in France, for instance, is probably six million strong. But when a Muslim family lives and works in a little town somewhere, they do not usually realize how many Muslims there actually are. Instead, they see themselves as a small island surrounded by a vast sea of non-Muslims.

Culturally, they are adapting. Even the most resistant Muslims cannot do much to stop their children or grandchildren from changing and following the patterns of the overwhelmingly non-Muslim society around them. Some adapt to the larger society by wearing Western style clothes, watching movies, and drinking alcoholic beverages. Others become part of the culture around them completely by marrying non-Muslims.

Negative View of Christians

Minority Muslims do not see Christianity in a good light. When they look at the "Christians" around them, they find much to criticize. They see low moral standards, pagan worship, and religious apathy.

Low moral standards. As we said before, Muslims do not differentiate between nominal Christians and those who are born again. If a Muslim sees the bar on his street full of people, to him this is standard "Christian" behavior.

Pagan worship. We have already discussed the Muslim misunderstanding of the Trinity. This misinterpretation makes Muslims think of Christians as pagans who worship three gods.

Religious apathy. Muslims look at the church buildings in the communities where they live and find them empty. They say: "These Christians are not interested in their religion. It must be boring to them. They prefer to go for a picnic or a ride or just stay home on Sunday."

We may not approve of how Christian minorities respond to Muslims or how Muslim minorities respond to Christians. The fact is, however, that attitudes and problems like the ones outlined here are commonly found. Later in this book, we will propose strategies for dealing with them. Before we do that, however, we need to examine three specific areas of conflict in depth. The first of these is what Islam thinks of the Bible. That is the subject of our next chapter.

11 | *The Bible*

"Heaven and earth will disappear, but my words
will remain forever....
Open my eyes to see
the wonderful truths in your law.
I am but a foreigner here on earth;
I need the guidance of your commands...
Keep me from lying to myself;
give me the privilege of knowing your law.
I have chosen to be faithful;
I have determined to live by your laws."

(Matthew 24:35; Psalm 119: 18–19, 29–30, New Living
Translation.)

verage Muslims believe that the Bible has been tampered with.
Somehow, they think, a number of stories and truths that were
inspired by God were taken out of it and others that were not
inspired have been added to it. Based on this belief, they assert that
the Bible in its present form is an altered, corrupt book. Muslims,
educated and uneducated alike, think that this is a helpful argument
against Christianity and Christians. And they do make generous use
of it! On almost every occasion when they set themselves to oppose
Christianity, they refer to it; it is their last weapon.

In this chapter, we examine this claim. We show why it cannot be true and present facts that will help you when you talk with Muslims about the Bible's divine authority and infallibility.

WHAT THE QUR'AN SAYS ABOUT THE BIBLE

One must understand that the Qur'an does not mention the Bible as such; rather it refers to the Torah (Pentateuch), *Zaboor* (Psalms), *Injil* (Gospel), and the Book, meaning the Holy Scriptures of the Jews and Christians. With that in mind, let us examine what the Qur'an says about the Holy Scriptures (or the Bible). Six main statements identify its view.

1. The Qur'an clearly says that the Bible came from Allah (Sura 2:87; 3:3; 4:136; 163; 5:46, 47; and 29:46).

2. The Qur'an gives the Bible names that call for unusual respect and reverence (Sura 45:16; 35:25; and 37:114–117).

3. The Qur'an says that the Bible has direction, guidance, and light for people (Sura 3:4; 5:44; 6:91; and 7:157).

4. The Qur'an says that the Bible uplifts the lives of those who believe in it to superior levels of character (Sura 3:113, 114; 11:17 and 21:48).

5. The Qur'an calls on Jews and Christians to observe their Scriptures (Sura 5:68).

6. The Qur'an instructs Muslims to believe in the Bible, and it threatens those who do not believe (Sura 3:84; 10:94; 40:53–54, 70–72; 42:15).

THE ACCUSATION OF ALTERATION

Over the centuries, Muslims have tried to use the Bible as a witness to the validity of Islam. In order to achieve that, they claim that the original Bible had prophecies about Muhammad and Islam, but both Jews and Christians removed them! So we have a dilemma: Muslims want to call "a witness" to testify on behalf of Islam, but they say that the witness has already changed his testimony before even appearing on the stand!

Let us examine this line of reasoning. There are three main reasons why the Muslim accusation that the Bible has been altered cannot be true.

Alteration Is Logically Impossible

Here we ask the question, "Who changed or altered the Bible? The Jews or the Christians?" If the answer is the Jews, the Christians would not accept the alteration. If the answer is the Christians, the Jews would not accept the alteration. Furthermore, the Jews had many sects and the Christians had many sects. Which one of these many groups dared to change the Bible? Where were the others when the supposed changes were made?

The theory of alteration must overcome another difficulty. Centuries before Muhammad, the Bible was available in several languages. So, in which translation was it altered? How is it that all translations contain the same alterations? Did people from different nationalities and language groups get together with all their manuscripts in a conference to change the biblical text?

To find the answer, one needs to address the following theological question: Who is the real source of the Bible? The answer should be, "God." Well, is God able to protect and guard His Word or not? Jesus said, "I tell you the truth, until heaven and earth disappear, not the smallest letter, not the least stroke of a pen, will by any means disappear from the Law until everything is accomplished" (Matthew 5:18). He also said, "Heaven and earth will pass away, but my words will never pass away" (Matthew 24:35). The Psalmist declares: "Your word, O Lord, is eternal; it stands firm in the heavens" (Psalm 119:89). If God is not able to protect His precious Word from being corrupted by humans, He is a weak God, and I do not want to worship Him. But this is not the case. God has kept His Word from corruption, and I can rely on it completely.

Alteration Is Historically Impossible

Here we ask the question, "When was the Bible changed?" For instance, was it altered before Muhammad was born? But Muhammad witnessed to it in the Qur'an as we have just noted. After Muhammad? But our Bible today is the same that existed in Muhammad's time. Thousands of ancient manuscripts in libraries and museums in many parts of the world bear witness to this fact.

Alteration Is Philosophically Impossible

Here we ask these questions: If the Jews know that the Torah has been changed, why do they still believe it? If the Christians know that other Christians have added or taken away things from the Old or New Testaments, why do they still respect them as God's Word? Does it make sense that hundreds of thousands of Christians have sacrificed and continue to sacrifice their lives and die as martyrs in every region of the world throughout all the centuries Christianity has existed—all for a book that they know is not true and that *they* forged?

REASONS WHY MUSLIMS REJECT THE BIBLE

The accusation that the Bible is a falsified book is serious indeed. It is an indictment leveled at Christians accusing them of forgery, dishonesty, and lack of integrity. But from my experience of working with Muslims, I have discovered that many of them use this accusation more as a smoke screen than as an indictment. When they come face to face with the Bible, they feel threatened. They feel deeply troubled for two reasons.

The Bible Judges Them

The Bible judges people. It is God's Word. It is His message to humans. It is the yardstick for salvation, righteousness and holiness. Yet people in their rebellion do not accept God or His message. Jesus expressed these truths clearly when He said: "There is a judge for the one who rejects me and does not accept my words... For I did not speak of my own accord, but the Father who sent me commanded me what to say and how to say it" (John 12:48, 49).

To illustrate, here is a story from the Hadith that shows how Muhammad was agitated and upset when one of his companions tried to read from the Old Testament. In spite of some positive statements he made in the Qur'an regarding the Bible, Muhammad wanted nothing to do with the Old Testament!

One time Omar brought a copy of the Torah to the apostle of God and said, "Apostle of God! This is a copy of the Torah." Muhammad became silent. Omar started reading from the Torah, but Muhammad's face changed. Abu Bakr said, "Woe to you! Do you not see the face of the apostle of God?" Omar looked to Muhammad's face and said: "O I take refuge in God from the anger of God and the anger of his apostle. We have accepted God as our Lord, Islam as our religion, and Muhammad as our prophet." And here Muhammad said: "I swear by him who has Muhammad's soul in his hand! If Moses came to you and you followed him and left me, you would be going astray."[1]

There is no doubt that when Muslims encounter the Bible, they feel its convicting power. Like sharp arrows, its truths hit their mark, and Muslims take refuge behind the accusation that it has been corrupted.

The Bible Has Deep Spiritual Concepts

A second reason why Muslims reject the Bible is because it contains many deep spiritual concepts that they cannot understand. Even highly educated Muslims find these concepts incomprehensible.

Born-again Christians would agree that many truths in the Bible are above human reasoning. But the fact that they are is not surprising. Are they not incomprehensible to nominal Christians as well, including those with great intellects?

For example, Christ told His followers, "If someone strikes you on the right cheek, turn to him the other also" (Matthew 5:39). In my experience of evangelizing Muslims, this command has always caused a lot of amazement. It motivates the Muslim hearer to ask numerous questions and provokes hours of discussion. Many times I have pointed out that the "weakness" and "defeatism" Muslims see in the act of turning the other cheek should rather be understood as "strength" and "victory," since it shows the power of self-control and the triumph of patience, love, and forgiveness.

When Muslims object to the deep spiritual truths of the Bible, Christians must not be disturbed or try to argue with them. All people, Muslim or otherwise, who are controlled by their own fallen human nature, do not comprehend such matters until the Holy Spirit comes to abide in them and reveal biblical truths to them (1 Corinthians 2:14).

ALLEGED PROPHECIES ABOUT MUHAMMAD

Muhammad said that Jesus prophesied his (Muhammad's) coming. The Qur'an says:

> Jesus the son of Mary said: "O Children of Israel, I am the apostle of Allah to you, to confirm the Torah that we have and to announce to you that an apostle will come after me whose name will be Ahmad" (Sura 61:6).

Qur'anic interpreters say Ahmad is another name for Muhammad—though the meaning of Ahmad is "I praise" and of Muhammad is "a praised one." Because this passage is the only place the name Ahmad is mentioned in the Qur'an, some experts maintain that this is a later addition to the Qur'an.[2]

Further, some Muslim apologists argue that the Paraclete promised by Jesus in John 14:16 is none other than Muhammad the prophet. We noted before that some Muslim scholars have advanced the idea that the references reading *parakletos* ("counselor" or "comforter") in the gospel of John should read *periklytos* ("illustrious one" or "praised one"), which in Arabic is *Mahmood*, another alleged form of Muhammad.

The idea that only a slight textual change is required to transform *parakletos* into *periklytos* may make such a theory seem plausible to some. After all, minor textual variations do exist among the manuscripts of the New Testament. But even if the different word the Muslim scholars propose were to exist in some manuscript (which it does not), its existence would by no means be enough to support their claim. The fact is, *no* manuscript or text has *periklytos* in John 14:16. In addition, there are a number of other reasons why Muhammad cannot possibly be the fulfillment of Jesus' prophecy. Here are twenty such reasons.

1. The Counselor is a Spirit, not a human being. When we read the context of John 14:16, it is clear that the Counselor that Jesus talks about there is the Spirit of truth (v. 17) and plainly the Holy Spirit (v. 26). The same is true of John 15:26 and 16:7 when we read the context. This "Spirit of truth" is not a human being; while Muhammad was a human being.

2. Jesus made the identity of the Counselor clear and definite: "But the Counselor, the Holy Spirit, whom the Father will send in my name, will teach you all things, and will remind you of everything I have said to you" (John 14:26). The identification of the *parakletos* with the Holy Spirit in this passage is unmistakable and final. It cannot refer to Muhammad.

3. The verse mentioned above (John 14:26) says that the Counselor would be a teacher. "But the Comforter, the Holy Spirit, whom the Father will send in my name, will *teach* you all things" (John 14:26). He is the One to teach them. However, Muhammad never claimed to be a teacher and was never called teacher.

4. Again, John 14:26 indicates that the Holy Spirit would be the source of inspiration for the disciples. Muhammad denied such a role for himself. He declared in the Qur'an: "I do not say to you that I have the treasures of God or that I know the hidden things or that I am an angel" (Sura 6:50).

5. Further, John 14:26 states that the purpose of the promised Holy Spirit is to *remind* Christ's followers of *everything their Master said*. Muhammad did not remind anyone of the things Jesus taught.

6. Jesus told the disciples that the Counselor would be with them forever (John 14:16). Muhammad's life offers a striking contrast. He came, lived out his span of years, and died on 8 June 632 A.D. He did not stay forever.

7. Further, no mortal man can do what the Counselor was to do, for He would be in the disciples. "He lives with you," Jesus said, "and will be in you" (John 14:17). Muhammad could not and cannot be in anybody.

8. Jesus says that the world *would* not see the Counselor or accept Him (John 14:17). Yet Muhammad was flesh and blood, and the world did see him.

9. Jesus said that the world *would not know* the One who was to come. Only those who believed and accepted Jesus Christ would know Him. However, friend and foe alike knew Muhammad—that is, the world did know Muhammad.

10. Jesus said that the Counselor would be "the Spirit of Truth who goes out from the Father" (John 15:26). The Counselor would thus be a divine entity who would come from God. Muhammad had no such origin. He was born of human, mortal parents, Abdullah and Amena.

11. Jesus promised His disciples that the Holy Spirit would come soon after His ascension. He said, "For John baptized with water, but in a few days you will be baptized with the Holy Spirit" (Acts 1:5). The prophecy points clearly to a speedy fulfillment—"in a few days." But Muhammad came more than five centuries after Christ, not just a few days. Jesus said: "But you will receive power when the Holy Spirit comes on you; and you will be my witnesses in Jerusalem, and in all Judea and Samaria, and to the ends of the earth" (Acts 1:8). This prophecy was definitely fulfilled on the day of Pentecost.

12. The Muslim claim is refuted by the purpose of the prophecy itself. Jesus gave it the night before He was crucified in order to encourage His disciples. At that point, they were fearful and anxious because He had just warned them that He would be taken and killed. Jesus said that His disciples would not be alone because the Counselor would come to be with them. For both of these reasons, Christ could not have meant Muhammad. How could an Arab born more than five hundred years later and far away in another country possibly be of any help or comfort to His disciples?

13. The book of Acts plainly tells us that the prophecies about the Comforter who is the Holy Spirit were indeed fulfilled just ten days after Jesus' ascension. At that time, on the day of Pentecost, the disciples "were filled with the Holy Spirit and began to speak in other tongues as the Spirit enabled them" (Acts 2:1, 4). Here it suffices to note that the Holy Spirit's coming at just this time fits in perfectly with the previous prediction, as does the fact that He was God's own Spirit—not some mortal man. Muhammad could not fulfill this prophecy because it had already been fulfilled and because he was only a man.

14. Further, Jesus told His disciples they were not to begin their task of evangelizing the world (Matthew 28:19–20) until the Paraclete had come upon them. They were to remain in Jerusalem until the

promise had been fulfilled (Luke 24:49; Acts 1:4, 8). But the disciples went out evangelizing after the day of Pentecost. Did they misunderstand Jesus? Should they have waited in Jerusalem for almost six hundred years in spite of the fact that they did receive the Holy Spirit?

15. The Holy Spirit was to come upon the disciples in Jerusalem. Muhammad does not fit this requirement either. We know that Muhammad appeared in Arabia in Mecca.

16. In the New Testament, the title Paraclete is applied only to the Holy Spirit (John 14:16, 17, 26; 16:13) and by implication to Christ (John 14:16; 1 John 2:1). It never has any other reference.

17. The Paraclete of whom Christ was speaking here was to be sent by Christ (John 15:26; 16:7). No Muslim or Christian would say that Christ sent Muhammad.

18. The work of the Paraclete was not to gather armies and gain victories with earthly weapons, but to convict men of sin, the very essence of which is not believing in Christ (John 16:9). Muhammad's military career shows that he was not the Paraclete.

19. The teaching of the Paraclete was not to glorify Himself. It was to glorify Christ. And that teaching was not to be His own, but it was to be what Christ gave Him (John 16:14, 15). In contrast, Muhammad's proclamation was not from Christ nor did it glorify Christ.

20. *Parakletos* and *periklytos* are different words. For someone who is uneducated, they perhaps sound similar. The difference between them in Greek would be like the difference in English between "rest" and "wrist." Besides meaning "counselor" or "comforter," *parakletos* also signifies "advocate." The Qur'an denies the title of "advocate" to all but God Himself (Sura 2:48; 6:51, 70, 94; 32:4 and 39:44.) This shows that there is no way in which Islam could identify Muhammad with the Paraclete.

THE HOAX OF THE *GOSPEL OF BARNABAS*

Muslims often refer to a certain literary work known as the *Gospel of Barnabas* when they discuss the subject of Christianity. According to Josh McDowell and John Gilchrist, "Muslims hold that the Christian account of the life of Jesus in the gospels is not authentic, but rather that the truth is to be found in the Gospel of Barnabas."[3] What is the *Gospel of Barnabas* and what is its relationship to Islam and the Bible?

Origin and Identity of the *Gospel of Barnabas*

The issue of the *Gospel of Barnabas* is complicated by the fact that this same name has been used for two different books. In addition, another work entitled the *Epistle of Barnabas* also exists. The *Epistle*, however, has no relation to the two *Gospels of Barnabas* or to the Islamic community. So, what are the two so-called *Gospels*?

Church history reveals that an early *Gospel of Barnabas* probably existed which was falsely attributed to Barnabas, Paul's missionary companion. This *Gospel of Barnabas* was actually an apocryphal book of Gnostic origin which denied foundational, orthodox Christian doctrines such as the deity of Christ. Barnabas was most certainly *not* its author. Far from attacking Paul or his teachings, Barnabas befriended him and shared fully with him in proclaiming that Jesus is the Son of God (Acts 9:26–27; 13:33). In spite of a fifth-century papal decree against this false gospel, it is possible that it may have been in circulation during the lifetime of Muhammad. However, we have no copies of it today.

In 1709, an Italian manuscript bearing the same title, the *Gospel of Barnabas*, was found. This later *Gospel*, supposedly an authentic reproduction of the original, contains quotes from the Qur'an and from Dante's *Divine Comedy* (which Dante wrote in the thirteenth century). Based on these facts and other evidence, scholars have concluded that this Italian *Gospel* is a medieval forgery of the earlier book and was first composed sometime in the fourteenth century.

Nothing definite is known about the author of this later *Gospel of Barnabas*. In view of its content, however, some have suggested that it was written by a Spanish Jew who had converted to Islam and wanted to refute Christianity. Others think its author was a Spanish Muslim who wanted to take personal revenge against the Christians who had won his homeland back from the Muslims. No copies in Spanish have survived, though some may have been circulated. The author may have chosen to write it in Italian in order to give substance to the claim that it had been hidden in the Pope's library in Rome. In modern times, the work has been translated into several languages including Arabic, English, and Urdu, and has had wide circulation among Muslims.

Content of the Italian *Gospel of Barnabas*

What bearing does the Italian *Gospel of Barnabas* have on the Muslim-Christian debate? A study of its contents shows the following contradictions, discrepancies, and false teachings. (Note: The *Gospel of Barnabas* contains 222 chapters. In the following discussion, references to individual chapters will include the name "Barnabas" and the number of the chapter, such as "Barnabas 2.")

It contradicts the Bible

The *Gospel of Barnabas* departs from orthodox, biblical Christianity in several important ways. It strongly denounces Paul and his ministry. It rejects the deity and uniqueness of Christ. It even denies that Jesus is the Messiah. These features were common in most of the Gnostic writings that appeared in the early days of Christianity. In addition, the content of the book disagrees completely with what we know about Barnabas and Paul from the New Testament.

Here is a list of several specific features or statements in the *Gospel of Barnabas* that contradict the biblical text.

1. Jesus was born during the reign of Pilate (Barnabas 3).
2. Jesus appeared to the Magi warning them not to visit Herod (Barnabas 7).
3. While Jesus was harvesting olives on the Mount of Olives, God sent down the "gospel" to him through the angel Gabriel (Barnabas 10).
4. The list of the twelve disciples includes Barnabas instead of Thomas (Barnabas 14).
5. Jesus said that the greatest of all the prophets was still to come after him because he would be the Apostle of God (Barnabas 17, 36).
6. The man that was demon-possessed had 6666 demons, and the herd of pigs numbered ten thousand (Barnabas 21).
7. The fall of Satan is clearly a rabbinical legend. When God was about to create man, Satan spat on the lump of clay and that is how humans have a navel (Barnabas 35).

8. Adam saw bright words in the sky saying, "There is no God except God and Muhammad is the Apostle of God" (Barnabas 39).

9. God's covenant with Abraham is through Ishmael and not Isaac (Barnabas 13, 43, 44, and so forth).

10. Jesus says that He aspires to be worthy of untying Muhammad's shoes (Barnabas 44).

11. Eighty-three people in addition to Noah were saved from the flood (Barnabas 115).

12. Jesus declares that He was not crucified; rather, Judas Iscariot was the one who died on the cross (Barnabas 221).

13. Jesus said that falsehood spreads faster than the truth, which explains why the idea of the crucifixion spread all over the world and why people proclaim that He is the Son of God (Barnabas 222).

It contradicts the Qur'an

Not only does the bogus *Gospel of Barnabas* contradict the Bible, it also disagrees with the Qur'an. Muslims who want to use it as a weapon against the Bible should first try to reconcile it with their own holy book. There are glaring contradictions between this book and the Qur'an. Here are some examples:

1. Mary gave birth to Jesus with no birth pangs or pain (Barnabas 3:10). Compare this with Sura 19:23 which says she had pains of childbirth.

2. The *Gospel of Barnabas* repeatedly states that Jesus was not the Messiah but that Muhammad is the Messiah. The Qur'an calls Jesus the Messiah, not Muhammad.

3. Ways to despise the flesh and subject it to the spirit are described because the flesh is people's enemy (Barnabas 25, 64).

4. Muhammad will sit on a throne for the Day of Judgment and he will be like a madman. Then he will intercede for people (Barnabas 54).

5. The holy angels will die at the end time. As a matter of fact, no one will be alive except God (Barnabas 53:32, 33). The Qur'an does not say this (Sura 69:15–17).

6. God does not forgive the person that fasts, prays, gives alms, and does the pilgrimage to Mecca; rather, He forgives the person who repents (Barnabas 89).

7. There is a closing prayer with the intercession of Muhammad (Barnabas 122).

8. Those who believe in Muhammad will stay in hell for seventy thousand years (Barnabas 136).

12 | *The Trinity*

"Holy, holy, holy, Lord God Almighty!
All Thy works shall praise Thy name
In earth, and sky and sea;
Holy, holy, holy, merciful and mighty,
God in three Persons, blessed Trinity!"
(Bishop Reginald Heber, 1783–1826)

"The really simple religions are actually ones which have been invented by human beings... If Christians had just invented their idea of God, of course, they could simplify it enormously—but the point is that they haven't. They don't have control over God and the way in which he has revealed himself."

(Alister E. McGrath. Understanding the Trinity. Grand Rapids, Michigan: Zondervan, 1990, p. 145.)

Muslims are called to proclaim that God is One. They assert that none other is like Him; He has no equal. The first half of the Muslim witness, "There is no god except God," expresses this central doctrine of the Islamic creed.

To the Muslim mind, Christianity, because of the doctrine of the Trinity, is not monotheistic like Islam, but a type of polytheism in which three gods are worshiped. Christians know this is not true. But the misconception Muslims have does not go away no matter how much we assure them that we worship one God, not three. The doctrine of the

Trinity, a deep spiritual concept, is not easy to explain to people who do not trust you and your sincerity about the One True God! With Muslims, though, this issue cannot be avoided. Why? Because in the doctrine of the Trinity, the essence of Christianity confronts the essence of Islam. Either Jesus Christ is truly God, as Christians say, or He is just another prophet, as Islam maintains.

In this chapter, we discuss the doctrine of the Trinity as it relates to Islam. We summarize what Muslims think Christians believe and examine in depth the Islamic idea of oneness. We consider ways in which Muslim beliefs can be used as starting points for introducing Christian concepts. To conclude, we review the doctrine of the Trinity and make suggestions as to how the Christian witness can help Muslims understand it better.

ONENESS AND TRINITY IN MUSLIM BELIEF

The doctrine of God's oneness forms the most conspicuous chasm between Islam and Christianity. Why?

The Muslim Declaration that God Is One

There are two reasons why Muslims began to strongly assert God's oneness. First, the declaration was a vehement reaction to the polytheistic worship that was common in seventh-century Arabia. Second, it was a response to the information Muhammad had about the Trinitarian doctrines of Christianity. Against these plural notions of divinity, as Islam viewed them, Muslims proclaimed God to be One and only One. The Qur'an says, "Declare: He is God, the One, the Everlasting; He begat not nor is He begotten, and none is His equal" (Sura 112:1–4). Ascribing oneness to God is called *Tawhid Allah*.

> Muhammad's declaration that there is no God except Allah was a bold attack on the centuries-old beliefs of Meccan and Arabic polytheism. True, the worship of God alone was known among some Arabs when Islam first came on the scene, but it was not widespread.[1]

God's oneness is so important it is considered the most essential tenet of Islamic theology. "The central pivot around which the whole doctrine and teaching of Islam revolves is the unity of the Godhead. From this concept proceeds the fundamental unity of the universe, of man, and of life."[2]

All Muslim theology begins and ends here. Since God is One, all worship, all adoration, and all allegiance are due to Him and Him alone.

Muslim Ideas About the Trinity

Apparently, Muhammad did not have a correct understanding of the Trinity. It was very possibly misrepresented to him as a combination of three gods, and he mistakenly thought these were God, Jesus, and Mary. Based on this misinformation, he would have been convinced that Christianity was a kind of polytheism. We know that polytheism was Muhammad's enemy from the beginning of his mission, so it is not surprising that he would oppose what he misunderstood Christianity to be.

In any case, the position of the Qur'an is clear. It categorically rejects the idea of a triune God:

Believe in God and His apostles. Say not three..., for God is One (Sura 4:171).

They do blaspheme, those who say that God is Christ, the son of Mary... They do blaspheme, those who say that God is one of three in a Trinity. There is no god except one God... And Christ, the Son of Mary is no more than an apostle (Sura 5:17, 75–77).

Then God said, "O Jesus, son of Mary, did you say to people, 'Worship me and my mother as two gods rather than God?'" He answered: "Glory to you! Never could I say what I have no right to say" (Sura 5:116).

The concepts of the deity and Sonship of Christ are also unacceptable to Islam. For Muslims, Jesus cannot be God because there is only one God. Neither can He be the Son of God, since a son is seen as the product of a sexual act between a man and a woman, and the Qur'an says God does not beget. We mentioned earlier that pre-Islamic Arabs had idols called "daughters of God," supposedly the offspring of deity. Islam rejected these.

The Question of God's Attributes

While the doctrine of absolute oneness is essential to Islam, it has certain serious difficulties. For example, Islam admits that God has attributes. The belief that He does, though, opens Islam to the possibility of making out of those attributes real entities that have real existence (in theology, called hypostatizing God's attributes). And if God's attributes are real entities, therefore there are multiple persons within the Godhead—a notion which Islam absolutely rejects. Here is a simple illustration to explain this issue. Islam says God knows all things. God's knowledge is eternal. That means that God's knowledge existed with Him from eternity. And if that is the case, is this knowledge a God since it is eternal?

The *Mu'tazilah* school tried to solve this problem by declaring that God's attributes are not in His essence; rather that they are His essence. Thus, compassion is His essence; likewise, knowledge is His essence. In other words, if God is absolutely one, no distinction can exist within Him between His compassion and His being, or between His knowledge and His being. The *Mu'tazilah* thus recognized God's attributes but denied that they were real entities that had been "added" to God. If God's compassion were eternal, they maintained, then it would have to be God. Since God is absolutely one, no division can exist between His attributes and His essence.

> The [*Mu'tazilah*] argument against the existence of eternal real attributes in God falls into two parts. First, it assumes that anything eternal must be God. Second, it assumes that the unity of God excludes any internal plurality in God, even if these plural parts are inseparably united from eternity.[3]

The controversy shows the difficulty of the problem. Orthodox Muslim theologians reject the interpretation of the *Mu'tazilah* and argue that God's eternal qualities exist *in* His essence. In the orthodox view, these eternal qualities are not God; but at the same time, they are none other than God! There is no analogy, human or otherwise, to explain them, because God has no resemblance (*shabih*).

POINTS OF TENSION AND RESOLUTION

The doctrine of the Trinity relates to three concepts that are also found in Islam: (1) God's immutability, (2) Jesus as the Word of God, and (3) the Spirit of God.

Absolute Oneness and God's Immutability

A study of the doctrine that God is immutable supports the principle of plurality in the oneness of the Godhead. God's attributes are eternal and unchangeable. If any of His attributes were ever to change, that would mean that He Himself changes. But God is unchangeable. To illustrate, let us consider two of God's attributes: God hears, and God loves. Both are affirmed by the Qur'an.

The Qur'an states that God hears: "And God always hears... for God hears and sees" (Sura 58:1). The question here then is: before the creation of angels and humans, whom did God hear? Hearing requires three elements: a speaker, speech, and a hearer. If God did not hear anything before He created angels and humans at a certain point in eternity past and then He started hearing when He created them, that means He has changed. But how can such a thing happen since God does not change?

The Qur'an also teaches that God loves: "Do good, for God loves those who do good" (Sura 2:195) "God loves those who fear Him" (Sura 3:76). Now we must ask: Is love an eternal attribute of God? If not, that would mean that at a certain point He underwent a change when He started loving. Again, this cannot be because God does not change. But if love is an eternal attribute, whom did He love before He created angels or humans?

Only the principle of plurality in oneness of the Godhead solves such problems. There are three Persons in the Godhead. Thus God has always loved because these three Persons in the Godhead have always loved each other. And God has always heard because these three Persons in the Godhead have always communicated with each other. In other words, there are three ways in which God is God, revealing Himself to people and having fellowship with them. Because of that, God has always heard, and God has always loved.

Christians have conceived of the Godhead, or Divinity, as a Unity of Being, which, from all eternity, has been composed of three centers of personal consciousness, each in constant and living relationship with the other two. To speak thus of three Persons as forming a never-broken living unity may appear to some as a mere play on words, but reflection suggests that this is not so. Within the natural universe, there is no single thing which is a single undifferentiated item on its own: even the simplest of substances, such as hydrogen molecules are composed of electrical charges which are in a constantly moving but constantly unchanged relationship with each other...[4]

It seems that God has stamped His image on His creation. From the world of humankind, from the universe, and from things inanimate, we may draw a wealth of illustrations. At the same time it should be noted that illustrations are not proofs. Neither do they have all the dimensions of the reality they try to illustrate. Thus attempts at illustrating the Triune Godhead should not be carried too far. Here are four relevant illustrations.

First, man has a body, soul, and spirit. These are not separate personalities or independent entities. A man cannot lose his spirit and continue to be. Yet, he is not three men; rather, he is one. Second, the sun has mass (body), heat, and light; yet it is one. Third, a box or a book has three dimensions—length, width, and depth. Nevertheless, it is still only one. You cannot separate one of its dimensions from the others and still have a box or a book. Fourth, there are three ways in which water is water: ice, water, and steam.

It is worthwhile to emphasize here what the Trinity is not. It is not (a) three divine attributes, (b) three separate gods, (c) three united gods, (d) three parts of the one God, or (e) three degrees in the Godhead. Rather, the Trinity implies three ways in which God is God. A famous Catholic theologian puts it this way: "These three self-communications are the self-communications of the one God in the three relative ways in which God subsists."[5] There is more than one way in which God is God. He can be God in all the ways that He is God, and at the same time, revealing Himself to people and having fellowship with them.

Absolute Oneness and the Word

The use of the term "Word" to refer to Jesus Christ in both the Bible and the Qur'an forms a second bridge between Islam and the doctrine of the Trinity.

The Qur'an states that Jesus is the Word of Allah: "Christ Jesus, the son of Mary, is the apostle of God and His Word which He cast to Mary, and [also] a Spirit from Him" (Sura 4:171). Several important truths about Jesus are conveyed through the use of the title, "Word of God." We will look at five of these and discuss what they teach us and how they can be used to help Muslims understand the Christian concept of the Trinity.

1. A word is a necessary means of communication. God is invisible, but He reveals Himself in His Word whom He sent to the world. Jesus Christ, the Word made flesh, was God's means of communication. He is the way God chose to tell us of His love. In the New Testament, John uses the term Logos for Jesus. This Greek term for "word" emphasizes the content of the spoken word. Its use highlights the fact that Jesus is God's message to us.

> The Word is, by definition, immanent [existing] in the divinity and active in the world, and as such the Father's revelation. A revelation of the Father without the Logos and his incarnation would be like speaking without words.[6]

2. A person's word expresses his or her disposition. If I say something good, people are pleased with me; if I say something bad, they are displeased with me. Why? Because my attitude is revealed through my words. In the same manner Jesus, the Word, displays the mind and will of God the Father.

The Old Testament points toward this truth. For example, the statement, "the word of the Lord came to..." is usually found whenever God reveals Himself. This means that God reveals Himself through His word that expresses His mind. Although His word is revealed, He Himself (the Father) remains unseen. Thus the word is God's mind revealed in action. Whenever there is a revelation of God, this revelation has come by or through His word. Justin Martyr explains this truth as follows:

When God says, "The Lord spoke to Moses" you should not imagine that the Unbegotten God Himself came down or went up to any place. For the Ineffable Father and the Lord of all neither comes to any place, nor walks, nor sleeps, nor rises up... Yet, He sees all things and none of us can escape His observation. Nor is He moved or confined to a spot, not even in the whole world, for He existed before the world was made. How then could He speak with anyone, or be seen by anyone, or appear in the smallest portion of the earth, when the people of Sinai were unable to even look on the glory of Him who was sent from Him? Therefore neither Abraham, nor Isaac, nor Jacob, nor any other man ever saw the Father and ineffable Lord of all... but [saw] Him who was according to His will His Son...[7]

While the Old Testament shows us certain facts about the Word of God, the New Testament is the place where we actually learn who the Word is. There we read that in the fullness of time, God appeared on earth in the person of Jesus. John says, "The Word became flesh and lived for a while among us" (John 1:14). Jesus is God's Word who expresses to us God's disposition and attitude. He reveals to us the mind of the Most High.

3. People cannot be separated from their words. It seems a mystery to me how my word and my being are so much a part of each other that they cannot be separated. Before a person uses a word, where has it been? You may answer that it was in the person's mind or thought. But is a surgeon able to extract a person's speech and place it by itself outside his or her being? No. Words are a part of our being. It is impossible to separate the two. If Jesus is God's Word, how can we separate Him from God? It is impossible.

4. God's Word has been with Him from all eternity. There has never been a time or even a moment when God was expressionless. Therefore, God's Word is eternal. The Gospel of John says: "In the beginning was the Word, and the Word was with God, and the Word was God. He was with God in the beginning" (John 1:1–2).

To help us understand this, theologian Orton Wiley makes these comments about God's thoughts or expressions:

Ideas are generated in the mind as truly as plants produce plants and animals generate animals. The difference lies in this, that in the mind the generation is spiritual. An idea or a thought is, before its expression, an internal work; and while distinct from the soul, it is not separate from it. The mind can generate thought without losing anything of itself.

Thus the Word or the Son is coetaneous [of equal age or antiquity] and coeternal with the Father. The Father does not exist first and then thinks; for as a Person, God is never without a thought. And this thought or Word of God as the Son is likewise distinct from the Father without being separated from Him, in the same manner that my thought is distinct from my soul without being separated from it. As an object held before a mirror reveals itself without destroying the original, so in an infinitely sublime manner the Son is eternally generated from the Eternal Father; and while distinct though not separate, the Son never diminishes the perfections of the Father.[8]

5. The Word has creative power. The Qur'an repeats several times that when God intends to create something, all He has to do is just speak a word, and that thing will come into existence. Here is one such reference: "He is the Creator, the Omniscient. Truly, when He intends a thing, He commands. 'Be,' He says, and lo it is" (Sura 36:81, 82; see also Sura 2:117; 3:47; 6:73; 19:35; and 40:68).

The Bible also states that God's Word has creative power. Here are some references: "By the word of the Lord were the heavens made, their starry host by the breath of his mouth" (Psalm 33:6). "Through him [the Word] all things were made; without him nothing was made that has been made" (John 1:1–3). "He was in the world, and though the world was made through him, the world did not recognize him" (John 1:10). Since Jesus Christ was involved in the act of creation as the Word of God, this means He existed before creation and is superior to all created beings.

The Qur'an contains accounts of Jesus Christ acting as a creator. Consider these references.

I [Jesus] have come to you with a sign from your Lord: I create for you the figure of a bird out of clay, and I breathe into it and it becomes a bird, by God's will (Sura 3:49).

Then God said: O Jesus, the son of Mary! Remember my favor to you and to your mother since I strengthened you with the Holy Spirit.... you create the figure of a bird out of clay by my will, and you breathe into it, and it becomes a bird (Sura 5:110).

Most Christian scholars agree that the incident described in these references has no historical authenticity. However, the references are useful in that they can provide a foundation to build a case when presenting to Muslims what the Bible says. The fact that the Word of God creates is significant, for only God has the power to create. Thus the Word who creates must be God.

To summarize, the use of the term "Word" in the Qur'an is highly significant. Christians should be aware of the points of contact it offers when witnessing to Muslims. As Thomas O'Shaugnessey observes:

In the opinion of several Christian writers who have commented on Muhammad's use of "word" to indicate Christ, the Prophet, indeliberately perhaps, but implicitly, admits our Savior's divinity... the very use of *Verbum Dei* necessarily implies a divine nature in [Christ].[9]

Absolute Oneness and the Spirit

The Qur'an states that Jesus is a Spirit from God. Consider this qur'anic verse: "Christ Jesus... a Spirit from Him [God]" (Sura 4:171). Although I do not agree with this concept, I use this Islamic teaching as a springboard to construct an argument, as follows.

What is the difference between you and your spirit? Can I ask you to have your spirit leave the room so that I can tell you a secret? Of course not. Such a question seems ridiculous. Yes, God's Spirit must be God. Now, consider these two qur'anic references: "Into her [Mary] we breathed our Spirit, and we made her and her son a sign to the worlds" (Sura 21:91). "And Mary... we breathed of our Spirit into her and she believed the words of her God" (Sura 66:12).

Spirit in both Hebrew and Greek means breath or wind. Without breath there can be no life. And without life the mind does not function. The Word of God is articulated by the breath of God, His Spirit. The Spirit represents the life of God (see Psalm 104:29, 30). The Scriptures often tell us that the Spirit of the Lord came upon someone so that God could communicate with His people. The Spirit of God is not a created spirit or an angel. He is God Himself.

CONCLUDING OBSERVATIONS

In plain and clear words Alister McGrath observes, "Who God is and what he is like—these are matters on which God himself has decided to have the final word."[10]

God's Sovereignty Is Displayed Through His Redemption

God's sovereignty is clearly illustrated in His stooping down to help His creation through love, sacrifice, and redemption. Indeed, He ties in His majesty and Lordship with His redemptive work, saying: "I am the Lord your God, who brought you out of Egypt, out of the land of slavery" (Exodus 20:2).

Belief in the Trinity Is Not a Denial of God's Oneness

The same passage in which God reminds His people that He has saved them goes on to say, "You shall have no other gods before me" (Exodus 20:3). The New Testament exhorts us in these words: "For there is one God and one mediator between God and men, the man Christ Jesus" (1 Timothy 2:5). These Scriptures connect God's saving work with the fact that there is only one God, and that all worship must be given to Him.

There are many verses in the Bible that emphasize that God is one and that worship is due to Him alone. Here are some: Deuteronomy 4:35, 39; 6:4; 2 Samuel 7:22; 22:32; 1 Kings 8:60; 1 Chronicles 17:20; Psalms 18:31; Isaiah 45:14, 22; Mark 12:29, 32; 1 Corinthians 8:4; Romans 3:30; Galatians 3:20; Ephesians 4:6; 1 Timothy 1:17; 2:5; James 2:19; Jude 25.

This one God reveals Himself in three Persons or three distinct manners of subsisting or three modes of existence. These three are the Creator, His Word, and His Spirit. They have always existed. If we were to say that only the Creator existed first, would we not imply that for a certain period of time He was speechless or lifeless? But that could not be. God's Word and His Spirit have been with Him all the time.

Biblical Christianity is monotheistic, teaching the existence of one God. The dogma of the Trinity neither endangers nor detracts from the oneness of God. True, the doctrine is a mystery that we cannot fully understand and one that we may never understand as long as we are still in this life. As humans, we are limited and conditioned by intellectual, cultural, and sociological factors. But even so, we can accept the biblical evidence that tells us that God the Creator has spoken to us by His Word and breathed into us by His Spirit—three in one and one in three.

God Has Revealed Himself to Be Father, Son, and Holy Spirit

The Bible refers to the three divine Persons in additional terms. They are called the following.

The Father. This term does not suggest in any way that God is a natural or biological father of Jesus. It is human language that helps us understand through metaphor or picture the spiritual relationship God has to Christ.

The Son. The Bible refers to Jesus Christ as the Son of God. Again, this is human language that is a metaphor of a spiritual reality. (It is worthwhile to note that people use similar metaphors, for example, when they say that someone is the son of a certain country or city.) In this case the expression points to truths about the relationship between Jesus and God. It means that Jesus is God's Son in some of the ways we understand the term "son" to include. But like other human concepts, we must set limits on the ways it can be applied to divine truths.

For instance, the Bible does not use the name "son" to imply that Jesus was the product of a marriage relationship and human procreation. Jesus had no human father—He came directly from God. In this respect biblical Christianity agrees with the Qur'an when the latter says: "And our Lord is so exalted, He has never had a wife or a child" (Sura 72:3). What the name "son" does mean is that Jesus has His source in the eternal Father, that He has the same nature as the Father, and that He is the perfect representative of the Father.

To help us understand some of the meaning of "Son of God," the Bible refers to Jesus in such terms as: "the image of the invisible God" (Colossians 1:15), "the radiance of God's glory" (Hebrews 1:3), "the exact representation of God's being" (Hebrews 1:3), and so forth. Theologian Karl Barth points out that it is in God that the original Father-Son relationship exists.[11] Human fatherhood and sonship are limited echoes of that divine relationship, similar to it in some ways, but unlike it in others.

The Holy Spirit. The Holy Spirit is the Lord God. He is the presence of the transcendent Being of God.[12] Karl Rahner says that through the Holy Spirit, God

> communicates himself to us in immediate proximity and through him he causes us to accept this self-communication... As self-communication of God he is God as given in love and powerful to us in love. Hence he possesses the one and same essence as the Father, he is God, yet distinct from Father and Son. He proceeds from the Father and the Son through an eternal communication of the divine essence as the act of the Father and the Son.[13]

The Holy Spirit guides us to the truth. He is the Comforter, our Advocate. "No one can say, 'Jesus is the Lord' [or the Word of God is God] except by the Holy Spirit" (1 Corinthians 12:3). Professor and theologian Thomas F. Torrance states:

> The Holy Spirit is the eternal Communion of the Father and the Son and therefore when He is sent into our hearts by the Father in the Name of the Son we are made partakers with the Son in His Communion with the Father and thus of God's own self-knowledge... This activity of the Spirit is not independent of that of the Son but is carried through only in fellowship with His saving work in which He exchanged His riches for our poverty that we might exchange our poverty for his riches.[14]

We have looked at several important theological issues concerning the Triune nature of God. Now we turn to an equally significant topic in the next chapter, one that also lies at the heart of Christian belief. That issue is the crucifixion of Jesus Christ. We will consider what it means and why Muslims find it difficult to accept.

13 | *Muslims and The Cross*

God's wonderful message of salvation through the cross of Jesus Christ is the Christian's priceless trust.

"Who would have thought God's saving power would look like this? ...There was nothing attractive about him, nothing to cause us to take a second look... a man who suffered, who knew pain first hand... it was our sins that did that to him, that ripped and tore and crushed him—our sins! He took the punishment, and that made us whole. Through his bruises we get healed..."

(Isaiah 53:1–6, The Message.)

The Bible states that humans are sinful, doomed to judgment and eternal perdition. It declares that God offers people forgiveness and acceptance through the death of Jesus Christ. Also, it proclaims that on the cross, Jesus bore the sin of the whole world and provided atonement and forgiveness for people's enmity, hatred, and rebellion.

Muslims reject all this. First, they cannot grasp the urgency of human sinfulness. Second, they cannot understand how the sacrifice of one man could atone for the sin of the world. And third, they insist that God rescued Jesus, sparing Him the shameful death of the cross.

These objections obviously deserve careful attention. As we deal with them in this chapter, we shall begin by exploring the historical context of the Islamic denial and the theological factors which are involved. I shall then offer my response to the Islamic rejection, giving reasons why the sacrificial death of Jesus was both possible and necessary. Finally, we shall conclude by identifying the true meaning of the crucifixion.

THE ISLAMIC DENIAL OF THE CRUCIFIXION

The Qur'an presents Muslims with a problem concerning the crucifixion of Jesus Christ. Islam's holy book seems to flatly deny that Jesus actually died on the cross. Muslim commentators have proposed a wide range of interpretations in an effort to explain away what happened at the crucifixion. As a result, most Muslims deny that Jesus actually died as the Bible says He did.

Roots of the Qur'anic Denial

Most qur'anic interpreters seem to agree that another person was crucified in Jesus' place. As for the identity of this alleged substitute, however, there is little agreement. Some of the individuals suggested are Judas Iscariot, Simon of Cyrene, Sargus, Titanus, Ashyu, and Faltayanus.

This substitute theory is in line with the logic of the Qur'an and general Islamic thought which claims that God the Just would never have allowed such a good prophet as Jesus to be crucified. Further, He could not have died on a cross, for the cross is a sign of weakness and cowardice. As Muslims see it, Jesus would have or should have been able either to defeat His enemies or to escape from them as Muhammad did whenever he encountered enemies. God would not have let Him die. Muslims reason that when the Jews rejected Jesus' message and tried to crucify Him, God in His might must have acted to rescue Him.

How does one account for this qur'anic denial of the crucifixion? If both Jews and Christians historically claimed that Jesus died on the cross, how could Muhammad proclaim the opposite?

It appears that some Gnostic, heretical ideas and pseudo-Christian teachings made their way into Muhammad's area of the world.

Several of these declared that Christ was never crucified. There are striking similarities between some of the heresies and the qur'anic view under examination. Here are some of the false teachings that circulated before and during Muhammad's time.

1. Basilides who lived in Alexandria, Egypt, c. 100–138, taught that Jesus could never have suffered because suffering always implies sin, while Jesus was righteous and sent from God. At the arrest and crucifixion, Jesus took on the form of Simon of Cyrene and Simon took on the form of Jesus. Hence the Jews crucified Simon in the place of Jesus, who looked at them and mocked them without their seeing Him.[1]

2. Docetism (the name comes from the Greek *dokeo* meaning "to seem") taught that Jesus was only a spirit, a phantom. What we hear about Him relative to human activities such as His birth, growing to manhood, eating, drinking, sleeping, and dying, are all illusions. These never actually happened but only "seemed" to happen. Note that the Qur'an uses the same word for "seem" to describe Christ's death. A maxim of this heresy went like this: "If he suffered he was not God; if he was God he did not suffer." If we replace the word "God" with "prophet" in this maxim, the docetic statement then becomes the Islamic teaching![2]

3. Cerinthus who lived in the Roman province of Asia in the early second century taught that at Jesus' baptism, the divine Christ descended on the human Jesus in the form of a dove. As the divine Christ, He worked miracles and proclaimed the unknown Father. But at the time of the crucifixion, the spiritual Christ flew away and the human Jesus died and then rose again.

4. Manichaeism was one of the ancient Persian religions. It was started by a self-proclaimed prophet called Mani who lived in Babylon (c. 210–276 AD) and claimed himself to be the Paraclete that Jesus promised. Manichaeism maintained that it was not Jesus who died but the "son of the widow" (possibly the widow of Nain mentioned in Luke 7:11–17). This religion was known in some other parts of the Roman Empire such as North Africa. St Augustine, before he came to faith in Christ, was Manichean.

5. Carpocrates of Alexandria founded another Gnostic sect around the middle of the second century. He taught that Jesus' soul was so

pure that He did not suffer death. Rather, one of Jesus' followers was crucified. Jesus despised the Jews, overcame the sufferings they wanted to inflict on Him, and then ascended to the Father.

It is very possible that such heresies did influence Muhammad's thinking concerning Christ. Currents of conflicting religious thought traversed his own country, nearby Hawran, and the Nabataean district where he would have traveled as a cameleer. True, these areas formed a natural network for the trade routes that linked Syria, Egypt, and Persia. Further, they became a refuge for many groups whose teachings had been outlawed by the Eastern Church authorities. Side by side with orthodox Christianity, heresies flourished to such an extent that orthodox Christian writers of the day described the region as teeming with heresy.

So the pagan Arabs of Muhammad's time must not be considered void of religious ideas. They were in frequent contact with some of their own countrymen who had adopted one form or another of Christianity. Further, they lived in an environment penetrated by Jews and Jewish teachings.

Reasons for the Islamic Denial

There are two principal reasons for the Islamic denial of the death of Jesus. First, Muslims deny the crucifixion based on their interpretations of the Qur'an; second, they deny it based on the implications of the cross.

Interpretations of the Qur'an

As we have said, many Muslim commentators on the Qur'an interpret its statements to mean that Jesus did not die and was not crucified. Here is the qur'anic statement about the crucifixion:

> They [the Jews] broke their covenant, disbelieved the signs of God, killed the prophets without cause, and said: "Our hearts are wrapped up in covers [uncircumcised]," while God sealed them up because of their disbelief, so that they believe but little. They disbelieved, saying against Mary great injustices… "We killed Christ Jesus, son of Mary, the Messenger of God." Yet, they did not kill him, nor did they crucify him, but it was made to appear so to them. And those who differed in [the matter] are certainly in

doubt about [it]. They have no knowledge of [it] except to follow conjecture. They did not really kill him. Rather, God lifted him up to Himself, for God is mighty and wise (Sura 4:155–158).

In studying various commentaries on this statement, we are faced with ambiguity, confusion, and contradiction. The overwhelming majority of Muslims interpret the passage as an absolute denial that Jesus was crucified or that He died. A very small minority interpret it to mean that Jesus was indeed crucified. I will briefly summarize these majority and minority views.

The majority view: Jesus was not crucified. Those who adopt the view that Jesus was not crucified are divided into two different groups. The first claims that a substitute was crucified in Jesus' place. I call this teaching the substitute position. The second group claims that no one was crucified at all and that the whole ordeal was imaginary. I call this teaching the illusion position.

1. The substitute position. The proponents of this position maintain that although the Jews claimed they had killed Jesus, in fact they did not. God miraculously hid Him, and someone else was crucified. Certain commentators say that the soldiers who went to arrest Jesus got confused in the dark. Through a miracle, God cast the likeness of Jesus (*a shabih*) on another person. That person was then arrested and crucified instead of Jesus, who escaped. In this way the Jews thought they had gotten rid of Jesus. But what had actually happened was that a substitute was killed instead. It only appeared to the Jews that they had crucified Him.

2. The illusion position. In the opinion of those who hold this view, no one was killed. They point out that the existence of a substitute is not mentioned or implied in the qur'anic statement. Hence, no "likeness" of Jesus was cast on anyone. They suggest that what happened was that the Jews were made to imagine that Jesus was crucified. But no one was actually crucified and the Jewish claim to have killed Jesus was false. Thus, the whole thing was nothing more than a mere illusion.

While these two different positions exist, their conclusion is the same: Jesus was not crucified and the Jewish claim to have killed Him is false. The minority view disagrees somewhat with this conclusion.

The minority view: Jesus was crucified, but He did not die. A group known as the Ahmadiyyas holds this view. The Ahmadiyyas believe that Jesus was indeed crucified but was still alive when He was taken down from the cross. The spices and perfumes in the tomb revived Him. He then got up and traveled to Kashmir, India, where He married, had children, and died at an old age.

How could a person, even if he were not dead, be embalmed in seventy-five pounds of a mixture of myrrh and aloes that is very gummy and live for three days? How could he be wrapped in burial cloth with that sticky substance, placed and sealed in a tomb, and then walk out three days later (see Luke 23:55–24:10)?

Though the qur'anic verses about the crucifixion create serious problems for Muslim interpreters, few are prepared to explain them away and accept the biblical teaching that Jesus did indeed die on the cross. As a rare exception, though, there is the view of the thinker Mahmoud M. Ayoub of the University of Toronto. He comes very close to the biblical teaching with this courageous statement:

> The Qur'an... does not deny the death of Christ. Rather, it challenges human beings who in their folly have deluded themselves into believing that they would vanquish the divine Word, Jesus Christ the Messenger of God. The death of Jesus is asserted several times and in various contexts.[3]

As we have noted, however, very few Muslims would adopt this line of reasoning. Most are convinced that the Qur'an denies the crucifixion. Thus, they are left with a holy book that contradicts a major historical fact that is attested to by Christians and non-Christians, relatives of Jesus and close friends, followers, and critics of His. Faced with this dilemma, only a scant few of them attempt to find a way to harmonize the qur'anic stand with history!

Implications of the Cross

What does the cross of Christ imply that makes a Muslim categorically reject it?

First, the cross implies the execution of an offender. The cross is a repugnant idea. Even in the Roman civilization where its use was the most widespread, crucifixion was considered the cruelest and harshest means of execution. Josephus the Jewish historian (A.D. 37–97) describes it as the most wretched of deaths.[4] To die on a cross was to die in the most barbaric and obscene way possible. The victim, hanging naked, was subjected to gruesome, tortuous, and shameful indignity. If he died within a few hours, he was fortunate; but usually he would hang on the cross for as long as ten days.

To Jews and heathen alike, to Greeks and Romans, Persians and Phoenicians, Carthaginians and Egyptians, to both the civilized and uncivilized, crucifixion was execution in an utterly offensive and totally humiliating way. In the Roman Empire, it was a means of punishment for foreigners, criminals, robbers, slaves, evil-doers and deceivers, but rarely for Roman citizens or individuals of class. Cicero (106–43 B.C.) called it the cruelest and most hideous of punishments.[5] He also said that not so much as even the thought or mention of the word "cross" should come near a Roman citizen.[6]

The ancient Roman world would never have viewed the cross in a positive light as Christianity now does. No national figure, philosopher, or person of repute was ever sentenced to death by crucifixion.[7] The cross was an abomination, a horror. It was a place of scathing mockery and bitter rejection. There, totally stripped of human dignity, the victim was discarded, dismayed, helpless, and hopeless.

Because overwhelming dishonor was heaped on those who were crucified, Muslims reject the notion that a good prophet like Jesus would have been made to suffer such indignity and humiliation at His death. In Arabic there is a blasphemous curse used by Muslims that expresses their disrespect and ridicule of the cross: "Cursed be the cross to which your mother belongs."

Sadly, Islam is unable to see in the cross anything beyond the curse. God's sacrificial, self-giving love is offensive. Redemption is unacceptable. Salvation through faith in a crucified, resurrected Redeemer is totally dismissed.

Second, the cross implies removal of a false prophet. During Old Testament times, death was the penalty for any person who tried to turn God's people away from Him by suggesting that they follow other gods. Even one who could perform signs and wonders in order to entice the people to rebel against God was to be killed. All those who followed such false prophets were also to be slain (Deuteronomy 13; 18:20).

When we examine the Gospels, we sense that some of the Jewish leaders saw Jesus as a false prophet. They viewed Him as a violator of the Law, a mocker of the traditions of the elders, and a blasphemer (Matthew 12:10; 15:2; Luke 5:20–21). Jealousy fomented in their hearts because they could match neither His powerful teachings nor His mighty works. This led them to assume that His miracles were part of His plan to lead the people astray—away from God and the prophets. They wanted to justify their stand. The reason He was able to cast demons out of people, they said, was because He used the power of Beelzebub, the prince of demons (Luke 11:14–16). These leaders became convinced that their religious duty called for action. They decided that they had to get rid of Jesus—both in spite of His miracles and because of them. They thought that to cleanse the nation of Him would be to obey what Deuteronomy 13 commanded concerning prophets who cause the people to forsake God.

While Jesus hung on the cross, the Jews' minds were filled with the notion that He was a false prophet. "Those who passed by hurled insults at him, shaking their heads and saying, 'So! You who are going to destroy the temple and build it in three days, come down from the cross and save yourself!'" (Mark 15:30). How could His prophecy about the temple come to pass now that His death was certain? In other words, at the cross they were finally able to assure themselves that He was a false prophet.

No Muslim agrees with the Jewish conclusion, for Islam states that Jesus was a good and righteous prophet. Muslims believe that Jesus is the righteous Servant of God. As we pointed out earlier, the Qur'an gives Jesus a greater number of honorable titles than any other figure mentioned in Islam's Holy Book. At the same time, since a Muslim uses reasoning similar to that of the Jews, "if he were to accept this story of crucifixion it means that he would have to delete the name of Jesus from the list of prophets"[8]. For Muslims to believe that He was crucified would be for them to accept the Jewish accusation that He was a false prophet. This they cannot do.

Third, the cross implies atonement for sin. This point is of the greatest importance! The cross of Jesus Christ demonstrates that in order for men and women to be put right with God, a sacrifice had to be made for their sins. A vital fact to emphasize here is that GOD instituted the rite of sacrifice, not man (see Genesis 3:21; 15; and Exodus 12).

Islam, however, teaches that humans have no inherited sin, no sin in their heart. Therefore Muslims see no need for redemption or salvation.

During Old Testament times, sacrifices served several important purposes. They acted as vivid reminders of the seriousness and reality of sin, and they were a means through which God sealed His covenant with His people. Through them the Israelites were assured of God's acceptance and forgiveness. But at the same time, sacrifices were limited in their scope, for they had no power to actually remove sin (Hebrews 10:4). Like prophetic pictures, they pointed beyond themselves to the true, eternal sacrifice that was to be made. In fulfillment of prophecy, Jesus Christ came to be that sacrifice. He was the Lamb of God who gave Himself completely on behalf of humankind.

While some Muslims understand this Christian doctrine of sacrifice, they do not accept it. Abdullah Yusuf Ali says that in orthodox Christianity, the death of Jesus "is necessary for the theological doctrine of blood sacrifice and vicarious atonement for sins, which is rejected by Islam."[9] The Muslim objections to the doctrine are many. We quote again from Muhammad Din:

> No sane person will, for a single moment, entertain the idea that the blood of one can atone for the sins of others. It is against nature, it is contrary to human experience... it makes the Supreme Being a bloodthirsty and vindictive tyrant, it is opposed to divine ideas of Mercy and Righteousness, and it sets at naught the divine reign of law that we witness all about us... it is against the holiness of God.[10]

Thus, the doctrine that God saves men and women through the sacrificial death of Christ upon the cross, one of the most basic themes of Christianity and the theological center of the New Testament, is rejected by Islam. Muslims consider it to be folly, nonsense, scandalous, offensive, unjust, unworkable, and impossible. It is an incomprehensible notion. As a matter of fact, though, their attitude should not take us by surprise. Parallels to it are found in the New Testament, a point we will explore later on when we present the Christian defense of the doctrine.

Fourth, Christ was declared to be the Son of God when He was raised from the dead. This is a subtle but very important reason for the Islamic denial. The Bible says that "Jesus Christ our Lord was shown to be the Son of God when God powerfully raised him from the dead by means of the Holy Spirit" (Romans 1:4, New Living Translation). If the cross was the death instrument for Jesus and if He was declared Son of God through the resurrection, how then can Muslims accept the cross? If they would accept the cross they would have to accept the resurrection and the fact that Jesus is the Son of God.

RESPONSE TO THE ISLAMIC DENIAL

In this section, we briefly summarize the evidence that confirms the death of Jesus on the cross. Then we offer a reinterpretation of the qur'anic cross passage based on Arabic and qur'anic exegetical principles.

Evidence Which Confirms the Crucifixion

With intense, vivid language both the Old and New Testaments point to the cross. However, Muslims do not accept the Bible as God's final revelation to humankind. So in this section we shall present extra-biblical witness in the areas of history, experience, and logic. These confirm the biblical account.

The Witness of History

There are many historic witnesses to Jesus' suffering, crucifixion, and death. Here are a few examples.

Tacitus (A.D. 55–120). Tacitus was called the greatest historian of ancient Rome. He criticized Christians severely. In *The Annals* he describes Jesus' shameful death as follows: "Christus... suffered the extreme penalty during the reign of Tiberius at the hands of one of our procurators, Pontius Pilatus."[11]

Josephus (A.D. 37–97). The Jewish historian Josephus spoke very briefly about Christ in *The Antiquities of the Jews* saying:

At this time there was a wise man who was called Jesus. And his conduct was good and was known to be virtuous. And many people from among the Jews and other nations became his disciples. Pilate condemned him to be crucified and to die. And those who had become his disciples did not abandon his discipleship. They reported that he had appeared to them three days after his crucifixion and that he was alive; accordingly, he was perhaps the messiah.[12]

The Talmud. The Jewish Talmud is comprised of the Mishnah (Jewish oral tradition) and the Gemara (a commentary on the Mishnah). It was developed between the third and fifth centuries. Concerning the death of Jesus, the Talmud has this to say:

On the eve of the Passover Yeshu [Jesus] was hanged. For forty days before the execution took place, a crier went forth and cried, "He is going forth to be stoned because he has practiced sorcery and enticed Israel to apostasy. Any one who can say anything in his favor, let him come forward and plead on his behalf. But since nothing was brought forward in his favor he was hanged on the eve of the Passover![13]

Lucian (A.D. 120–180). Lucian was a Greek rhetorician and satirist. He often criticized Christians who, in his words, "worship a man to this day—the distinguished personage who introduced their novel rites and was crucified on that account."[14]

Mara Bar Serapion. Serapion was a Syrian prisoner who wrote his son to take heed and imitate wise teachers. The letter is preserved in the British Museum and dates back to about the second century after Christ. Here are his words to his son:

What advantage did the Jews gain from executing their wise King? It was just after that that their kingdom was abolished. God justly avenged [him] …he lived on in the teaching he had given.[15]

All these indicate that ancient extra-biblical sources do indeed talk about Christ's suffering and death by crucifixion.

Besides the significant presence of these witnesses, there is the striking absence of contradictory testimony. There is another important historical factor here. The Church from its beginning has clearly asserted that the Jewish priests and Roman rulers were guilty of crucifying Jesus. If those accused parties did not crucify Him, why did they or their successors not refute what the Church has been proclaiming? The fact is, not one line or even one word of defense exists anywhere in any writing of religious or historical value on behalf of those religious and military leaders.

The Witness of Experience

All the disciples deserted Jesus when the Jews arrested Him (Matthew 26:56). After His crucifixion, they hid behind locked doors in fear (John 20:19). But not for long! Soon they were out on the streets and in the marketplaces, boldly and fearlessly preaching His death and resurrection. Palestine and the whole known world rang with their mighty proclamations (Acts 17:6). What accounts for this radical change of attitude? As we have already mentioned, some propose that Jesus never died. They say He managed to elude His persecutors and flee to Kashmir in disgrace. There, supposedly, He lived in obscurity to an old age. Yet the disciples were completely transformed. Could belief in a miserable "escapee" accomplish this? The proposal cannot be justified.

What can explain changed lives? When people in their misery, dismay, and hopelessness come—as they have for the past two thousand years—and commit themselves to the crucified, risen Savior, and the burden of sin, shame, and guilt gives way to peace and hope, what is the reason? It must be the freeing power of the atonement, the liberating power of the cross. How, what, and who changed Saul of Tarsus, for example, from an enemy to a follower of Jesus, from a persecutor to a defender of the Church and from an abuser to a servant of Christians? None other than Jesus Christ with His grace. From generation to generation, the changed lives of millions of Christians testify to the power of the cross.

The Witness of Logic

What would make the disciples invent such a story, subjecting themselves to humiliation, ridicule, and persecution, if Jesus had not truly died on the cross? They were well aware of the Mosaic Law, which states that anyone who is hung on a tree is accursed of God. This blanket verdict allowed for no exceptions, no matter who the victim was or why he was hung. Death on a cross was a shameful disgrace, a terminal defeat, and a dreadful stigma!

So for the disciples, all from Jewish backgrounds, a crucified Messiah was a disturbing paradox. They would never have invented such an idea. In fact, they could not believe that Jesus would die on a cross and did not understand Him when He told them He would (Luke 18:31 – 34). Clearly they had to overcome many barriers in order to accept and proclaim what had really happened to their Master. No one could ever preach such a thing out of human pride.

Further, why would early Christians adopt the symbol of the cross, so degrading and humiliating for themselves and their Master, and choose to glory in it? A veteran missionary to the Middle East suggests that in our times, this would be the same as hanging a guillotine in the front of a French church or using an electric chair as a focus for worship in an American church![16]

Martin Hengel refers to two early, anti-Christian caricatures which express ridicule of a crucified Jesus. The first is a crucified figure that has the head of a donkey. The other is a person with his tongue hanging out, dragging a heavy cross.[17] Such derogatory notions are painful. If the early Christians had wanted to make up a story about their hero, would they have been so foolish as to invent one which would cause them extreme shame and unending pain? How foolish it would have been for them to say that their Master, who claimed to be the Son of God, died on a cross and could not or would not help Himself in His hour of greatest need.

The first Christians were well aware of what the crucifixion implied. The church in Corinth sought to escape the folly of the cross and spare itself the offense it brought. To talk only of revelations, ecstasies, mysteries and the like was more intelligent, more appealing, and more acceptable. This was the approach of the learned and the wise, they said. But Paul would have none of it. He knew what it meant to carry the cross daily and follow the Master. He pointed out to the Corinthians that new life in Christ came because of the power of the cross—the cross which was a stumbling block to the Jews (it was improper) and foolishness to the Greeks (it was unnecessary). Martin Hengel observes that a crucified Messiah was a contradiction in terms to everyone—Jew, Greek, Roman, and barbarian. It was offensive to be asked to believe such a foolish idea.[18]

Yet, the scandalous crucifixion became Christianity's central theme, and the Crucified One became our object of worship and adoration! How does one account for this, especially if Christ did not really die? On the other hand, if someone else were to have died in Jesus' place, or if the whole event were mere illusion, how welcome such news would have been for Jesus' disciples. What elation and gladness they would have felt to know that their Master, after all, had been saved the degradation, the humiliation, and the curse of the cross! From a human point of view, such a triumph over His enemies would have proved His claims to greatness.

Peter in Acts 10:38–41 and Paul in I Corinthians 15:5 state that Jesus appeared after His resurrection only to certain people—all of them His followers. Why? Why did He not appear to nonbelievers, particularly to the priests and elders who hated Him and to Pilate who sentenced Him? Why did He show Himself only to His followers? If Jesus were not crucified, as the Muslims claim, it would have been logical that He show Himself alive to everyone in order to refute the "lie" of the crucifixion. It would have been only reasonable that Jesus go to all and say to them: "Some people claim that I died, but it is not true. I never died. Here I am alive and well!" But He did die and rise again. And He knew that if He appeared to those who did not believe in Him, they would have no choice but to fall on their knees and worship Him. Their faith would then be forced and compulsory! But Jesus wants people to come to Him and believe in Him out of their own free will.

Yes, Jesus died on the cross. He did not choose the way of the world but the will of His Father. As the obedient Son of God, He came to be the sacrifice for the sins of the world. He did not die a helpless victim. He could have commanded heavenly hosts of angels to come to His aid (Matthew 26:53). He could have escaped His enemies as He had done before (Luke 4:29). But no, Jesus came specifically to offer Himself on behalf of fallen humanity. There is no logic in inventing the story that He was crucified if it never really happened.

Possible Reinterpretations of the Qur'an

The most important qur'anic verse about the cross is this:

> Yet, they did not kill him, nor did they crucify him, but it was made to appear so to them... They did not really kill him (Sura 4:157).

We have talked briefly about the two traditional interpretations of this verse. Now we will look at the problems with these interpretations.

Problems with the Substitute Position

This position claims that the likeness of someone else was cast on Jesus, that is, another person was made to look like Jesus and was crucified. So, in reality it was not Jesus who died.

But, if Jesus were rescued by divine intervention, what about the disciples? He had asked them to take up their crosses and follow Him. Was a *shabih* (a "look-alike") provided as a substitute for each Christian believer who was crucified? What about the thousands of crosses where followers of Jesus have hung from the time of Nero on? Would they not speak of God's lack of interest, since He did not rescue the followers of Jesus in the same manner as He did their Master?

There is another serious problem with the substitute theory. It claims the reason why Jesus did not die is because God is just and would not allow His righteous prophet to die for sins He did not commit. But if God did not allow Jesus to die, why would He cause another man to suffer and die unjustly, even for the purpose of saving Christ? This would indicate contradiction in God's character and purpose, making a mockery of divine justice. Such an idea is in fact repugnant, causing one to doubt God's ethical values.

Problems with the Illusion Position

This position claims that people imagined that things were happening while in truth they were not. No one was crucified, no one was killed. It was all illusion. So, Jesus did not die.

If that was true, some say, this means we cannot be sure of anything we handle or deal with, including tangibles. For example, how do I know that my wife is really the one I imagine her to be? Maybe she is in fact someone else. Further, if such positions are possible, doubt is cast on the credibility of all historical witnesses. How can I judge the truth or falsity of any book, sacred or secular that claims to report history? Could not everything simply be a mass confusion of identities and information?

To elaborate on the above point, let us ask these additional questions. If the whole event of the crucifixion were a mere illusion, why should other events, both serious and trivial, not also be illusions? Was Jesus a reality, or was He a phantom?

Limits of the Qur'anic Statement

Some Islamic scholars see the limits of the qur'anic statement. They point out that the Qur'an does *not* say that Jesus was not killed, nor does it say that Jesus was not crucified. What it *does* say is merely that the Jews did not kill Him or crucify Him. In other words, these scholars say that all the Qur'an denies is that the Jews crucified or killed Jesus. It does not deny the events of Calvary.

A literal interpretation of the historical account shows this viewpoint to be a valid one. The Jews demanded the crucifixion of Jesus, but the Roman soldiers actually did the work. Christ Himself predicted that His death would be at the hands of the Gentiles (Luke 18:32). The Jews were not their own masters at the time of Jesus' death. They were under the political authority of the Romans. Without the approval of the Roman governor, Jesus could not have been crucified. In addition, death by crucifixion was not a Jewish means of execution. The Jews used stoning, which they had threatened Jesus with during His ministry and actually used later to kill Stephen (John 8:59; 10:31–33; 11:8; Acts 7:54–60).

The Question of Responsibility

At times, debates arise as to who really was guilty of crucifying Jesus. Some point the finger of accusation at the Jews; still others at the system—political and religious. The Bible says that both Jews and Romans collaborated in the act. Yet it also says that Jesus was handed over to the Jews "by God's set purpose and foreknowledge" (Acts 2:23).

It is very reasonable to interpret the qur'anic passage on the crucifixion as saying that it was God who was acting, as the Qur'an says in other situations. That is, God, not the Jews, passed the verdict and carried the events forward by His will, according to His purpose, and through His provision.

Consider this qur'anic verse that talks about what Muhammad did in one of his wars: "It was not you [Muhammad] that killed them, it was God. And when you threw, it was not you, but it was God" (Sura 8:17). This passage refers to the Battle of Badr in which Muhammad and his troops were greatly outnumbered by the Quraysh army. Muhammad threw a handful of dirt at the enemy when the battle started, symbolically blinding them in preparation for their defeat. Although the odds were against the Prophet and his forces, the Quraysh were defeated. The Qur'an, therefore, could be interpreted as saying something like this: "It was not you who killed the enemies; it was God who killed them for you. It was not you, Muhammad, who threw that dust; it was God who threw it for you."

What if this same interpretive principle were to be applied to the controversial verse of Sura 4:157? In that case, the verse could read like this: "The Jews said, 'We killed Christ Jesus, son of Mary, the messenger of God.' Yet, it was not the Jews who acted at Calvary, it was God. They did not kill him nor did they crucify him, but it was made to appear so to them. Rather, it was God who prepared him for this very purpose; God sent him to die!"

The question of responsibility is not easily resolved. As in the other mysteries of the Incarnation, God and the human race are both involved. At the cross, the human race rejected its Creator. Yet theologians would agree that the awesome event of the crucifixion began with God, as the above interpretations suggest. The Bible reminds us that Jesus is the Lamb slain before the creation of the world (Revelation 13:8). In their preaching, the apostles declared that Christ was delivered up by the definite plan and foreknowledge of God. So, the truth is that Pilate, Herod, the Gentiles, and the people of Israel did only what God's power and will had decided beforehand (Acts 2:23; 4:27 – 28). "God is the actor," Kenneth Bailey says, "not Herod and Pilate. Indeed, it only 'appears to them' that they are acting."[19]

Additional Qur'anic Statements

In addition to Sura 4:157, there are three other qur'anic statements which explicitly talk about Jesus' death. These lend support to the crucifixion's historicity.

And [the Jews] plotted and God plotted, but God is the best among those who plot. Then God said: "O Jesus, I will cause you to die and will lift you up to me and will clear you from those who disbelieve" (Sura 3:54 – 55).

I [Jesus] watched over them [the disciples and followers] as long as I was present with them, but since you caused me to die, you have been the One to watch over them (Sura 5:117).

Peace was ordained for me [Jesus] the day I was born, the day I shall die, and the day I shall be raised to life [or be lifted up alive] (Sura 19:33).

Note that Suras 3:54 – 55 and 19:33 place the death of Jesus first, then His ascension or resurrection. Since Muslims admit that Jesus has already ascended alive to heaven, it follows that He must have died.

As we have mentioned, Muslims opt for the substitute theory because they say that God the Just would not let a righteous prophet like Jesus die at the hands of His enemies. Yet the Qur'an states that indeed some prophets get killed.

They broke their covenant, disbelieved the signs of God, killed the prophets without cause (Sura 4:155).

Is it that whenever there comes to you a prophet with what you do not like, you become arrogant and disbelieve some of those apostles and kill some others? (Sura 2:87).

Furthermore, several Muslim writers of antiquity as well as more recent ones state that the Prophet died from poison put in his food.[20] If the objection of "injustice" is raised about the crucifixion of Jesus, why not about the killing of other prophets and the reported poisoning of Muhammad?

WHAT GOD SAYS ABOUT THE CROSS

To demonstrate how strong the witness is to the crucifixion of Jesus Christ, we have drawn from the Qur'an and its interpretations, from history and thought, from experience, reason, and logic. All these offer response to the Islamic denial. However, no talk is complete and no decision is conclusive until the Bible has said its word. In the Bible, God speaks. We need to help Muslims hear what He says about the cross, as He opens their hearts to listen.

The Bible states that Christ died on the cross. He "who, being in very nature God... humbled himself and became obedient to death—even death on a cross!" (Philippians 2:6, 8). On the cross, Jesus suffered the basest of all humiliation and the lowest of all degradation. The crucifixion was not an afterthought. It was planned by God in eternity past for humanity's own benefit and God's own honor. At Calvary we are confronted by a mystery, for the cross of Jesus is a theme too high and too deep to be grasped by human minds or communicated by human words.

Some Muslims may say that the cross of Christ is not possible, since man must reap what he sows. This argument overemphasizes God's justice at the expense of His mercy. Others may say that the cross is not necessary, because God is too kind to punish sinners. This overemphasizes God's mercy at the expense of His justice. But the Bible says that the cross is necessary and possible—necessary because God is just, and possible because He is merciful (Hebrews 9:14, 26, 28; 1 Peter 2:24).

The cross, far from being unnecessary or impossible, was essential to the mission of Jesus Christ. It shows what He came to do. Mark 1:21–27 reports an encounter between Jesus and a demonic spirit. The spirit asked, "Have you come to destroy us?" (v. 24). This question sums up the purpose of Christ's ministry in one line. It was to bring about the ultimate destruction of Satan and his reign of darkness. This was why Jesus came to earth, He said. At the cross there is the most decisive battle ever fought and the most heartening victory ever won.

To assume the Islamic position, let us imagine that Jesus did not do what the Bible says He did, but avoided the mission for which He came, escaped the arrest, mocked His enemies and tormentors, and then went to heaven. *This* indeed would have been a defeat! Muslims do not accept that God allowed Jesus to suffer and die. Rather, the Almighty planned "operation rescue!" So, Islam maintains that the crucifixion was made to seem so to men because it could not possibly be so with God. But this claim is blind to the awesome power of God's love. The paradox is that through what seemed like a defeat in the eyes of the world, God won the victory. On Calvary, heaven's love bore the awful weight of man's sin and so broke its power forever. There is no shame in the cross. "May I never boast," said Paul, "except in the cross of our Lord Jesus Christ" (Galatians 6:14). It is the ultimate expression of God's self-giving love as Bishop Cragg states:

> The Cross happens on earth because it is inherent in Heaven. God was in Christ reconciling the world unto Himself. There was no rescue here—not because Heaven lacks the power or the will, but simply because it has the love.[21]

Prolific Muslim author Abbas al-Aqqad parts company with his co-religionists and says:

> It is not correct to claim that the Gospel records are an unworthy source [of information] about the life of our Master the Christ... Rather, the correct thing is that they are the only written source of that history... They are the source upon which those who were closest to the time of Christ relied. And we, about 2000 years later, have no better and more dependable source.[22]

Yet, Muslims are afraid of ascribing defeat to Jesus. But the cross did not mean defeat; it meant victory. It meant the defeat of the powers of darkness, not of Jesus. Satan's downfall was decreed and secured at the cross. It dealt him and all his followers a mortal blow from which they will never recover. Just as the cross was the acme of Christ's redemptive work in behalf of humankind, so also it was the pinnacle of His victory over the forces of evil. There, "having disarmed the powers and authorities, he made a public spectacle of them, triumphing over them by the cross" (Colossians 2:15). The conclusion is inescapable. The cross meant honor, not shame; victory, not defeat!

It is disappointing that Muslims are unable to see what a dying criminal, also on a cross and at Christ's side, saw. Definitely that thief received light from heaven that prompted him to acknowledge that the man dying beside him was the Lord and Savior, the Master and King! "How clear was the vision of the eyes, which could thus see in death life, in ruin majesty, in shame glory, in defeat victory, in slavery royalty."[23]

The cross is a threat to those who live for themselves. The cross is ridiculed by some, but Paul glories in it. The cross is paradoxical. It is an image of weakness and misery, a symbol of defeat and despair, a picture of punishment and death. But when attached to the name of Christ, it becomes the ultimate symbol of sacrifice, power, victory, life and glory! Natural man tries to escape the cross, but we, like Paul, boast in it!

The cross cannot be denied. There is no mercy away from it. There is no justice apart from it. Take away the cross, and earth will be the other half of hell. Take away the cross, and humans will die forever without faith, without love, and without hope. "For the message of the cross is foolishness to those who are perishing, but to us who are being saved it is the power of God" (1 Corinthians 1:18). God has entrusted Christians with this message. To our Muslim friends, let us explain it with clarity, teach it with patience, and preach it with authority.

PART FOUR

Challenge and Opportunity

14 | *Facing Difficulties*

> In my estimation, Islam has cruelly enslaved its
> followers! It is a system that has abused the spirit
> of its subjects and shackled their imagination.
> In Muslim societies, whether in the West or in
> Islamic countries, schools teach hatred, mosques
> preach contempt for and violence against non-
> Muslims, media glorify killing for the sake of God.
> I sympathize with Muslims as persons. On the
> human level, most of them are nice people. Many
> of them are kind and decent. But all of them are
> under a cruel and ruthless taskmaster. This is one
> of the multiple difficulties that face the Christian
> witness.

Now we are going to take a closer look at the actual work of evangelism. This chapter examines difficulties that arise because of the cross-cultural nature of the Christian witness' work and relationships with Muslims.

For Muslims in general, but especially for those in traditional Islamic communities, conversion is a serious matter with far-reaching consequences. Christians who share the gospel with them have their own convictions and values, based not only on their commitment to Christ but also on their cultural background. These factors can create serious obstacles.

Those hindrances, however, can be overcome! Remember this: when Jesus gave His disciples the mandate to evangelize the world, He also gave them the promise of His presence and power (Matthew 28:19–20).

DEALING WITH THE HINDRANCES TO CONVERSION

In Muslim evangelism, two main kinds of obstacles exist: the ones that most Muslims face when they try to leave Islam and follow Christ, and those that most witnesses face when they try to bring Muslims to Christ.

Obstacles for Muslims

Muslims are hindered from leaving Islam because of theological beliefs, cultural patterns, and socioeconomic factors.

First, Muslims' theological beliefs hinder them from leaving Islam. Muslims who are drawn to Christ face a dilemma: What are they going to do with the fourteen centuries of faith in Muhammad and the Qur'an? Muslim resistance to the gospel clearly derives from statements in the Qur'an. These pronouncements, in themselves, are not extremely inflammatory against Christianity. Yet Muslim writers and leaders have developed a theology based on these statements that is full of hostility towards Christianity. This is a way to "protect" Islam from Christianity. Added to this hindrance are those caused by the "offense" of the cross and "contradictions" a Muslim sees in Christian theology. We have already covered all these areas in detail.

Second, the strong grip Muslim society has on its adherents hinders them from leaving Islam. As we have seen, Islam is a communal religion. It takes pride in its solidarity as the community of the faithful. Anyone who is outside the community is considered part of the House of War. Individual Muslims are group-oriented. The influence of the group and the grip of the Islamic society on its individual members are tremendous hindrances to Muslims who would like to follow Christ.

As an example, from the Islamic society's viewpoint, conversion brings dishonor to the convert's entire family. So Muslims put tremendous pressure on converts. Many are disinherited. Their friends reject them because it is considered shameful to befriend a Muslim who converts to Christianity. Their very life is threatened, and sometimes when family members have carried out their responsibilities fully, converts have been killed. Serious threats also come against converts from Muslim religious leaders and government authorities. The Islamic law of apostasy, based on sura 2:217; 9:12; 16:106 is certainly a major block to conversion.

Islam and its defenders do not intend to allow their beliefs to be scrutinized. This means that freedom of thought is forbidden in Muslim societies. Over the centuries, any criticism of Islam has been dismissed as either a heresy from the inside or a malignant attack from the outside. Any deviation from the community's mainline beliefs is met with decisiveness and brutality. For instance, one hundred years after the death of Muhammad, a man dared to say that the Qur'an was created, not eternal. What happened to him? He was killed!

Third, strong socioeconomic factors hinder Muslims from leaving Islam. Muslim sheiks, imams, preachers, and qur'anic teachers and readers all see Christianity as a threat to their social and economic well-being. As leaders, they have positions of influence in the community. A Muslim who becomes a Christian no longer gives them allegiance or financial support. They accordingly resist and oppose Christianity and make it harder for a Muslim to leave Islam.

Barriers for Christians

When Christians witness to Muslims, they encounter tremendous barriers that frustrate their efforts to bring Muslims to the kingdom of God. There are basically three kinds of difficulties.

First, in Muslim-majority societies, Christians must overcome negative attitudes that result from their own minority status. We discussed this earlier.

Second, Christians must deal with a Muslim attitude caused by tragic historical events. The Crusades and colonialism have shaped the image Muslims have of Christianity. Which parts do they remember most?

The Crusades have made an indelible mark in the Muslim mind. As Islam surged forward, Muslim armies conquered areas that were formerly Christian. They forced Islam upon the people and transformed their churches into mosques. Many mosques today in Baghdad, Damascus, Izmir, Istanbul, Cairo, and other places were formerly Christian churches. The Christian West reacted violently. They organized the Crusades as a counter-jihad against the Muslims. The "victories" they won left irreparable wounds, lasting hurts, and bitter feelings in the minds and hearts of Muslim peoples. From that time until today, those hurts have marred the Islamic perception of Christianity. So in their conversations with Christians, most Muslims will eventually bring up the issue of the Crusades. When that happens, what should the Christian witness do?

Some Christians maintain that we should continue to repent because of the atrocities the crusaders committed against Muslims. While Nehemiah 1:6–7 provides a biblical base for repenting for the sins and ignorance of our forefathers, once we have acknowledged those sins, we need to go on with our commission, the task of winning Muslims to Christ.[1] God has entrusted this work to us, and it needs to be done.

Muslims who seem determined to blame Christians today for the Crusades of the Middle Ages show that they lack forgiveness in their lives. Their present attitude is what creates the difficulty, not what soldiers did hundreds of years ago in the name of Christianity. They cannot forget, and they do not want to forgive. There is a certain irony in their view. They remember with bitterness the hurts they suffered centuries ago, but they do not remember the ones they caused. This is not an attempt to vindicate the Crusades or the crusaders. But we must not allow ourselves or the Muslims we are seeking to win to become mired in the past.

The colonial era created another set of problems. While we cannot explore that history in detail, examples taken from North Africa and the Philippines indicate the difficulties it produced.

Throughout the French occupation in North Africa, French officials showed a complete lack of interest in evangelizing Muslims. Sometimes they even displayed outright hostility toward those who tried to convert Muslims. Their policy was based on the following rationale: first, they feared that a revived Christianity would arouse resentment among the Muslim nationals; second, they represented the government in France that was not particularly sympathetic with the business of evangelization. Sometimes it was even antireligious.

The Spanish occupation of the Philippines provides another example of the mistakes of colonialism. The Spanish had no interest in converting the Filipino Muslims to Christ. They simply wanted to dominate them politically. In certain cases the Spaniards did try to convert some Filipinos to Christianity, but they did so mainly to secure their loyalty. The Muslims who were converted even by those attempts suffered consequences of disastrous proportions. Fear of the same reprisals from their own people became an obstacle to other Filipinos who may have considered becoming Christians.

Third, Christians must deal with problems created by gospel witnesses who have used the wrong methods in their desire to evangelize Muslims. We will examine two main kinds of errors in order to help you avoid them.

1. Some gospel workers have presented Christianity as a "high religion" only. Thus, it appears impractical and inferior to Islam, which emphasizes "low religion." Let me explain what I mean.

The terms "high" and "low" religion refer to different features of a particular religion. High religion has to do with cosmic, eternal issues; low religion has to do with practical, everyday experiences. The way Christians communicate the gospel message shows whether they are emphasizing high religion or low religion. Sometimes the same truth can be presented either way. Consider Matthew 8:23–27, for example, where the disciples were frightened by the storm and Jesus ordered the wind and the sea to be quiet. As a title for this miracle one can say "Jesus, Lord of Nature " or "Jesus Calms the Storm." Both are correct. However, the first draws attention to the cosmic issue (high religion), while the second touches on a tangible issue and is close to people's experiences (low religion).

In a similar way, the miracle in Matthew 8:28–34 could be titled either "Jesus' Authority over Demons" or "Jesus Casts Demons out of Two Men." Again, the second title is clearly closer to people's experiences and needs than the first. In both cases, the truth is the same. The point is that while Christians must present the gospel in both forms, they must avoid a tendency to present it only as "high religion."

The difficulty the gospel witness faces is that some workers among Muslims have unintentionally emphasized only the cosmic and spiritual questions which Christianity answers—those which have to do with eternity, sin, salvation, and righteousness. Hungry stomachs, sick bodies, destitution, and other human ailments have been inadvertently overlooked. Thus the Christian gospel has been misrepresented. By contrast, Islam appears to Muslims more relevant to the immediate problems of everyday life since its principles seem more centered on answering questions of folk needs and practices. One of my personal experiences helps illustrate what happens when people hear only the "high religion" aspects of Christianity.

Sabah, a Muslim college girl, started coming to our meetings in a North African capital at the invitation of a friend. She started reading the New Testament, studying its teachings, and asking questions in the Bible study sessions. But a few months later, she stopped coming to the meetings. When I talked with her, she explained her problem. She thought Islam was more practical than Christianity. She found more in Islam that addressed itself to her down-to-earth, daily living, such as her need to keep her family's approval by finding a husband, securing a well-paid job, and maintaining a good reputation as a loyal Muslim.

I did not agree with her, of course, and what she said was not true. At the same time, I saw her point. When we explain Christianity, we often make the mistake of presenting only its spiritual and eternal remedies. For people caught up in the struggles of daily living, those solutions seem too remote to be of any immediate value. Most Western missionaries in Muslim countries are Christians who have come from a highly institutionalized system of Christianity. When they try to present the gospel to people who are more concerned with the pressing problems of everyday life, Muslims see their own religion as superior to Christianity, and Islam keeps its grip on its adherents.

Paul B. Smith warns against emphasizing the spiritual truths of the gospel while excluding or glossing over the areas concerned with human life on this material earth. Referring to an exclusive emphasis on the "spiritual" as opposed to the "physical," he says this:

Nothing could be farther removed from the real message of Christianity. By His presence at the wedding in Cana our

Lord put His seal of approval on the love between a man and a woman that leads to physical union in a marriage bond... Jesus blessed this wedding not only by His presence but also by His contribution of wine which obviously added to everyone's enjoyment.

When the Bible talks of the deity of Jesus it is telling us that Christianity has to do with life in the future. When it emphasizes the humanity of Jesus it is reminding us that Christianity is concerned about life here and now. The average Christian goes through life dividing it into two parts. On one side of life he writes the heading *Secular*, and under it he thinks of a great many things—business, social life, recreation, friendships, education, family, home, etc. On the other side of life he writes the word Sacred, and under that heading he thinks of his church, Sunday school, choir, family altar, salvation, heaven, eternity, his soul, etc.

If we really understand the Christian faith, then we must realize that it involves every area of our lives. For the Christian all of life is sacred. His faith ties together in one bundle the entire gamut of his life, because Jesus Christ is both God and man, both human and spiritual...[2]

Christianity is not philosophy, theory or academics. It is life in Christ. And that is how the gospel witness should present it to Muslims.

2. Some Christian witnesses have used ineffective and offensive methods. We will look at three of these faulty approaches.

a) Using abrasive means of evangelism. Some people confuse rudeness with boldness. Some time ago, I was ministering in India. I was speaking to a group of Christian leaders about some counterproductive methods of evangelism, methods that hurt rather than help. I call this abrasive evangelism. I encouraged my audience to show sensitivity in the way they present the message of God's love.

A young minister did not like what I was saying. He enthusiastically announced: "I should proclaim the truth, all the truth, and tell Muslims in market places or wherever that Jesus is the only Lord and Savior. He is the Son of God. And if they do not believe what the Bible says, they will perish."

How can we be effective? Should we do as the young minister suggested? Should we begin witnessing to Muslims by insisting that they first fully accept the ideas they find the hardest to understand (Jesus' divine Sonship and crucifixion)? Should we openly ridicule Muhammad and deride Islam? Before we answer these questions, we should reexamine the methods of Jesus. His example is our guide. A study of the New Testament reveals many similarities between His situation and gospel work among Muslims.

When Jesus called His disciples, they had much to learn. They were more fanatic and more narrow-minded than many Muslims are today. A.B. Bruce makes this observation about the disciples:

> They were indeed godly men… But at the time of their call, they were exceedingly ignorant, narrow-minded, superstitious, full of Jewish prejudices, misconceptions and animosities. They had much to unlearn of what was bad, as well as much to learn of what was good, and they were slow both to learn and to unlearn. Old beliefs already in possession of their minds made the communication of new religious ideas a difficult task.[3]

And yet Jesus called these people, accepted them, and worked with them. True, He accepted them because they believed in Him. But that belief or faith was not mature, although it was genuine. They were indeed godly men—honest and sincere—but they were slow to understand and conceive spiritual things. Jesus had to work patiently with them to till their hearts.

Compare the disciples' concept of Jesus before His death and resurrection with the Islamic concept of Jesus.

Disciples	Muslims
Jesus is a prophet	Jesus is a prophet
Jesus is the Messiah (military leader)	Jesus is the Messiah (uncertain meaning)
Rejected the idea of the cross (out of respect and honor for Jesus and the lack of understanding its necessity)	Reject the cross (out of respect and honor for Jesus and the lack of understanding its necessity)

The similarities are striking. For the disciples, it took three years of the personal teaching of Jesus, the miraculous signs of His authority, the cross, the resurrection, and the coming of the Holy Spirit before they were able to fully grasp the message of salvation. Some still had many prejudices to overcome even then. Is it fair to demand more of Muslims than Jesus did of His disciples?

b) Borrowing foreign church patterns. It is tragic to present Christianity to any people in foreign garments. Jesus never intended eternal life in Him to be culture-bound. Christian witnesses to Muslims need to guard against thinking that the way things are done "back home" is the only way they can be done. What about the North American custom of having the weekly worship service on Sunday morning at eleven o'clock, for instance? Surely we would agree that what happens at a worship service is far more important than *when* or even *where* it takes place.

If gospel witnesses simply try to duplicate their home church organization and pattern on foreign soil, they will be left with a stymied, stunted product. About the kind of church such efforts produce, Dr. Alan Tippet says,

> Instead of being indigenous, it is only a foreignized church in the midst of a hostile heathenism... Instead of being a native plant growing under normal conditions, the church becomes an exotic hothouse growth, always needing shelter from cold blasts of heathen hatred.[4]

c) Failing to let converts assume responsibility. Another mistake gospel workers must avoid is the tendency to keep the reins of authority in their own hands. We have to learn the risk of faith. Until we delegate authority to Muslim converts, there will be no church growth among Muslims. We have to trust them—their ability to understand the Word of God, their ethical conduct, their capacity to handle finances, their moral standards—all in the light of the Bible and with the help of the Holy Spirit. Trusting Muslim converts to carry responsibility is trusting the Holy Spirit. True, some might fail the test of leadership, but great successes far outnumber and outweigh failures.

The example of Jesus again instructs us. Only forty days before Jesus ascended to His Father, Peter had clearly denied Him, and all the rest of His well-trained disciples had completely deserted Him. But without hesitation, He delegated to those same men the authority to carry out the huge responsibility of the most important mission in human history.

Paul provides us with another example. Phygelus, Hermogenes and other leaders deserted him. Demas, Hymenaeus, and Alexander failed, and Paul had to deal with their failures. But in spite of all this, he continued to advise his assistants and associates to delegate authority to others (1 Timothy 1:19–20; 2 Timothy 1:15, 4:10; Titus 1:5).

It is easy for leaders to be plagued with self-sufficiency. People called by God to be leaders are always in danger of trying to take on more than they can handle. It is a common mistake to think that because you are called to lead, you are also called to do everything yourself.

As a gospel witness in North Africa, the Holy Spirit taught me how to trust Muslim background believers to carry responsibilities that I enjoyed doing myself. Trusting them was not easy. It involved the possibility of failure, and I had to exercise faith. But with God's grace, I saw the necessity of delegating authority to converts even at the very beginning of their walk with Christ. I saw that my role was to win Muslims to Christ and immediately train them to be leaders.

For example, I administered water baptism only once to show Muslim converts how to do it. Several baptismal services took place after that, but they administered the rite to their compatriots. I administered communion only a few times to show converts how to serve communion. Afterward, serving it was their responsibility. Today, those trainees are the leaders of the church in that area.

Muslims emphasize their equality and brotherhood. This fact, as well as the biblical pattern seen in the examples given above, makes it essential to delegate responsibility to new Muslim background believers.

15 | *A Sensitive Strategy*

Raymond Lull (1232–1315) was one of the most notable intellectuals of his day. He came from a noble Spanish family from Majorca. He led a life of immorality and debauchery. When he saw a vision of Christ, he decided to follow the suffering Savior. Immediately God called him to give his life to win Muslims to Christ. He exhorted the Church to bring the Mongols to the Christian faith before they convert to Islam or Judaism.

His missionary strategy was to prepare hosts of men of God to be knowledgeable in Christian doctrine, fluent in the language of the people they would evangelize, and skilled in Muslim culture and beliefs! Also he indicated that he himself might someday lay down his life for the sake of Christ.

He established a missionary school to train the workers who would reach Muslims. He went to North Africa three times and led to Christ some notable people. There he was stoned at least twice. He died as a martyr.

(For details about Lull's life, see: Liam Brophy, *So Great A Lover*, Franciscan Herald Press, 1960.)

For centuries the Muslim world has been stamped as "resistant" to Christian missionary efforts. The description certainly seems to fit. Many missionaries have gathered their belongings and gone home in disappointment because, for them, it was impossible to convert Muslims to Christ. But why? Why have Christians failed to bring thousands and even millions of Muslims to be reconciled with God at the cross of Calvary? Why is the harvest from among the Muslim people so meager?

When Muslims come to Christ, it is the Holy Spirit who draws them. But Christian witnesses are responsible to plan and effectively strategize the part God gives them to play in the process. Missions executive Raymond Davis as he speaks of the great mid-twentieth century awakening in Ethiopia and concludes:

> there are factors that one can discover, effects of the wind that can be observed. When we try to trace out the pattern of God's working, we do not minimize His sovereign grace—we magnify it. As those who are responsible, under God, for the development of a successful strategy of world evangelization, we owe it to God, to the Church, to the world, to discover the means God used in Wallamo.[1]

So, in this chapter we seek to discover effective means of winning Muslims to Christ. We explore several practical, positive steps to help you develop a strategy that works.

PREPARE YOURSELF FOR MINISTRY

Evangelism among Muslims requires a sensitive strategy that is marked by deep, sacrificial love. To win their confidence, gospel workers must show them that they understand their religion, their culture, their way of thinking, and their grievances. How can we do this? We must first be sure that we ourselves are prepared.

Commit Yourself to Prayer and Fasting

God works miracles to confirm His Word in answer to the prayers and fasting of His people. There is no activity that needs our intensified, concentrated prayer and fasting as much as missionary work does. And one of the neediest areas of missions today is the Muslim world. By His example, Jesus taught us to pray and fast. And by His words,

He taught us how to pray and fast. Praying and fasting for Muslims is a very rewarding ministry, because God answers prayers and Muslims do get saved.

To go to Muslims with the message of the cross is to mount an open attack on the territory of Satan. The enemy does not stand there as an onlooker while the Christian witness tries to win them to Christ. He will come full force against you. Therefore, it is naive, rash, and presumptuous to try to win Muslims to the kingdom of God without first wrestling in prayer and fasting and prevailing.

It is important that we intercede for individuals and groups of people, for tribes and nations, for cities and countries. When we pray, we are able to bind the demonic powers that close doors and hinder the harvest—people are freed from bondage to receive Christ and the new life He offers. That is why the Word of God instructs us to pray. Paul says, "Devote yourselves to prayer" (Colossians 4:2).

Henry Martyn, possibly the first Protestant missionary to Muslims, said: "Oh, that I may be a man of prayer." Martin Luther said: "As it is the business of the tailor to make clothes and the cobbler to mend shoes, so it is the business of the Christian to pray." And the apostle James said that "the prayer of a righteous man is powerful and effective" (James 5:16). We move mountains not when we talk about prayer, not when we study prayer, not even when we believe in prayer, but when we pray.

Unless Christians rethink their prayer practices and discipline themselves into serious, intense prayer for Muslims, they should not be surprised when Islam resists missionary efforts and even tries to conquer a tired Christendom and take over a spiritually destitute and wayward Western world. I say "a tired Christendom" because it is overburdened by the trappings of past success, by a form of godliness that has long since lost its power, and by hollow rituals that have no life. I also say "spiritually destitute and wayward Western world" because it trivializes faith in Christ and because its mainly neo-pagan population is pagan by choice!

Depend on God's Word and God's Spirit

Rely on the power of the Word of God. Our weapon, our sword is the Word of God. We have to speak the Word of God simply and clearly, counting on the power of that Word. When someone who is shallow in the knowledge of God's Word tries to win a Muslim to Christ, often there are no results.

Gospel witnesses to Muslims should be well-established and deeply rooted in the Word. They should use the Bible with competence. As a missionary and communications professor observes:

To change a world, politicians have the tools of public opinion and the power of privileges given and withheld; generals have the might of armies, disciplined men and unbelievable powerful weapons; administrators have systems with objectives, accountability and the flow of money and benefits. But what does the Christian have with which to change the world? Only a Message.

Whenever the Church has depended on the tools of generals, politicians or administrators as [its] primary force, the Church has slid into decay and even extinction in areas of the world. And whenever the Church has failed, for any reason, to give the Message truly and understandably, the Church has been ignored in its obscurity. The Message is all we uniquely have; it is all we need to transform the world.[2]

Rely on the Power of the Holy Spirit. We must be filled with the power of the Holy Spirit to be able to help Muslims make the exodus into the freedom of Christ. Muslims will come into the Kingdom only by the power of the Spirit of God, not by our own strength or wisdom. The Bible says: "'Not by might nor by power, but by my Spirit,' says the Lord Almighty" (Zechariah 4:6). It is when Christian messengers forget about their resources in Christ, the power of the Spirit of God, that they come from the Muslim harvest empty-handed. When the Church of Jesus Christ forgets about her rights in Christ to manifest and operate the gifts of the Holy Spirit she becomes ineffective in Muslim evangelization.

If we depend on human wisdom and methods, what we accomplish will have no lasting value (John 15:5). It is true that we are responsible to carry on the task, but it is really the Holy Spirit who does the work of changing people's lives (Titus 3:5). In the next chapter, "Forces at War," we will say more about how the gifts and power of the Holy Spirit relate to Muslim evangelism.

Use Your Mind and Heart

Know them. There is no substitute for knowing your Muslim audience. While this text has given you some help, you should consider it to be only an introduction. Some areas will require your continued attention. Know the following:

1. Their book and beliefs. Become familiar with the Qur'an and the significance it holds for Muslims. Acquaint yourself with their beliefs.

2. Their culture and practices. Study their way of life and try to understand it. Know their likes and dislikes. Observe and understand the impact of folk religion on everyday life.

3. Their literature and stories. Acquaint yourself with some of their literature and stories. These tell a lot about the people, about their society and how it works. That is why, for example, the stories of the popular character Goha (sometimes called Joha or Mulla Nasrudin) shed an incredible light on interpersonal relations and cultural traits of the society where these stories are created![3]

Love Them. Muslims, like any other people, need to be loved, accepted, and understood. The gospel witness must be permeated with genuine, sacrificial, self-giving love for Muslims. We greatly manifest God's love to them when we are gentle, kind, and forgiving, and when our interest in them is genuine and we intercede for them in prayer. We do have something precious that we can give them, and they can get it from no one else—the gospel of Christ. The Lausanne Committee for World Evangelization makes this comment:

> Over the centuries Christians in both the West and the East have all too readily cherished and cultivated an antipathy towards Muslims and have expressed it by essentially neglecting their obligation under God to share Jesus Christ with them.[4]

Muslim individuals are not enemies to be conquered. We will never be able to win them to Christ unless we befriend them and with gentle love try to bring them to meet our Savior at the cross.

Our love and obedience to God and our love and interest in our Muslim friends compel us to help them see the importance of the gospel message. Our motivation then is not contempt or condemnation, but rather love and commitment. We are not in the business of religious confrontation; rather, we are messengers of reconciliation. Our life among them should be marked by the kind of love described in 1 Corinthians 13.

Be a Credible Messenger

As you go to Muslims with the gospel of Christ, they will watch your lifestyle closely. They will be very curious to know your eating and drinking habits. They have heard that "Christians" get drunk and eat pork, that their women have loose morals and appear half naked in public. Although under grace you are free, if exercising that freedom is your first priority, you will offend Muslims rather than win them.

COMMUNICATE WITH YOUR AUDIENCE

The Christian witness must also learn how to communicate effectively with Muslims.

We are offering Muslims the message of God's love revealed in Christ on Calvary. It is so simple, but we often make it hard to understand. The way we present the gospel of Jesus Christ—the words we use and the content and structure of the message we offer—decides whether or not Muslims will hear the truth we offer.

Make the Meaning Plain

What the Christian witness says can be easily misunderstood. A Muslim who "agrees" with what I (the Christian witness) say may not be agreeing with me at all. Because when I say something, the hearer interprets it, and he agrees with what he thinks I mean. This happens because when I speak, the words my listener hears are translated in his mind within the sphere of his own word meaning, life experiences, cultural traits, and religious beliefs. Therefore my words are translated into the same meanings I intended sometimes and other times they are not.

So when I make a statement, I am responsible for the kind of words I choose as well as the meanings my words bring to the hearer's mind. When I say "sin," for example, my Muslim friends hear the word, but is the meaning that their brain receives the same meaning I intended? Certainly not. I mean "sin" in the biblical sense, while their concept of sin is totally different. So I need to find out what meaning my hearer will attach to the words I say.

The incident described in John 18:28—19:16 shows that Jesus understood this principle. In His brief exchange with Pilate over the meaning of the word "king," Jesus showed His awareness that the word had two different meanings. To Pilate it had a political meaning. If Jesus said He was a king, Pilate would interpret Him as saying that He was a rival to Caesar, a pretender to the throne of Judea. To the Jews it had a militant meaning. If He said He was a king, the Jews would interpret Him as saying that He was a revolutionary, a Messiah who would over-throw the yoke of Rome. Both meanings are defective. Yet Jesus is King, but in a sense different from both and more sublime than both.

When Pilate asked Jesus if He were a king, Jesus did not answer yes or no. "Yes" would have meant that He was a political rival. "No" would have meant that He completely denied being any kind of king at all. So Jesus wanted first to establish a common understanding of the word "king". He asked Pilate: "Is that your own idea... or did others talk to you about me?" To put it another way, He was asking something like this: "What is the source of your information? Who told you that?" In other words, "How do you understand the word 'king,'—in the Roman or the Jewish sense?"

Pilate did not like the question. He protested that he was not a Jew to use the word in a Jewish sense. He pointed out to Jesus that it was His own nation and the religious leaders of His people who were accusing Him. That is, it was a Jewish allegation. Then Pilate asked Jesus, "What have you done?" But Jesus took him back to the essential issue, telling him that He was a king in a different sense, and that His kingdom was not of this world.

As a matter of fact Pilate's source of information is mentioned explicitly in Luke 23:1–3. The Jewish priests and elders said: "He claims to be the Christ [that is, a king]." I believe Pilate understood Jesus' answer, that He was truly a king, but not over Palestine or Rome or a piece of land in the Roman Empire; rather over a heavenly realm. Thus Pilate felt that Caesar's throne and his own position were not threatened. That explains the ruler's statement, "I have found no basis for your charge against him" (Luke 23:14–6).

Like Jesus, we must be sure that we have made our meanings clear. Good communication with Muslims is indispensable in order to drive home the gospel truths we want them to accept. If we give confused signals, how can we expect positive responses? Some say, "Muslims reject Christ," but what kind of Christ have they "rejected"? What do they think when we say, "Christ"? What do *we* mean when we say "Christ"? Is He the same Christ as the Christ of the Bible, or is He a Christ of our making? Have we hidden Him behind cultural traits and expressions that may be meaningless to our Muslim friends at best, or frustrating and disturbing to them at worst? Like Paul, we must avoid such distortions and set forth the truth plainly (2 Corinthians 3:2).

Avoid Common Misconceptions

Christians are used to using certain words and phrases when they talk about spiritual things. Often they are unaware that many of those expressions have very different connotations for unchurched people and particularly for Muslims. So the gospel witness may have to state things in a different way in some cases so that Muslims will understand. It is also true that some words Muslims themselves use may work very well. Following are some areas of possible controversy or misunderstanding and how to deal with them.

The question: "Are you a Christian?" Most Muslims use the word "Christian" to mean someone who comes from a culture that is broadly labeled as Christian. They get their information about what a Christian is from books, movies, and tourists from places like Europe and the United States. With that in mind, they conclude that a Christian is a person who has base morals, eats pork, and drinks alcohol (both forbidden by the Qur'an). In other words, Muslims often associate with the term "Christian" the things that born-again believers from the West often associate with the term "non-Christian"!

How should one respond to this question? To answer, let us look at the history of the term "Christian." The Greek word *Christianos* occurs in only three places in the New Testament: Acts 11:26; 26:28; and 1 Peter 4:16. In all three contexts, Christianos is a description of the followers of Christ by non-Christians. It is chiefly used to designate a person as a member of a particular group, not to indicate anything significant about his way of life and religious convictions. When the writers of the New Testament wished to refer to the followers of

Christ, they used other terms, such as "disciples," "believers," "those who are in Christ," or "God's people."

In the context of Muslim evangelism, are we obligated to use the term "Christian" to identify ourselves? The answer depends on the meaning that particular society has for "Christian"! If Muslims ask us, "Are you a Christian?" we first need to find out what the term means to them. Here is a sample of the kind of conversation that avoids misconceptions.

Muslim seeker: "Are you a Christian?"

Witness: "What do you mean by Christian?"

Muslim seeker: "I mean Westerner, European, non-Muslim, someone who does not follow the teachings of the Qur'an. I mean someone with low morals like the people I see in the movies and read about in the books that come from Europe and the United States."

Witness: "If that is what you mean, my answer is 'No.' In fact, I was that kind of person you have described, but I got converted! Now I follow Christ according to the Bible."

The question: "Do you believe in the Trinity?" Again, the gospel witness must find out what the Muslim means before he or she gives an answer. By asking this question, the Muslim may be seeking to know whether the witness believes in a trinity of Allah, His wife (Mary), and their son (Jesus), or in a trinity of God, the Son, and the Holy Spirit as three separate gods. If the gospel worker says "yes" without clarifying the meaning of "Trinity," the Muslim will conclude that the missionary believes in three gods! If the witness says "no," he or she will be denying what the Bible teaches and the Muslim will not learn the truth. When this question comes up, you must explain what you mean by the term "Trinity" before you answer it.

The question: "Is Jesus the Son of God?" Again, this question can lead to miscommunication. If a Christian witness says "yes," a Muslim may think that God had a wife, and Jesus is their offspring. This is what he or she has been taught.

The question: "Did Christ die?" For the Muslim, the Christian belief in the death of Christ means that Jesus' followers worship a God who is weaker than Satan, a God who was defeated by Satan.

Instead of answering "yes" at first, the witness might respond with another question in order to provoke a deeper examination of the death of Jesus (to show that the cross demonstrates God's love). For example, the Christian witness might ask the Muslim something like this: "If your child's life were in danger, and your death could save him, would you give up your life?"

The use of the name "Allah" for God. While I do not intend this to be an exhaustive study of the subject, I would like to shed some light on it to help us understand the issue.[5]

In recent years, some people have said that since the *Allah* of Islam is not the same as the God of the Bible, Christian witnesses to Muslims should use a different name to refer to God, our Creator and Savior.

Some have also written articles stating that when a Muslim comes to Christ, he should do away with the name *Allah* and use some other name for God. One of those articles, written by an American missiologist of renown, went so far as to claim that *Allah* is a created angelic being who ended up as an agent of darkness just like Satan did! Question: Where did the author obtain such blatantly false information? He did not tell the readers!

The name *Allah* comes from the Arabic *al* and *ilah* meaning "the god" and signifies the most high God. This is, in reality, not a name coined by Muhammad or Islam, nor is it an exclusively Muslim name for God. This point is very important. *Allah* is an Arabic name. It existed before Islam. Muhammad's father who died some months before the birth of Muhammad and forty years before Islam came into existence was called Abdullah, meaning "servant of Allah."

At that time and even earlier, *Allah* was the name used by Christians in Mecca and throughout Arabia (as well as by pagans in those lands). So, the Christian Church among Arabs worshipped *Allah* long before the coming of Islam. That church knew even better than we do today that there were erroneous teachings associated with the word *Allah* as it was employed among pagans. Nevertheless, they still felt it was the word to use.

The problem with the name *Allah* is not the word itself. The serious problem is in the wrong concepts attached to it. When Muslims say *Allah*, they mean the remote Deity, the vengeful God, the Lord of the Day of Judgment, and so forth. On the other hand, when I as a born-again Christian say *Allah*, I mean the loving heavenly Father who cares for me, who sacrificed Jesus for my sake, and so on.

The truth is that no matter what name one gives the Creator, the Islamic concept of Him will remain flawed and sub-biblical. A missionary from the 1800s expresses it this way:

> the just Judge [will be] lost in the Sovereign, the Father lost in the King, the prayer-hearing Parent lost in the dread of the Fearful, the Person lost in a grand pantheistic Negation, the ever-present One in a universal Nothing. All these fearful misconceptions must be corrected, but we cannot change the name by which He is known.[6]

So changing the word *Allah* will not change the concept Muslims have for the Supreme Being. It is the concept that needs to be changed.

Another question: If we did decide to substitute another word for *Allah*, why not do the same thing for "Jesus?" After that there are others like "Abraham" and "Moses" and so forth. Certainly Muslims' understanding of Abraham and Moses and many other biblical personalities is defective when held up to the light of the Scriptures.

In many languages, people use names for God that may have pagan associations. Bible translator and author Eugene Peterson notes that

> *El*, the regular Canaanite term for god, was also a term freely used by the Hebrews. Among the Canaanites *El* was the head god, the father of the gods, who with his wife Asherah fathered a vast progeny of gods and goddesses. The Hebrews seemed unembarrassed to share the word, tainted as it was, with their neighbors.[7]

Studying the etymology of the English word "God," we find that it is an Indo-Germanic word. In Europe it referred to a northern European deity. So it became God in English; *Gott* in German (akin to Persian *Khoda* and Hindu *Khooda*); *Gud* in Swedish, Norwegian, and Danish; and *God* in Dutch. All these are names that Christian believers have used for many generations.

Zeus was the chief of the Greek gods. This name became *Theos* in Greek, *Deus* in Portuguese, *Dios* in Spanish, *Iddio* in Italian, *Dieu* in French, and *Dia* in Irish and Gaelic. Again, all these are names that Christian believers have used for many generations.[8]

The English word *God* or any other of the names listed above is not necessarily superior to the Arabic word *Allah* from a linguistic point of view. In fact, one could make a case that the reverse is true. Since both Hebrew and Arabic are Semitic languages, the Arabic name *Allah* is virtually the same as the Old Testament Hebrew name *Eloah*.

Even today, *Allah* is still the only Arabic word for God. That is why both Christians and Muslims use it. More than ten million Christians in the Middle East and North Africa use the word *Allah* to refer to God. When I read my Arabic Bible, *Allah* is the word for God there. All Arabic Bibles in various translations produced over many centuries use *Allah* for God. He is to them the triune God—the Father, the Son and the Holy Spirit. I have more than twenty-two of those translations, some of which were done by Jews in Arab lands!

When Paul preached to the Athenians in Acts 17:22–31 he used the Greek name for God which is *Theos*. He used it even though their concept of the Supreme Being called by that name came very short of our Christian concept of God and was, in fact, scripturally outright erroneous! Paul's speech was aimed at correcting those errors.[9]

Paul's discourse serves as an example to encourage gospel witnesses among Muslims to use *Allah* because it is the Arabic name for the Supreme Being, and to clothe that name in the biblical meaning they seek to project and teach. By doing that they will find it easier to establish a bridge of communication with their audience.

The question: "Do you believe that Muhammad was a prophet?" How should you respond to a friend who asks that question? To answer, let us first investigate the meaning of the term "prophet." You need to be sure you know two things about this term: a) how the Bible uses it, and b) how most Muslims use it.

The Bible does not give us a definition of "prophet," but it shows us what a prophet does. Consider the following:

1. A true prophet speaks God's words to people (Deuteronomy 18:18).

2. The test of a person being a true prophet or not is whether or not his prophecies are fulfilled. Moses said to his people:

You may wonder, "How will we know whether the prophecy is from the LORD or not?" If the prophet predicts something in the LORD's name and it does not happen, the LORD did not give the message. That prophet has spoken on his own and need not be feared (Deuteronomy 18:21–22, New Living Translation).

When God gave messages to the prophet Ezekiel, He assured the prophet that those messages would come true. God said that would be the sign that He had indeed sent Ezekiel to His people. "When all this comes true—and it surely will—then they will know that a prophet has been among them" (Ezekiel 33:33).

3. Not all prophets are true prophets. A prophet can also mislead people and speak his own words rather than the words of God. He may even speak on behalf of other gods (Deuteronomy 18:20, 22)! For instance, Nehemiah prayed to God to remember the evil deeds of "the prophetess Noadiah and the rest of the prophets who have been trying to intimidate me" (Nehemiah 6:14). Hananiah, son of Azzur, was called a prophet, yet what he prophesied was clearly not from the Lord (Jeremiah 28:1, 3 and 15–17).

4. To confirm his mission, a prophet may have a dream or a revelation or may also offer a miracle or a sign (Deuteronomy 13:1–2). However, the test of such a prophet is not what he can do but which God he preaches (Deuteronomy 13:3; see also Galatians 1:8).

5. The term "prophet" is sometimes used as synonymous with poet or philosopher (Titus 1:12).

Now let us consider what the term "prophet" means to Muslims. Some meanings are similar to those found in the Bible. For instance, some Muslim commentators consider Aesop[10] to be a prophet. This meaning would correspond to the general sense in which Paul used the term (Titus 1:12). Some Muslims also consider Alexander the Macedonian to be a prophet. The term has a military and political connotation in this case. Supremely, though, Islam considers Muhammad to be a prophet. The term has a wide, inclusive meaning when applied to him. It means that Muhammad received a message from God, which made him the final messenger from God and the military, social, and political genius who forged the nation of Islam.

Muslims consider Muhammad to be their hero. Should a Christian witness try to discredit him? History acknowledges that Muhammad accomplished much. Here are some of his qualities and accomplishments. He was a champion of the weak, a skilled statesman, and an innovative soldier. He often showed himself to be a fair, honest man. He brought the Arabs out of the darkness of idol worship into monotheism. He was a man of unusual literary gifts who had words and expressions fit for the occasion, and his oratorical skills endeared him to his people. From the standpoint of human achievements, he was the founder of perhaps one of the greatest political and social movements the world has seen.

My point is this. There is no call for you to needlessly insult your Muslim friend by denigrating Muhammad or by saying he was not a prophet. To any Muslim, that would come across as aggressive and hostile. It could also signal to your Muslim friend that you reject and hate all Muslims, since they admire Muhammad so much.

Artemis was the goddess of Ephesus. When Paul brought the Gospel to that city, he did not attack or discredit their goddess. The city clerk testified to that fact when he said: "You [Ephesians] have brought these men here, though they have neither robbed temples nor blasphemed our goddess" (Acts 19:37). We do not need to blaspheme or discredit Muhammad or attack Islam in order to be able to win Muslims to Christ. The Bible teaches us to lead a quiet life (I Thessalonians 4:11–12), to respect everyone (I Peter 2:17), and to be ready to give an answer about our faith with gentleness and respect (I Peter 3:15–16).

MAKE THE TRUTH AVAILABLE

Our great example for ministry is God Himself. The Bible shows us that He starts with men and women where they are. Consider Israel in Egypt. At first the people were not willing to leave. But kindly and patiently, God used a series of circumstances to gradually change their minds. The inspired prophets, apostles, and writers followed the same principle. Drawing close to their audiences, they expressed themselves in stories, parables, and illustrations drawn from the familiar scenes of everyday life. God wanted to be understood, so He met His people at their level.

Ultimately, God became man—a human being like us. The Son of God walked where we walk, felt what we feel and took our sins and diseases on Himself. If our goal is to minister to Muslims, we have to meet them at their level, wherever that is. Our success or failure to meet them where they are is the factor that will decide whether or not they understand our message. There are three ways in which we must meet them.

Meet Them at Their Theological Level

We must meet Muslims at their theological level. Your Muslim friend will bring up certain serious differences, misconceptions, and questions as you talk with him or her. These, as we mentioned, relate to the deity and Sonship of Jesus Christ, the Trinity, the cross of Jesus, and the inspiration of the Bible. It is your responsibility to answer the questions in a way that brings glory to the name of our Lord. Previous chapters have suggested ways to do this.

However, when you talk with your Muslim friend, it is better to start on common ground. There are several items in the Muslim faith that can be used as bridges. As you have discovered, Muslims believe in one God who is the only Creator. They also believe that Jesus Christ was born of a virgin, did miracles, was sinless, and ascended to heaven. These beliefs and others make good starting points. Then you can proceed to gradually explain the full gospel message.

What you want your Muslim friend to realize is this: You are not in a "war of religions" against him or her. You are not trying to win a theological debate or a talking competition! Rather you have a message that you believe God sent you to offer to others. It is the message of God's love to all people. So, this is not about Muhammad or Islam. It is not even about Christianity or any other religion. It is about eternal life with God offered free to everyone through the grace of our Lord the Christ.

I usually refuse to get involved in arguments regarding Christianity versus Islam, Jesus versus Muhammad, the Bible versus the Qur'an, and so forth. Seldom have such arguments brought forth positive fruit. Rather, the damage they cause is often irreparable. That is why gospel witnesses should never lose sight of what their mission is about—helping precious souls find peace with God.

Even Jesus did not start to train his disciples by first presenting hard, deep theological issues.. It took Him some time to drive home to their minds and hearts who He really was. He did not offend them at the beginning of His ministry by talking about the cross or sending them out to evangelize the Gentiles.

Your Muslim friends need salvation from sin. Your goal is to help them, not defeat them. They have spiritual needs. They need peace of heart and mind. They need the baptism in the Holy Spirit. They need divine healing and deliverance from satanic power and fear. Your task is not to win arguments but to lead them into a living relationship with Jesus Christ.

Meet Them at Their Cultural Level

What is culture? A missionary and brilliant author of the twentieth century answers that question:

> When we speak of culture in its broadest sense, we are speaking about the sum total of ways of living that shape (and also are shaped by) the continuing life of a group of human beings from generation to generation. We are speaking about the language that enables them to grasp, conceptualize, and communicate the reality of their world; about law, custom, and forms of social organization, including marriage, family, and agriculture. These things shape the life of each member of the society. They are also shaped, modified, and developed from generation to generation by the members of the society. From the point of view of the individual member they are given as part of the tradition into which he or she is born and socialized.[11]

So, culture is the system of traits, actions and responses characteristic of a group of people. In brief it is their way of life. Every culture has its own set of rules. Cultural rules are not learned from a book; they are learned mostly by being in the culture and participating in it.

To make the truth available to Muslims, we must meet them at their cultural level in three basic ways.

1. *Understand how Muslims tend to view Christianity in relation to their culture.* Traditional Muslims see Christianity as a danger to their way of life. In many cases they do not even want to hear the gospel because they believe it is a threat to the solidarity of their Islamic

community, a force that will destroy the fabric of the society of the "faithful."

What causes this negative viewpoint? Sometimes gospel witnesses themselves are to blame. Many have not tried to adapt their message to the Muslim culture. The Lausanne Committee says that in work among Muslims, "missions agencies continue to conduct… culturally insensitive, unplanned missionary work…"[12]

Like every culture, Muslim culture has its accepted styles of communication. Gospel witnesses should not be surprised that their Muslim audience responds unfavorably if these communication patterns are ignored. In other words, the problem is not so much that the gospel looks "wrong" to Muslims, rather it looks alien. It strikes them as distinctly foreign, and they want nothing to do with it.

Muslims see the Christian evangelist as trying to impose on them strange new customs and traditions. They imagine that in order to be a Christian they must renounce their own culture, lose their own identity, and betray their own people. They look at fellow Muslims who have become Christians as traitors to the House of Islam. In their society, such converts have forfeited the privileges of belonging to the Community of the Prophet, the ummah. They have become defectors who must be eliminated as sources of pollution and corruption.

However, the truth is that the gospel of Jesus Christ is not out to destroy or defeat Muslim culture—or any other culture. God has created a colorful mosaic of human races. In the words of the Lausanne Committee:

> This rich variety should be preserved, not destroyed by the Gospel. The attempt to impose another culture on people who have their own is cultural imperialism. The attempt to level all cultures into a colorless uniformity is a denial of the Creator and an affront to His creation.[13]

We need to emphasize to the Muslim seeker that belonging to Christ does not mean abandoning his society or converting to a different culture.

2. *Recognize that ideas of cultural superiority are hindrances to effective cross-cultural ministry*. British theologian John Stott points out

a significant truth about the cultures of humankind: "Because man is God's creature, some of his culture is rich in beauty and goodness. Because he is fallen, all of it is tainted with sin and some of it is demonic."[14] Many of us have grown up with the idea that our own culture is the best. We are often blind to our own faults, faults that others often see very clearly. For example, Christian believers in developing countries are often shocked at the blatant materialism which is all too common among Christians in the affluent West.

Paul said that he had a lot to boast about in regard to his culture. Jesus had to deal with Paul's attitude to be able to use him effectively among the Gentiles (cross-culturally). Literally, Jesus had to strip Paul of the pride he took in his Jewish ancestry and way of life.

In order to win Muslims to Christ, we must respect their culture. We must discover how to offer them the gospel in a way that attracts their attention and appeals to them. We have to wrap the gift of salvation in a manner that fits their way of doing things. At the same time, we should be careful not to distort the gospel message. The need to maintain this balance leads us to our next task.

3. *Evaluate cultural traits in the light of the Scriptures*. What about Islamic culture itself? As Muslims are attracted to Christ, accept Him, and start to live for Him, how do we deal with the customs of their culture? There are various traits which must be considered in the light of the Scriptures. They can be grouped into the following categories.

a) Cultural traits that should be renounced. These are the ones that should be rejected and discontinued immediately because the Word of God regards them as sinful. This category includes traits such as swearing, cheating, or lying. Teach Muslim converts what the Bible says about such issues.

b) Cultural traits that may be tolerated. Certain traits are part of a culture's social fabric. In order to avoid serious disruption, they must be changed slowly and gradually. An example of this is polygamy. It is the author's opinion that a man who has more than one wife is free to accept the Lord with his whole family. They can all become church members. However, polygamous unions should not be encouraged for converts who are not already involved in them.

c) Cultural traits that can be retained. In my opinion, some of the features of Muslim society can be kept as they are, such as the emphasis on Allah in everyday life. Others can be kept but transformed, such as the practice of setting aside a month for fasting.

No one can give absolute rules for these issues. These observations are offered to show how to evaluate and deal in a sensitive way with the various patterns of Islamic culture. As you encounter specific situations, you will need to seek the wisdom and guidance of the Lord.

Present the Gospel in Muslim Garments

The Christian witness who communicates the gospel to Muslims must also find culturally sensitive ways of fostering their spiritual growth. We need to present the gospel message in Muslim garments. Following are some guidelines for doing this.

Use familiar forms of worship. The Muslim form of worship, called "prayer," is different from what we are acquainted with in our churches. While it is our custom to enter church with our shoes on and sit on a bench or a comfortable seat, these are unacceptable forms in Islam. To pray, Muslims take off their shoes, wash according to formal rituals, and sit and pray on the floor, usually using a prayer mat. I have prayed with Muslims to God in the name of our Lord and Savior Jesus Christ on straw mats. On the other hand, I prayed recently with a Muslim high government official in his living room without having to take off my shoes. Why? Because he has visited several churches and knows how services are conducted. Therefore he expected me to behave in that way. It was touching to see tears in his eyes when I finished.

Recognize that for Muslims, conversion is usually a process rather than a crisis experience. Many of us from nominal Christian backgrounds have a limited view of conversion. We have come to interpret it only as a sudden, crisis experience. Is this interpretation biblical? The Lausanne Committee says that "elements in our traditional evangelical view of conversion are more cultural than Biblical and need to be challenged."[15] We must recognize that a process form of conversion is equally valid. It would be extremely difficult for Muslims to be converted without going through a long period of change (much longer than the conversion of nominal Western Christians). They must study, weigh matters in their own mind, repent, believe on the Lord Jesus Christ, change some of their ways, and renounce their past allegiance.

Speak their language. To help Muslims hear the gospel and understand it, we must speak their language: not only Arabic, Urdu, Turkish, Farsi, or other languages used by Muslim peoples, but also the daily language common to all Muslims—the words and phrases which show that life and religion are all part of the same whole. This language comprises the words *Allah*, *Isa* (Jesus), *masjed* (place of worship), *djamaa* (mosque), *subhan Allah* (praise or glory be to God), *bismellah* (in the name of God), and other similar expressions.

Respect their social ties. We have noted that Islam is a community religion. Generally speaking, Muslims are group-oriented. In this they vastly differ from the Western ideal of individuality and personal independence.

For example, in most of Europe and the United States, marriage is an individual's personal matter. It is no one else's business for the most part. Even the parents are often not consulted. Advice may sometimes be offered, but the final decision is almost always the couple's. This is not the case in Muslim communities. The marriage of a young man or woman involves basically and primarily the two families. Western individualistic behavior is not encouraged and sometimes not even tolerated.

What does this group orientation of traditional Muslim society mean for Christian witnesses? It means that we must be sensitive to the strong links that bind people together. Be careful not to break down what ties the family has. Encourage the converts to make changes in a way that causes minimum rejection for them; and foster the changes collectively whenever possible (hopefully the whole household or social unit together). Realize that to build the Church of Jesus Christ only on individuals will result in a weak establishment that is foreign to the culture.

We do not deny the fact that accepting Christ in one's life is a personal matter that concerns the transformation of one individual life. In evangelizing though, we must constantly aim to bring groups, families, and communities into the body of Christ. Let us pray that group movements from within Islam will bring hundreds of thousands and millions of Muslims to give their total allegiance to Jesus Christ.

Meet practical needs. Like everyone else, Muslims need to be loved and accepted. It is our duty to seek to know their felt needs and respond to them as much as possible. Maybe someone we know needs food, a doctor's care, clothes or a spouse. When we are deeply involved with people and show them love and care, they are more open to the message of life we proclaim.

Find functional substitutes. Religion fills the life of the traditional Muslim. Converts need institutions and forms that fit within their culture and fulfill the social functions that were met by the old forms.

For instance, devout Muslims will sacrifice and save money in order to make a pilgrimage to Mecca at least once in their life. Such a pilgrimage has a powerful effect on them as they feel the excitement of joining in international brotherhood with Muslims from all over the world. What in Christianity corresponds to this powerful ritual? Christians do not revere holy sites, of course. However, they do recognize the value of gatherings that draw many people together as part of a large Christian family whose membership crosses political and social barriers. In many parts of the world, prayer conferences, camp meetings, conventions and the like are organized to bring believers together. Similar conferences could be organized with the purpose of serving as functional substitutes for some Muslim celebrations.

THINGS TO AVOID

A sensitive strategy for winning and discipling Muslims has some "don'ts" as well. Following are three serious errors that Christian witnesses should avoid in their ministry among Muslims.

Avoid Promoting Your Own Cultural Traits

There is always a strong tendency for the surrounding culture of any particular group of Christian believers to shape its understanding of Christian standards and behavior. We must recognize this and avoid imposing our particular cultural "hang-ups" on a church made up of Muslim converts.

When we look at Christianity worldwide we see differences among Christian believers on a variety of issues. The use of alcohol is a good example. To evangelicals in France, the drinking of alcoholic beverages "soberly" is accepted and considered natural. Most evangelicals in the United States abstain totally from alcohol.

Standards of dress provide a second illustration. Ladies in the United States may have short hair and wear sleeveless dresses in Pentecostal churches without causing any offense. In Italy, in some rural areas, many Pentecostal churches would find such behavior unacceptable.

The form of worship gives us a third illustration. The Christian Church definitely has its roots in the Jewish synagogue. A comparison of Christian forms of worship with Judaism shows that many Christian customs can be easily identified as extensions of Jewish culture. Even the buildings in which Jews and Christians worship often show a striking similarity.

A fourth illustration is the naming of children. In Christian circles, children's names often follow Jewish preferences, such as Isaac, Rebecca, or Jonathan rather than Ishmael, Khaled or Hagar, which are common names among Muslims. Significantly, all these names are biblical! Workers among Muslims show prejudice and lack of love if they ask Muslim converts to change their names. They also show prejudice if they imply that converts should select Jewish names for their children.

Avoid Removing Converts from Their Society and Culture

Muslims who commit their life to Christ are tempted to escape persecution and leave their society altogether to live in freedom. We cannot understand the pain and suffering converts encounter. Under the Islamic law their very life is threatened. But it is a big loss for the converts' community if they decide to leave—loss of witnesses for Christ; loss of believers' impact on the society; and so forth. Christian workers need to discourage such a move without judging those who choose to make it.

We also need to consider what happens to a group of Muslim converts that is grafted into a group of ethnic Christians. Some of the results, in my estimation, are negative. I will mention a few.

Such a group will consistently take the form of worship and use the behavioral patterns and theological expressions of the ethnic Christians. This is not just in church meetings and spiritual matters. The effect shows also in everyday life of these converts. They talk and behave as if they were ethnic Christians. I am not referring to the work of God's Spirit in changed lives; rather, the adopting of a culture that is not originally theirs. Even the music they start using is not genuinely from their culture. It is the music ethnic Christians use (and even some of that has been translated from English and uses Western tunes). Muslims who place their faith in Christ and who are grafted into ethnic Christian groups put aside their own culture and adopt totally different cultural traits.

In such a situation Muslim converts are usually stymied in their Christian growth. They look up to the ethnic Christians and are awed by their seniority in Christ. These Muslim believers reason that since they themselves are new to the faith, the Christians know much more and can therefore run things more efficiently. New Muslim believers in these situations have little chance to develop into leaders.

What can gospel workers do to prevent Muslim converts from losing their cultural identity? I suggest that Muslim converts have their own separate meetings. This will give them the opportunity, under the guidance of the Holy Spirit, to develop patterns of worship that are meaningful to them. Christians in many parts of the world often divide believers into age/gender groups (men, women, young people, children) or ethnic groups (the Hispanic meeting, the Korean meeting, the Vietnamese meeting) in order to build their sense of worth and achieve specific goals. I am of the opinion that this should be done with Muslim converts. If the group is truly their group, they will feel freer to develop their own music and worship forms and promote responsible leadership among themselves.

Avoid Spoiling Muslim Converts

Gospel workers need to be very careful about the way they treat Muslim converts. Giving too much attention to new converts can cause as many problems as giving them no attention at all. You may very possibly lose them either way.

Because Christian witnesses have frequently found it difficult to win Muslims to Christ, we hardly know what to do when we succeed. When miraculously one does come to Christ, we find this so unusual and so historic that the convert becomes the focus of an enormous amount of attention. This extraordinary "status" can prove to be suffocating and spiritually fatal. Sometimes the Muslim convert becomes a spoiled child who makes arrogant demands of his or her spiritual parents and gets by with all kinds of wrong behavior. This goes on until an explosion takes place and either he rebels against them completely or they desert him. In either case, the outcome is tragic.

God will help us as we develop a sensitive strategy for winning Muslims to Christ. As we follow the guidance of His Spirit, we will learn how to fully enter their world, yet remain true to the gospel. What we say and how we say it is important.

16 | *Forces At War*

Christians who seek to win Muslims to Christ must understand that the conflict with Islam is a spiritual warfare. For the true Christian, this is an inspiring and challenging thought. Indeed, the Commander-in-Chief of our armies is none other than the Ruler of the universe, the Absolute Sovereign over all kings and chiefs.

Yet, for secularists, non-religionists and many others, the prospect of spiritual warfare should be sobering indeed. For such people, to confront Islam is disheartening, overwhelming, and even frightening. Why? The weapons available to them are philosophical and humanistic arguments on one hand and arsenals of military hardware on the other.

If they are armed only with these, they have no chance to stand up to Islam. Neither philosophy nor military force can defeat the spiritual powers behind Islam.

Something much greater is needed.

We have observed that traditional Muslims accept the reality of what is not seen as well as what is seen. In contrast to secular materialists in the West, average Muslims not only believe in the supernatural but also are involved, to a greater or lesser extent, with spiritual forces and phenomena.

Their belief system includes a particular understanding of invisible entities and the powers of the underworld.

For this reason, gospel workers among Muslims must be fully prepared to back up their message by dealing with the invisible forces that oppose the good news of Jesus Christ. If they are unable to do this, they will find that their ministry is severely limited. But evangelists have no reason to be handicapped. Jesus Christ has provided for victory on every level. The confrontation between opposing forces, good against evil, is called "power encounter" or "showdown of powers."

WHAT IS POWER ENCOUNTER?

Ahmad (not his real name) was a Muslim college student. He accepted Christ. Six months later, he was baptized in water and filled with the Holy Spirit on the same day.

He liked to skin dive. One day after he was converted, he was skin diving in the Mediterranean Sea. Down under the water where he was diving, he caught his foot in the crevice of some rocks. He tried and tried to get free, but nothing worked. Finally, he said he actually began to feel the life leaving his body. Then he said in desperation, "Jesus." Just His name. But he said it as a prayer. And he still doesn't know how it happened, but he found himself at the surface of the water.

This was clearly a miracle.

After Ahmad graduated from college, he was appointed to a very good position with the government. A few months later he was called in for military service. Since there was no guarantee that he would be rehired after serving in the military, he had to confront the real possibility of losing his good job. But he had to go.

On his first day at the military camp, they shaved his head and gave him military fatigues. During a break, he sat under a tree, discouraged and despondent. He said that he tried to pray, but words would not come. Yet his soul was crying out to God for help. All of a sudden, he heard a voice from behind him saying: "Where is Jesus whom you have been following? Ha! Jesus is not the mighty God. Muhammad is the prophet of God. Can Jesus help you now? Renounce your faith in Him and call on Muhammad." He said that the voice was almost audible. He immediately rebuked the voice and said: "Satan, get away from me. You're a liar." Then he continued, "Jesus, I believe in You. You are the Son of God. You are my Lord, my Savior, my everything. I love You Jesus. Help me." Only a few hours later the young man was discharged from the military and was able to return to his job. No explanation was given for his release.[1]

This was a power encounter.

A power encounter or showdown of powers is an open, public confrontation between opposing forces. The outcome of this clash is often demonstrated in some tangible form—practical, audible or visible.

In Muslim evangelism, the opposing forces involved are: on one side, the Spirit of God acting in power through the gospel that the Christian witness proclaims; and on the other side, the unregenerate hearts of people along with the spiritual forces of evil opposing the gospel.

These evil forces act through beliefs and traditions. In an average Islamic society, they are backed by a host of other factors, such as the tight grip of religious, political and social authorities; the influence of the Qur'an; the sayings of the Hadith; and the impress of Muhammad. The evil forces involved instigate bitter conflict, spread hatred and animosity, and blind people to spiritual truths by closing their minds and searing their consciences.

The Bible tells of power encounters that gave men of God an open door to speak on God's behalf and declare His glory (I Kings 18:36–39; Acts 28:3–10). These encounters also motivated people to listen to the message (Acts 8:6–7).

Power encounters have the same results today. Through them, people see the power of God at work as they hear the good news of Jesus. The Holy Spirit ministers to needs, alleviates pain and suffering, dispels fears, grants security and assurance, and fills hearts with Christ's love. The living Christ is recognized as having the ability to help people in their everyday needs and difficulties.

That Muslims are impressed by a powerful showdown of forces is not surprising. Their belief system and their heavy involvement in

folk practices make them more open to be influenced by power encounters. As David Burnett says:

> If one believes in a world of unseen powers, it is logical that one
> would want to see the reality of a greater power before changing
> allegiance to another god. Can this new god meet my basic needs?
> Or, more simply, does this new religion work? ...The demonstra-
> tion of the power of the gospel and the communication of its
> message must lead to a personal commitment to the gospel.[2]

Kinds of Power Encounters

The term "power encounter" has a narrow as well as a broad meaning.
In its narrow sense, a power encounter is a debate in the mind and
heart of a person whether to accept Christ or to remain loyal to his
or her own religion. The Holy Spirit confronts and woos the person.
But he in turn resists, opposes, and often rejects the Word of God,
unaware that what he is being offered is eternal life. In its broad sense,
a power encounter refers to visible demonstrations that prove the superiority of Christ over old lords. In other words, there is a primary
and subtle encounter in the minds of Muslims being evangelized as
they compare Islam and Christianity. Then there is a secondary but
open and visible clash of forces. The bulk of this chapter deals with
the latter—the demonstrable kind of power encounters.

When we offer Christ to a Muslim, Satan and his hosts try to
keep a tight grip on that person's life. At the same time the Holy
Spirit seeks to draw him or her to Christ. All this is nothing less than
an intense spiritual warfare for the person's soul. It is extremely important that Christian workers know how to involve themselves in
this conflict. They must learn to gear the warfare so that the encounter takes place at the level which most concerns and affects the person
they are dealing with. They should seek to manifest Christ's power,
sometimes through answering immediate needs, and other times by
working signs and wonders to confirm the Word of God.

Scriptural Foundations for Power Encounter

Since the scope of this subject is very broad, a comprehensive discussion is not possible here.[3] But demonstrations of God's mighty acts
and His power to meet people's felt needs in the name of Jesus are

important catalysts to quell antagonism and hostile feelings toward the gospel and help people to take a step of faith toward Christ. The Scriptures provide us with a solid foundation for such use of power encounter. Consider the following verses.

1. "Tongues, then, are a sign, not for believers but for unbelievers" (1 Corinthians 14:22). They are something miraculous—a sign that God is present in the person speaking. Also they are an impressive sign if the person who gives the message does so in a language that the unbeliever understands! To Muslim seekers who continue to question the Christian faith, tongues are a sign that God is speaking to them and that they should heed the truth. Judging from the context of this verse, one should not stop at speaking in tongues; rather there should be an accompanying interpretation in order to present the truth of the message (1 Corinthians 14:24–25). I tell Muslims that I want to pray for them in languages I have not learned. I do explain what that means and then proceed to do it.

2. "'Unless you people see miraculous signs and wonders,' Jesus told him, 'you will never believe' " (John 4:48). These are not words of exasperation. Jesus is not refusing to heal the man's son or perform a miracle. Rather He is confirming that miracles inspire faith.

3. "My message and my preaching were not with wise and persuasive words, but with a demonstration of the Spirit's power..." (1 Corinthians 2:4). The Greek word translated here as "demonstration" literally means proof—something that is forceful enough to bring conviction.

4. "The apostles performed many miraculous signs and wonders among the people. And all the believers used to meet together in Solomon's Colonnade... more and more men and women believed in the Lord and were added to their number" (Acts 5:12, 14). "The things that mark an apostle—signs, wonders and miracles—were done among you with great perseverance" (2 Corinthians 12:12).

Signs, wonders, and miracles do not describe three categories of miraculous acts. Rather, they are mighty deeds seen from three different aspects: a) in their ability to authenticate the message, they are signs; b) in their power to evoke awe and astonishment, they are wonders; and c) in their capacity to display divine supernatural power, they are miracles. Paul states that these are the things that mark an apostle. Indeed, they should mark an apostle to Muslims.

When people are sick, they can be ministered to through the gift of healing. Needs may also be met through a message in tongues and interpretation or through a prophetic message which exposes sin or unspoken thoughts. Such miracles can lead nonbelievers to soften their antagonism toward the gospel and consequently place their faith in Christ. When in the name of Jesus an evil spirit is exorcised or a taboo is broken; when the sick are healed, the blind see, the deaf hear and the lame walk; the Lord is exalted, and people will be disposed to put their faith in Him.

We must realize that Islam will continue to have the upper hand in the hearts and minds of Muslims unless Christ's mighty power is demonstrated clearly. Their traditional religion of many generations past will continue to claim their allegiance until challenged by the Holy Spirit. Through mighty acts the Spirit validates the message we preach and manifests the power of the gospel to break Satan's chains.

Some Muslims are afraid to convert to Jesus Christ because they fear that God will punish them. They think He might strike them dead if they turn away from Islam. But when one or more Muslims accept Christ without incurring God's wrath, those watching see the mighty power of Jesus in action. They can witness for themselves that one may convert to Christ and stop following the religion of Islam without suffering divine wrath. Testimonies of specific experiences like the following speak to them: a) converts who receive God's blessings although they no longer go to the patron saint, sheik, *marabout*, or *wali*; b) families who have healthy babies although they no longer go to the saints' festivals (*mowled*); or c) converts who omit the Ramadan fast without suffering terrible consequences.

WHY POWER ENCOUNTERS ARE NECESSARY

What does a power encounter mean to a Muslim? What effects does the confrontation of spiritual forces—Christian versus Muslim—produce, both in the society and for the gospel witness? Is power encounter biblically warranted? Does the Bible speak of it, and if so, in what terms? I will deal with these questions and the need for power encounters from two perspectives: factors within Muslim culture and patterns from the Bible.

Sociological Reasons

There are two main cultural factors within Islam that point to the necessity of the power encounter. These are folk Islam and the Islamic concept of power.

Folk Islam

In our examination of folk Islam we saw how Muslims are involved with the supernatural, the transempirical, and the underworld to various degrees and in multiple forms. These practices demonstrate needs that are not answered or fulfilled by the orthodox beliefs, the religion according to the book. That is why people resort to folk practices such as wearing an amulet so that their baby will live; visiting a sheik's tomb so that a suitor will come to their daughter; going to the fortune-teller to know which neighbor stole the silver necklace; and so forth. In such a context, presenting Christ as the loving and the all-powerful will meet receptive hearts. It will create favorable attitudes and positive responses.

The Islamic Concept of Power

The Islamic concept of power also shows the need for this kind of spiritual confrontation. This concept includes the following ideas, some of which we have already considered.

Triumphalism. Victory over one's foes and a subsequent triumphalism were major themes in Muhammad's wars and have been for Muslims ever since. We have looked at the Islamic conquests during Islam's first century and noted that these successes apparently instilled in Muslim minds an indelible impression that such triumphalism is God's only way. In any situation where there is conflict, less than victory, less than a show of power, is not worthy of Islam. That is why bringing about a power encounter is often an important part of evangelizing Muslims. It demonstrates that Christ's power far exceeds that of all others, including Satan.

Jihad. Jihad or holy war is another facet of the Islamic perspective of power. This warfare, commanded in the Qur'an, is seen as a legitimate means for ridding the world of infidels and spreading the religion of Islam. All adult Muslims are required to answer summons to war against unbelievers. Paradise is believed to be the automatic reward for any Muslim who dies fighting for Allah.

These strong factors all reinforce the Muslims' desire for triumph. Muslims respect power. Earlier I explained that for them, weakness is not a virtue; rather it is despicable. The signs of God's approval are unity, power, and victory. Their view is that God favors people with power. They regard the tremendous expansion of Islam as the supreme proof that their religion is chosen by God.[4]

Although Muslims know that Jesus Christ never carried a sword or fought a war, they have deep, though mostly unexpressed, veneration for Him. They respect His superiority of character and His purity. But above all, they respect His outstanding miraculous power, a quality on which the Qur'an and the Hadith both elaborate.

For Christians, Islam's respect for power forms a bridge for witness which opens a door for ministry to Muslims. The fact that Christ is mightier than the jinn and spirits, that sickness and disease can be cured in His name, and that real spiritual victory is available through His eternal triumph on the cross will all command their attention.

The Bible teaches that we are involved in warfare against the spiritual forces of evil in the heavenly realms and against the rulers of this dark world (Ephesians 6:12). Nothing less than the power of the Holy Spirit working in us and the authority of Jesus' name is able to defeat these forces.

Final victory is not in doubt, for Satan is a defeated foe. He was cursed in the garden of Eden (Genesis 3:14, 15). He was cast out of his exalted position in heaven, an event that the Son of God Himself witnessed (Isaiah 14:12–14, Luke 10:18). His purpose was thwarted and baffled in the wilderness temptation (Matthew 4:11). And at the cross of Calvary, Jesus made a public show of Satan and his hosts (Colossians 2:15). There Satan's judgment was declared and his ruin was decreed. Indeed, his defeat is incontestable.

But if Satan has been defeated, why is he still on the scene? Why is he allowed such freedom of activity? Why is he still called "the god of this age" and "the ruler of the kingdom of the air" (Ephesians 2:2; 2 Corinthians 4:4)? Here is an answer from two Pentecostal theologians:

There is a vast difference between a judgment gained and the carrying out of the penalty. There is no doubt of the judgment rendered against Satan at the Cross; but for good reasons, best known to Himself, God has seen fit to allow the enemy a degree of freedom. It certainly is not for lack of power that God has not dispensed with the Devil already. The time for his final dispersal will come; its time has already been set.[5]

In other words, the sentence has been pronounced, but not yet delivered. Lesslie Newbigin says:

The powers were disarmed, but they were not destroyed... the principalities and powers... which were unmasked and robbed of their pretensions to absolute authority when they put Jesus on the Cross... still continue to function after Christ's decisive victory, yet only under his authority...[6]

We may not know all the reasons why Satan is still at large, but we do know what can happen in the hearts of people who actually see him defeated. When God heals the sick, liberates the demonized, and meets felt needs after prayer in the name of Jesus, these graphically declare to Muslims that Jesus is greater than Satan. They see that the "strong man" has been overcome by One who is stronger yet (Mark 3:23–27). Indeed, Satan's defeat in a power encounter can be a tremendous encouragement to a Muslim moving toward the gospel.

Biblical Reasons

Now let us look at some biblical reasons for using power encounters as an integral part of evangelizing Muslims.

A Witness to God's Love

Power encounters demonstrate God's love. He comes to meet people's needs—to cast out fear, bring healing, deliver from demonic possession and oppression, supply a job, send rain, provide a spouse, and help in many other ways. Such divine intervention shows that He is a God who is concerned about and interested in His creation and who cares for people. The Bible tells us that because of His compassion and love, Jesus performed such supernatural works (Matthew 20:33, 34; Mark 1:41; 5:19; 8:2–10; Luke 7:11–17).

A Confirmation of the Claims of Christ

Power encounters confirm the claims of Christ. In one of the Jews' heated debates with Jesus, He told them that His works were a clear confirmation of who He claimed to be (John 10:36–38). He cites His works as a witness to His divinity, for they showed that He was exercising divine, supernatural power. His ability to command the winds and the waves, to heal the sick, and to raise the dead all proved that His claims were divinely supported and accredited (John 14:11). No one else could do the same works. They were His distinctive acts (John 15:24).

Miracles were God's endorsement of Jesus. They were like a certificate of accreditation. In Acts 2:22 Peter declares: "People of Israel, listen! God publicly endorsed Jesus of Nazareth by doing wonderful miracles, wonders, and signs through him, as you well know" (New Living Translation). The New International Version says that God "accredited him" by miracles.

John sent his disciples to ask Jesus: "Are you the one who was to come, or should we expect someone else?" Jesus did not answer by giving logical proof, rather He demonstrated His mighty power (Matthew 11:3–6).

Nicodemus said to Jesus: "Rabbi, we know you are a teacher who has come from God. For no one could perform the miraculous signs you are doing if God were not with him? (John 3:2). When Jesus fed the multitude, the people who saw the power of God working through Him concluded: "Surely this is the Prophet who is to come into the world" (John 6:14).

Manifestations of divine power confirm Christ's claims and point people to Him. An African Christian song from the Transvaal says:

Jesus Christ is the conqueror;
By His resurrection He overcame death itself;
By His resurrection He overcame all things;
He overcame magic;
He overcame amulets and charms;
He overcame the darkness of demon-possession;
He overcame dread.
When we are with Him,
We also conquer.[7]

This is what we need to teach: Christ has the power to set people free and liberate them from the dread and power of Satan. Christ is the conqueror of all opposing forces and He grants us this same victory.

A Manifestation of the Kingdom in Power

Power encounters show that the kingdom of God has come among men. The Bible and the experience of the Church demonstrate that the advance of the kingdom of God has always provoked a confrontation of forces and will continue to do so.

Old Testament examples. In the Old Testament, power encounters took place in various geographic areas, at different times and with various peoples. These were important confrontations in which the only true God showed the superiority of His might and strength over all else. As examples, note the following passages: Genesis 3:1–5; 6:1–4; Deuteronomy 17:2–7; 18:10; 1 Samuel 28:13; 1 Kings 18:16–40; Job 1:6–12; 2:1–7; Psalm 89:6, 7; Isaiah 8:19 and Daniel 10:13, 20.

The ministry of Jesus. The opposition to God's rule reaches new levels of intensity in the New Testament. Jesus' ministry was characterized by many power encounters. Satan, the prince of demons, certainly dreaded the coming of Christ. It seems that he used every evil trick he knew, even to the point of unleashing hoards of demons and spirits to prevent the fulfillment of the promise of the Messiah. In the words of Arthur F. Glasser:

> When God identified Jesus as "my beloved Son, with whom I am well pleased" (Matt. 3:17) open warfare began. That Satan immediately counterattacked was inevitable after such an identification. But he was quickly repulsed... Even the demons joined in the struggle for they too had heard the Voice, and they trembled over its implications (Mark 1:24).[8]

When Jesus read Isaiah 61:1–2 at the synagogue in Nazareth, He commented: "Today this scripture is fulfilled in your hearing" (Luke 4:21). In other words, the final act in the unfolding of the divine drama had already begun. Christ had started to set up His kingdom.

Jesus' ministry was often projected as twofold: first, He preached; and second, He cast out demons. Mark says that Jesus "traveled throughout Galilee, preaching in their synagogues and driving out demons" (Mark 1:39). That put the kingdom of darkness on the defensive on two fronts: the preaching of the gospel and the demonstration of Jesus' divine power. John Bright observes that Christ's miraculous acts were:

> a taste of "the powers of the age to come" (Hebrews 6:5). In them the grip of the Adversary—who has enthralled men in bonds of disease, madness, death, and sin—begins to be loosened. When the Pharisees accused Jesus of casting out demons by the power of Satan, he replied that if that be so, Satan's house is divided and cannot stand; "But if it is by the finger of God that I cast out demons, then the Kingdom of God has come upon you" (Luke 11:20; Matthew 12:28). In the mighty works of Jesus the power of that Kingdom has broken into the world; Satan has met his match (Luke 10:18; Mark 3:27); the cosmic end-struggle has begun.[9]

The experience of the early church. Since its very inception, the Church has experienced power encounters. Consider what happened on the Day of Pentecost and how people heard their own languages spoken by a group of "unlearned" followers of Jesus. The outcome was powerful indeed. Three thousand people believed in Christ and were added to the Church (Acts 2:41).

The story of Ananias and Sapphira shows that opposition to the kingdom of God did not cease when Jesus ascended to heaven (Acts 5:1–11). Their plot provoked an important power encounter in the early history of the Church. The resulting judgment showed that the coming of God's kingdom would continue to bring conflict and victory. What happened?

The Holy Spirit had granted the young church many victories over hostile Jewish religious authorities. In their relations with each other, believers were characterized by openness, generosity, and an understanding of each others' needs. Against this background, Ananias and his wife schemed to deceive the church. But as Peter pointed out, they had lied not only to people and the church, but also to God. They had agreed "to test the Spirit of the Lord" (Acts 5:3, 9).

What challenge did the plot of Ananias and his wife present? It was an encounter between Satan acting through the couple, and the

Holy Spirit acting through Peter and the church. It's important to note that Peter was not the agent of death. Rather, he was the prophet who revealed the sin and pronounced the sentence. What was the outcome of this confrontation? The church was afraid to lie to the Holy Spirit, and outsiders were afraid to plot against the church.

Many other power encounters took place in the ministry of Peter, John, Philip, Paul and others. Spiritual power is an important manifestation of the kingdom of God. The apostle Paul identifies the kingdom as more than mere talk; it is a matter of power (1 Corinthians 4:20).

The pattern now. Power encounters occur today. God rules as the eternal King over the universe and over people's hearts. Because He does, there is a relentless conflict between His reign and the temporary rule of Satan, the prince of this world. With every advance the kingdom of God makes, Satan and his forces come under renewed attack and suffer shame and defeat. He desperately tries to keep his grip on people's hearts, thoughts, beliefs, and practices as well as on their systems, institutions, organizations, and groupings.

A friend who is a pastor in Brussels, Belgium tells the story of a dying lady who requested his visit. He knew she was heavily involved in sorcery, magic and other demonic activities. As a young pastor, he felt he needed the support and company of two of the church elders. He asked them to go with him for that visit. But the elders declined. They said they were scared of that lady. The pastor had no choice but to go by himself. God did a miracle. The lady started crying upon hearing the message of God's love. She repented of what she had done and accepted Christ as her Savior. On the basis of His finished work, Christ delivers people not only from sin, but also from bondage to the evil authorities and powers (Colossians 2:13–15).

As God's kingdom advances, the Lord continues to work out His purpose, triumphing over satanic opposition. He is at work now to free men and women from bondage. Their deliverance from evil spirits in the name of Jesus is proof that His kingdom has come among humans. The coming of the kingdom of God to the Muslim people is no exception. Its breakthrough should be emphasized and sustained by power encounters that engage all the forces involved and confirm the victory of the Church.

HOW POWER ENCOUNTERS ARE CONDUCTED

Now we will look at how power encounters work.

Aspects of Power Encounter

The issue. As we have noted, in a power encounter the forces of righteousness confront the forces of evil. The outcome determines whether God's name is honored or Satan temporarily achieves his objectives. The issue is the glory of God.

> Satan is gripped with envy, desiring to have the glory that God has. He realizes that he will never have this glory; so he is now determined to gain all the satisfaction he can by depriving God of as much of it as possible. From an eternal perspective, he is doomed to failure. But in the present order of things, he can partially achieve his objective. He can gain some satisfaction by causing men to live at a level below their privileges as God's children—children by creation or redemption.[10]

The strong opposition. Satan does not calmly watch the demise of his kingdom. At times he brutally assaults Christians; at others he counterattacks their blows and struggles to keep his foothold. In all this, our Lord and Savior has given us his word: "I will build my church, and all the powers of hell will not conquer it" (Matthew 16:18, New Living Translation). Ultimate victory, achieved and secured by Christ's death and resurrection, belongs to God's kingdom.

The battlefield. The battlefield is the soul of an unregenerate person who hears the message of Christ. For example, consider the incident in Acts 13:6–12 which involved Sergius Paulus, the governor who heard Paul (Saul) preach. Note the following: Elymas was a Jew; he was a sorcerer (Jewish sorcerer—absolutely forbidden!); he was a false prophet; he was a court official (attendant of the governor); he opposed the apostles; he tried to turn the governor from the faith. Paul called him a child of the devil and an enemy of everything that is right. He also said that Elymas was full of all kinds of deceit and trickery, that he was perverting the right ways of the Lord, that the hand of the Lord was against him and he would be blind.

Notice that the power encounter was for the soul of the governor, not Elymas. Also, the governor was an intelligent man, yet it was not a rational argument that brought him to faith.

We must understand the seriousness and gravity of our task as we approach a Muslim with the gospel of liberty. As Alan Tippett says, "There is no way out in this war, no compromise, no friendly agreement to engage in dialogue, no mere Christian presence."[11] John Calvin sounds the alarm, declaring that the devil's position as God's adversary and ours ought to "stimulate us to a perpetual war" with him:

> If we feel the concern which we ought to feel for the glory of God, we shall exert all our power against him who attempts the extinction of it. If we are animated by becoming [appropriate] zeal for defending the kingdom of Christ, we must necessarily have an irreconcilable war with him who conspires its ruin.[12]

The foundation for victory. As Christian witnesses and workers, our victory over the authorities and powers of evil is based on an unshakeable foundation. First, it is rooted in God's love for us. Paul makes this clear:

> In all these things we are more than conquerors through him who loved us. For I am convinced that neither angels nor demons, neither the present nor the future, nor any powers, neither height nor depth, nor anything else in all creation, will be able to separate us from the love of God that is in Christ Jesus our Lord (Romans 8:37–39).

Second, it is secured in Christ's position. He is seated at the right hand of God in the heavenly realms, "far above all rule and authority, power and dominion, and every title that can be given, not only in the present age but also in the one to come" (Ephesians 1:21). With these facts in mind, we can replace cowardice with confidence. "If God is for us, who can be against us?" (Romans 8:31).

Who Takes the Initiative?

We can divide power encounters into two categories according to who takes the initiative. In the first, the Christian takes the initiative and attacks Satan's domain. Here, Satan finds himself on the defensive. In the second, Satan initiates the attack against the kingdom of God. The Christian has to stand firm in Christ's victory and in so doing counterattack the enemy.

Timothy Warner talks about taking the initiative, stating that there are

ways in which missionaries take the initiative in claiming territory held by Satan. This begins with evangelism (bringing people "from the power of Satan to God"), but it also includes the destruction of occult objects or paraphernalia [used to bring about] healing, confrontation of practitioners of the black arts and the casting out of demons. I do not suggest that missionaries go on a "lion" hunt trying to set up a series of dramatic power encounters. But neither do I suggest that we back off in fear when the power and glory of God are being challenged by men under the power of demons.[13]

Regardless of who takes the initiative, both types of power encounters have similar aims and results. In his contest with the prophets of Baal on Mount Carmel, Elijah had a particular goal. He wanted

to put before the eyes of the whole nation a convincing practical proof of the sole deity of Jehovah and of the nothingness of the Baals, that were regarded as gods... Through this miracle Jehovah not only accredited Elijah as his servant and prophet, but proved Himself to be the living God, whom Israel was to serve; so that all the people who were present fell down upon their faces in worship...[14]

The ten plagues inflicted upon Egypt were offensive attacks sent by the God of Israel against the gods of Egypt.

The New Testament also gives some examples of this kind of power encounter. We already looked at the encounter between Paul and Barnabas and Elymas the sorcerer. When Jesus cast out the evil spirits from the men in the region of Gadarenes, He did not wait for the demon-possessed men to seek Him out. He went to where they were, boldly entering territory dominated by Satan (Matthew 8:28–34).

Church history contains many accounts similar to those in the Bible of how a confrontation of forces caused people to convert to Christ. Kenneth S. Latourette includes several in his report on the phenomenal growth of Christianity during the first five hundred years of its existence. He indicated that entire families and communities embraced the faith because a case of demon possession was cured in the name of Jesus, a dying child was restored to life, or an entire village escaped a plague.[15] At these encounters, the power of Jesus' name was very effectively demonstrated to the people at the level of their needs.

Around 725 A.D. the missionary monk, Boniface, initiated an historic confrontation with the forces of evil at Geismar, Germany. While a large crowd of hostile pagans watched, Boniface began to cut down an oak tree dedicated to the worship of the god Thor. After only a few strokes, a powerful blast of wind blew, hit the tree, and completed the task for Boniface. The giant oak fell and shattered into four pieces. The pagan bystanders' faith in this tree-idol was also shattered. They had believed that anyone who tried to destroy the tree would be struck by lightning and killed. But Boniface was untouched, and there had been no lightning at all. Gradually the people became convinced that Boniface's God was mightier than theirs, since their god could not even defend or protect his tree! Consequently, they converted. Boniface used the timber of the tree to make a place of prayer. After further ministry, he reported the conversion of over 100,000 pagans to Christ.[16]

Christian workers among Muslims should regard any situation of illness, demon possession, idolatry, personal need and so forth as possible settings in which God can bring deliverance and mighty answers to prayers. If there is sickness and the Lord reveals that it is caused by demonic forces, it is our duty to pray for the sick and rebuke those powers in the name of Jesus. If a person is demonized, it is our responsibility as soldiers of the kingdom of God to cast them out. In most cases, those who suffer from possession by demons have not welcomed their intrusion. Expelling the evil spirit or spirits in Jesus' name restores the sufferer to a normal state, and Christ is glorified. Seeing demons exorcised may cause some onlookers to shift their allegiance from Muhammad to Jesus, and it will cause others to at least begin to think more seriously about the gospel.

There is no specific formula for exorcism, only a command to the spirits to leave the person on the authority of the name of Jesus. African Professor Andrew Igenoza points out that the expulsion is through an authoritative command and not through an adjuration which suggests begging or seeking the consent of the spirits to be expelled on oath... The Christian human instrument of exorcism does not use magical rings, herbs, roots, incantations or other rituals. Like Jesus, he is first of all spiritually commissioned and empowered (Luke 11:20; Mt. 12:28; Acts 1:8) and he uses no other name apart from the name of Jesus in addressing the spirits.[17]

Another kind of power encounter that can advance the kingdom of God is the one that takes place when a convert or believer makes a confession of faith. This confession can be made as a response to questions. Its form may be declarative: "Yes, I believe." Rather than asking Muslim converts to recite a creedal statement, and in place of or in addition to telling the story of how they accepted Christ, I suggest that they be asked questiozns. The early church used this system in the years prior to A. D. 200 (before they developed the "Apostles' Creed"). Here is an example of this kind of confession.

Minister: Do you believe in the Almighty God, the Father, and that He loves you?

Believer: Yes, I believe.

Minister: Do you believe in the Lord Jesus Christ, the eternal Son of God, and that He came to earth, suffered and died for you?

Believer: Yes, I believe.

Minister: Do you believe that He rose from the dead, ascended alive to God the Father, and today He is alive in heaven appearing before God's throne on your behalf?

Believer: Yes, I believe.

Minister: Do you believe that the Holy Spirit is the Spirit of God Himself, and that He now abides in you to teach and strengthen you?

Believer: Yes, I believe.

This is not a complete confession, just an example of a possible model. Such a statement of faith could be used at the baptism of converts, when they are accepted as church members, or at every communion service.

The advantage of this question-answer form is that every time a believer says, "Yes, I believe," he is emerging triumphant from a power encounter in which Jesus' name is glorified. It is certainly meaningful for the convert to participate in such a confession. Alan Tippett emphasizes: "The power encounter for the new convert is both a symbolic act and a step of faith."[18]

Modern Examples of Power Encounters

I personally know of and have witnessed many power encounters. Following are several I want to share with you to show what God is doing among Muslims.

A young man whom I shall call M. M. is a believer. He was raised in a conservative Muslim family in a country where the national population is 100% Muslim. He got in touch with us and started receiving the Bible lessons for evangelizing Muslims. In the course of the study, he received lesson six of the series. The lesson challenged him to a power encounter with Jesus. The following morning he wrote this in a letter to me: "Last night I saw Jesus. He came to my room. He asked me to sit by Him, gave me water to drink, and taught me how to praise God." That, to him, did it. He accepted Christ as his Lord and Savior.

As we were pioneering a church in a North African city, the country was going through a severe drought. They had had almost no rain during the fall and winter. During one of the church meetings, we prayed for rain. The same day God answered our prayer. Rain started falling, and the drought was over.

When I was teaching at a Bible College in Europe, one of my students, a young lady, was a missionary to Muslims. She told the class that once she was invited to a Muslim home for dinner. The people were pleasant to her. They served her a plate of rice in a mold form. She dug into the middle (which she normally would not do) and found a small three-pronged fishhook. The man of the house was very embarrassed. His wife's face turned red and there was a long silence. Then they apologized to her. The young lady told them, "It is Jesus who protects me. He takes care of me." Apparently they wanted to kill her. They hated the fact she was a missionary to Muslims.

This kind of experience is more than inspiring. Such displays of God's power are a real encouragement for Christian workers and for Muslim converts.

What Comes After a Power Encounter?

What should a Christian witness do after a power encounter?

Give God the Glory

It is God who acts in His mercy to challenge satanic forces and grant salvation, restore health, and bring dignity to humans. The Christian evangelist is only His minister of deliverance, a mere tool in His hands. All glory and gratitude are due to Him.

Proclaim Christ

In every power encounter we need to offer the message of Christ in words that are clear and that the audience understands. It is true that the power of the Holy Spirit must be at work and that the name of Jesus should be glorified by demonstrative acts. But our responsibility does not stop here. The message that Jesus Christ is Lord should be declared clearly and simply, directly and plainly.

Seek a Decision

The ultimate goal of a power encounter should always be the glory of God and the eternal well-being of those involved in or watching the encounter. The Christian witness should ask those present to make a decision for Christ—give their hearts to Him and crown Him King and Lord over their lives. A power encounter should lead people to commit themselves to God, to love Him, to obey Him and to live for Him.

Incorporate the Convert into a Body of Believers

People who commit themselves to Christ need to grow in their Christian life and faith. They need to be discipled and learn how to live victoriously. Incorporation into a body of believers is essential for any convert, including those from a Muslim background. Muslims coming from the ummah of Islam need to be a part of the ummah of God, the body of Christ!

Possible Pitfalls of Power Encounter

Dangers face those who wage war against Satan. If the evangelist is not careful, frustration and defeat can replace the hope and victory gained in a power encounter! Here are some possible pitfalls one should be aware of.

Eclipsed Message

When signs and wonders take the limelight, the gospel message seems secondary. The Christian witness must be sure that miracles fulfill their intended purpose—confirmation of the gospel message. Sri Lankan author and noted Christian leader Ajith Fernando says:

> The demonstration of power is very spectacular and effective in attracting crowds, but this could dethrone the Gospel from its place of supreme importance in evangelism. Power ministry must always be viewed as a servant of the Gospel and aimed at pointing people to the Gospel. Paul said that it is "the gospel" that is the power of God to salvation (Rom. 1:16). What follows that statement in Romans shows that by "gospel" Paul meant the work of God in justifying those who believe by the grace that flows from His cross (Rom. 1:16–5:21).[19]

This is a dangerous trap. Our human experience cannot and should not determine what the truth is. The truth of God's Word is the measuring stick by which we judge experience. When people are deceived, sliding blindly toward eternal ruin, nothing can open their eyes and set them free except the truth—the gospel is the truth. Power encounters are only an effective accompaniment (Mark 16:17). They are not the message.

Flawed Healing Theology

God sometimes heals without medicine, but He also uses medicine to bring healing. Richard Foster says:

> There may be times when God asks us to rely upon prayer alone for healing, but this is the exception, not the rule. The refusal to use medical means to promote healing may be a gesture of faith—more often it is a gesture of spiritual pride.
>
> It is just as possible to err in the opposite direction, of course. Many trust in medical means exclusively and turn to prayer only when all available medical technology has failed. This only betrays the materialistic base of so much of our think-

ing. Normally the aid of prayer and the aid of medicine should be pursued at the same time and with equal vigor, for both are gifts from God.[20]

Disappointment and Sense of Failure

The gospel witness must be careful not to instill a sense of failure and guilt feelings in those who are not healed or delivered. Unrealized expectations and dashed hopes can cause disappointment.

Pride

Success in power encounters and positive supernatural interventions can lead to pride. This is the same sin that caused Satan, once an angel of light, to be what he is today—enemy of man and God (Isaiah 14:12–15; Ezekiel 28:2). We quote again from Fernando:

> As this ministry deals with power, it is possible for the evangelist to be corrupted by power and give in to pride. The taste of power may cause him or her to become authoritarian in his or her other dealings... the prayer of all those involved in such "power ministries" should be for humility. They should seek to train themselves (1 Timothy 4:7) in humility.
>
> An effective antidote to the abuse of power is accountability to a community. An active and loving biblical community would not let one of its members persist in pride without battling the pride. It is a source of grave concern to us that many who are engaged in power ministries have not submitted themselves to the discipline of accountability to a community. They are in danger of shipwrecking their ministries.[21]

Christian "Magic"

Christian workers need to beware of using the name of Jesus like a magical incantation. The book of Acts tells us the story of seven sons of a Jewish priest who tried to exorcise an evil spirit using Jesus' name as a magic spell! The demon-possessed man beat them, stripped them of their clothes, and sent them running nude out of the house (Acts 19:16–19)! Jesus' name is not a magic formula. His name is the expression of His person and His presence in power and love.

Preoccupation with the Demonic

Our ministry, both the message and the methods, should be Christ-centered. If the Christian workers become preoccupied and obsessed with struggling against the forces of evil, they can lose their focus on Jesus and unwittingly exalt Satan. That can also encourage people to avoid personal responsibility for their sins and attribute everything to the works of the devil. Let us not blame Satan for our sins of the "flesh."

People seen as the enemy

Christian workers need to make it clear that this combat is not against people. They should always remind themselves and their audience that we are not warring against people, but against spirit powers. We do not condone violence, the use of force, or aggression. We seek the eternal well-being of all men and women of all religions and beliefs and hold dearly the dignity of all.

Possibly, because of misunderstanding this warfare (and a subtle fear of the enemy, Satan) there has now arisen an anti-spiritual warfare movement in some Christian quarters. It is important to remember that in our stand against satanic forces, there is a place for war-like language; but in our relationship with other people, the language of peace and reconciliation should be prominent.

The Value of Power Encounters

In Muslim evangelism the Church faces spiritual warfare of a magnitude unknown in encountering any other religion or faith. This warfare is against spiritual forces of evil in heavenly realms and against the rulers of this dark world. Nothing less than the power of the Holy Spirit and the Word of God will be able to defeat these forces.

The gospel is God's power for salvation (Romans 1:16). However, if it is offered to Muslims without the confirmation of signs, wonders, and miracles, as is the biblical pattern (Acts 14:3; Hebrews 2:3–4), it often appears superficial, limp, and unattractive. In most cases they reject it. On the other hand, the gospel that brings with it healing for the sick, deliverance for the demonized and oppressed, and victory in the name of Jesus is more appealing. It makes sense to Muslims. Indeed, it is the gospel Christ commissioned His disciples to preach (Matthew 10:1).

Christian witnesses will advance triumphantly, unchecked by satanic opposition, when their work follows the twofold pattern shown in the ministry of Jesus and the apostles. On the one hand, we must courageously preach the gospel of salvation. On the other hand, we must avail ourselves of our spiritual resources in the Person of the Holy Spirit—His mighty power, manifestations, and gifts. When we do these things our dynamic message will communicate Christ's victory to millions of Muslims.

Power encounters have value for Muslim converts as well. As a result of seeing God defeat the forces of evil, they become more convinced that the Christian message is true. They also learn of the spiritual resources they can draw upon as they seek to live for Jesus and testify of His love to others.

The church of Jesus Christ in Muslim communities, more than anywhere else, faces a difficult task. It must preserve its faith in the absence of external supports, symbols, and institutions. It must be able to survive and practice biblical ethics in the midst of an ocean of humanity that at best does not understand those ethics and at worst is set against them. To do these things, the church must know that God is alive.

Like other born-again Christians, Muslims who put their faith in Christ realize that they are under divine orders to propagate their faith. But the hard reality is that they have to discover how to do so in a society that vehemently opposes them. To succeed, they must have the power of the Holy Spirit. They must know that in an actual showdown of forces, God can and will give victory. This knowledge will enable them to carry out the commission of Jesus to spread the gospel to the ends of the earth.

17 | *Christa As An Experience*

> "I desperately wanted to learn more about this Jesus... [So] I traveled to Europe hoping someone would talk with me about [Him]. But no one did. I used to wish that someone would sit next to me on a plane or in a restaurant and bring up the subject of Jesus so I could get some answers... I decided to come to America, what I perceived to be a Christian country. Surely someone there would tell me about Jesus. I lived in an apartment complex in the South. It seemed that everyone around me was into parties, alcohol, drugs and women. And I wondered how on earth I was going to find Jesus. It didn't appear that anyone I saw knew Him."
>
> (From an interview with a Muslim man from the Middle East.)

This chapter looks at the importance of presenting Christ "as an experience." What does that mean? Simply this: biblical Christianity is not a dogma to be learned but a Person to be encountered. It is a living experience of the living Christ. All dogmatic odds were against any possibility of Saul of Tarsus, a strict Pharisee, becoming a Christian. But when he saw Jesus, he did convert—and what an extraordinary Christian he became!

Cultural factors as well as biblical principles make a strong case for using evangelism methods that bring Muslims face to face with the incomparable Savior, not into a debate about Christianity. For Muslims, practical needs—not cosmic theological questions—are uppermost. In addition, Western "logic" does not usually make sense to them. All this means that, in general, we should set aside such unproductive methods as debate and dogmatic reasoning. Rather, we must present Jesus to our Muslim friends as He really is, the One who is able to help them with their daily problems. If we fail to do this, they will continue to view their religion as superior, and Islam will keep its grip on them.

John says that certain Greeks once came with a request to Philip, one of the Lord's disciples. "'Sir,' they said, 'we would like to see Jesus'" (John 12:21). I believe that the Holy Spirit is stirring many Muslim hearts today to make this same plea.

OFFER A PRACTICAL ENCOUNTER WITH CHRIST

Some time ago a pastor in California called me to ask for advice because he had been sharing the gospel with a Muslim lady. He wanted to know how to prove to her that the Qur'an was false. I said: "Tell her about Christ. Preach to her the power of the name of Jesus!"

While there are various methods and strategies to bring Muslims to Christ, there is only one name by which they will be saved and that is the name of Jesus. Argument and theological debate never give people life. Show Muslims the face of God in Jesus Christ; show them God's mercy and grace in the words and actions of Jesus; tell them of the greatest love ever known and of Jesus' ultimate sacrifice; describe to them what happened to His hands, feet and side at Calvary—and Muslims will be disposed to believe in Him!

Recently I was talking with a young man about his call to missions. He told me about his family: he is the youngest of eight siblings; two of his brothers are drug traffickers; two other brothers committed murder; and two of his sisters are prostitutes! Many people would see no hope for someone from such an environment. But the power of the name of Jesus has saved him, transformed him and brought him into the Kingdom. Today he is Christ's servant and a preacher of the gospel.

There are two strong reasons for offering Christianity to Muslims as a living, practical encounter with Christ. The first is cultural; the second is biblical.

Culturally, It Is the Right Place to Start

First, Muslim culture shows that a practical encounter with Christ is the right place to begin. Efforts to lead Muslims to Christ have often been unproductive because of the serious theological disagreements between Christianity and Islam. These controversies touch some of the most fundamental tenets of the faith—the divine authority of the Bible, the Trinity, the deity of Christ, the divine Sonship of Jesus, and the crucifixion.

In addition, discussions of these doctrines bring into focus some Islamic teachings which Christians find totally unacceptable. These include the Muslim belief that the Qur'an is God's final revelation to humans; that Muhammad was the last, the greatest, and consequently the "seal" of all the prophets; that the Shari'a is the divinely sanctioned law for humanity; and that God wants all people to convert to Islam.

As serious as these issues may be, they do not form an insurmountable hurdle. But it is usually not helpful to begin evangelizing a Muslim by confronting these issues. Rather, in the beginning stages of a Christian-Muslim encounter, it is more important to show a Muslim Jesus Christ than to try to smooth out theological difficulties.

One of the first stages in ministering to a Muslim, I believe, is to take him by the hand and introduce him to Jesus. I want my Muslim friend, in a sense, to walk with Jesus on the hills of Judea, sit with Him by the Sea of Galilee, listen to Him teach, watch Him do miracles, hear Him pray, talk with Him, see Him crucified, and watch Him come to the upper room alive after His resurrection. I want my Muslim friend to see that Jesus is unique, but like us; matchless, but not aloof; far above all, yet close to us. I want him to realize that Jesus is in heaven, but also on earth, that once He died, but now He is alive.

It Is the Biblical Perspective

The second reason why we should offer Christ as an experience is that this is the essence of biblical Christianity.

Human nature clearly hungers for an encounter with God. To know God, rely on Him, call on Him, talk with Him, please Him, be assured of His acceptance—all these are basic, spiritual longings.

Because they exist, there is religion. In fact, religion is the human response to the supernatural; it is an attempt to satisfy the deep desires of one's heart.

Christianity, then, as seen in this light, is a person's positive reaction to the claims of Christ. First there is the person of Christ. Then there is the response a man or woman makes. To put it another way, I could say that God takes the initiative by providing Jesus, and people make the response by accepting or rejecting Him. True religion starts with what God does. People then respond to His divine provision through faith, repentance, worship, joy, baptism communion, and other ways.

The view that practical experience is the essence of religion has not been typical of modern Western society which places more emphasis on what can be "proved" by using the scientific method of experiment and observation. This emphasis has pervaded all of Western life, and it has even influenced the way the gospel has been presented.

In my estimation it is a pity when gospel workers present Christ shrouded in rational arguments. They generally come back from the harvest empty-handed because Christianity, when reduced to dogmatic reasoning with no place for the ecstatic and mystic, becomes a kind of "lame creature"—a cold, impersonal catalog of beliefs. What a difference there is when Christian witnesses offer people the evidence of the eternal power of Christ which changes peoples' lives, heals the sick, delivers the demonized, and fills the hearts of the sad and destitute with joy and peace. The Bible says, "*Taste* and see that the Lord is good" (Psalm 34:8).

When I talk about the need for the ecstatic and mystic, I do not mean a need for the irrational. Psychologists differentiate between the rational and nonrational components of religious experience.[1] The first is related to reason, logic, and theological thinking. The second has to do with feelings and personal involvement. Psychologists also distinguish between the irrational (unreasonable) and the nonrational (neutral as far as rationality). Christianity is rational as well as nonrational, but it is not irrational.

My point is that although Christianity is certainly rational, we will be more in tune with how Muslims think if we will emphasize its "nonrational" side. Let me quote Kenneth Nolin, a man who spent several years as a missionary in the Middle East and who has special insight regarding Islam. Although I disagree with him on some issues, here he is particularly astute.

Many Christians think of their faith in Jesus as a dogma to be accepted rather than a reality to be experienced. In doing so they simply perpetuate the dogmatic conflict, and in effect prevent the very discussion they profess to be encouraging, about who and what Jesus really is.[2]

People, as intelligent beings, use their intellect to respond to and cope with life situations. But intelligence alone does not govern humans, nor is it the sole component of their personalities. If we are to truly reach them for Christ, we must present the gospel in a way that involves all their being. People need a personal encounter with Jesus in order to be touched and transformed. They need a dynamic experience with Christ that goes beyond theological arguments and intellectual reasoning.

I am not calling for an irrational existentialism that leaves no place for reason. Rather, I want to emphasize that people need to experience a fervent relationship and true identification with Jesus Christ. The gospel projects Him as a real person, able to relate to people at their level. Only this kind of message is able to penetrate the hearts of Muslims. Anything less will fail to bring them into a living relationship with Christ so they can communicate with Him in human terms as their hearts long to do.

Blaise Pascal (1623–1662), the noted French philosopher, inventor, and mathematician, said, "It is the heart which experiences God, and not reason. That is what faith is; God felt by the heart and not by reason."[3] He also states: "If we submit everything to reason, our religion will have no mysterious and supernatural elements. If we offend the principles of reason, our religion will be absurd and ridiculous."[4]

Missionary anthropologist Paul Hiebert also talks of the need for religion to relate directly to people's lives. He says that religion is "based on the human need to 'make sense' out of human experience and find some order and significance in the whole human situation."[5]

Oswald Chambers (1874–1917) has this to say regarding people who are contemplating conversion to Christ:

There must be a surrender of the will, not a surrender to persuasive power, a deliberate launching forth on God and on what He says until I am no longer confident in what I have done, I am confident only in God. The hindrance is that I will not trust God, but only my mental understanding… my relationship to [God] in the first place is a personal one, not an intellectual one. I am introduced into the relationship by the miracle of God and my own will to believe, then I begin to get an intelligent appreciation and understanding of the wonder of the transaction.[6]

All of this shows how important it is to use evangelism methods among Muslims that help them discover who Jesus is right in the beginning rather than relying on logical arguments to win them to Christ..

TAKE INTO ACCOUNT THE CHALLENGE OF MUSLIM LOGIC

Now we look at the problems that can arise if a Christian worker tries to follow a Western type of logic when witnessing to Muslims. Many Westerners who have worked in Islamic contexts have discovered that Muslim logic defies what Westerners believe to be rational reasoning. In other words, Muslim logic does not necessarily follow the reasoning pattern Westerners often use which depends heavily on formal deductive arguments and linear logic. (When I say "Muslim logic," I mean the way the general populace thinks, not the way Islamic apologists think. The latter represent the elite, not the average.) The fact that Muslim logic does not follow Western patterns does not mean there is an absence of logic in Islam. Rather, it means that linear logic is not automatically the basis Muslims use for reasoning.

Linear logic (where A leads to B and B leads to C) is not particularly a characteristic feature of Muslim reasoning. Sociologist and scholar Edward Westermarck, relates the following incident and betrays his frustration at not understanding Muslim logic which differs from his own way of thinking. The story is about a Moroccan *sharif,* a revered descendant of Muhammad considered to be a holy man. This *sharif* was fond of alcohol and often got drunk.

When I expressed to some natives my surprise at so holy a man constantly transgressing the law of the Prophet, I was told that he did not really drink wine; because when the wine touched his saintly lips it was transformed into honey. "But how could the honey make him drunk?" I asked. The answer was, "Anything is possible for a saint." Here we have two miracles at the same time: the wine became honey, and the honey made the saint drunk.[7]

Westermarck's dilemma was that he tried to match Muslim logic with his own.

Muslim writer Aida Barkan strongly warns Muslims against Christian evangelism. She balks at bold efforts to convert her coreligionists to Christianity. She says that "evangelism is closely related to colonialism. They are two sides of a coin finally aiming at political, economic, and military subjugation of Muslim peoples..."[8] Barkan goes on to "expose" what she considers to be imprudent activities of Christian missionaries in Muslim countries. She wants to mobilize Muslims to combat such efforts.

The reader may view this as a normal response from an average Muslim. But the very next article in the same issue is a detailed report about the new Islamic center in Toledo, Ohio. The magazine's cover photograph depicts the new building. The report reveals that Muslims responsible for the center want to send Muslim missionaries to American institutions, convert American Christians to Islam, and help new converts understand Islam and be firm in their religion. The center includes a mosque that seats two thousand people, a lecture hall that seats six hundred, and several other buildings.

Muslims see no incompatibility between the two articles or the two attitudes. For them, publishing those two together shows no discrepancy, bigotry, or injustice. But to the Westerner, it is illogical for Muslims to condemn Christians for doing what they themselves proudly do.

Consider another example. In his work, *When Horses Entered Al Azhar*, Sheikh Kishk, an Egyptian imam, explains away the fact that Egypt was in fact occupied by the Turks when Napoleon conquered Cairo in October of 1798. The Sheikh argues that there is no such thing as a colonization relationship between two Muslim countries. In his view, the Turkish sultan merely had the right to appoint the ruler and control taxation. "Would that make Egypt a Turkish colony?" he asks. No, is the reply. He claims that it was impossible for the Muslim Turks to be considered colonizers of Muslim Egypt, even though they did everything which colonial rulers do. Yet, when he reports Napoleon's occupation of Egypt, the Sheikh furiously "shakes his fist" and describes the French forces as barbaric. Of course they were. They were not Muslims![9]

Sandra Mackey in her insightful book *The Saudis*, tells of a British man who once was drinking alcohol at a Saudi friend's home. The house, made of mud, stood alone on the edge of town at the end of a small road. Suddenly the front wall of the house collapsed as a car driven by a Saudi hit it. The three men were taken to jail. When the case was heard the following day, the judge passed this sentence:

> The British guest: twenty days in jail and 20 lashes for drinking alcohol. The owner of the house: twenty five days in jail for locating his house in such a place that the driver could run into it. The driver of the car: no punishment![10]

While these apparent contradictions make sense to Muslims, they certainly seem illogical to most Westerners. In my opinion, they show that Islamic logic is not based on the same kind of rational reasoning used in the West. This cultural feature points to the fact that, in drawing Muslims to Christ, a practical religious experience with Jesus is far more important than theological reasoning and rational argumentation.

ANSWER FELT NEEDS

We know that Christianity deals with spiritual issues. It talks about God, angels, and eternal life. Nevertheless, we must constantly remember that it is also deeply concerned about human life on this material earth—problems people face here and now. As the New Testament reveals, the gospel addresses itself to people's immediate as well as spiritual needs. Christ not only forgave sins, He also healed the sick, fed the multitudes, and restored joy to broken hearts.

We unintentionally misrepresent Christianity at times by failing to explain the answers it gives to practical problems. We talk only of spiritual issues that lie beyond people's sense experience. Our message falls short of its mark as a result, particularly when we are dealing with Muslims.

When Watchman Nee, the famous Chinese preacher and author, visited some churches in England in 1933, he was impressed by the Christians' purity of doctrine but grew impatient with their complacency and lack of faith. He declared to a conference at Park Street, Islington:

"My dear brothers, your understanding of the truth is vast, but in my country it would avail you so much," and he brought finger and thumb together, "if when the need arose you could not cast out a demon!"[11]

Let us not fail to present the full gospel to Muslims. Islam is mainly based on practices and issues related to everyday life. So when gospel workers present Christianity as a religion that meets only spiritual needs, they make it appear unconcerned with immediate needs, focusing only on remote, transcendental, and "spiritual" questions—eternity, sin, salvation, righteousness, and so on. It is made to look "so heavenly-minded that it is no earthly good." Consequently, Muslims see Christianity as impractical by contrast, and consider it inferior to Islam. We referred to this earlier when we discussed obstacles that hinder Muslims from accepting Christ.

Christ is the answer to the cosmic questions of spiritual and eternal dimensions; but He is also the answer to felt needs. Muslims, like all other people, have immediate needs that compete for their attention. As Christian witnesses we are obligated to empathize with them in their everyday circumstances and show them how Christ can meet all their needs.

In the Lord's Prayer (Matthew 6:9–13) there are seven petitions. Only three of these have to do with cosmic issues: "hallowed be your name, your kingdom come, your will be done." Four, however, are about immediate personal needs: "give us this day our daily bread, forgive us our debts, lead us not into temptation, and deliver us from the evil one."

The New Testament vividly shows the way people's needs are met through an experience with Jesus. It often speaks about how people received a personal touch from Him and had a personal encounter with Him. Nathaniel, Nicodemus, the Samaritan woman, and the man born blind were a few of these. Jesus healed people when they were sick, fed them when they were hungry, and comforted them when they needed solace. I believe we need to follow this pattern. As we expose Muslims to who Jesus really is, as they learn and read about Him, they will feel His closeness. They will sense the reality of His person and the warmth of His love. They will experience His patience, His tenderness, His purity, and His power.

Christ has all authority both in heaven and on earth (Matthew 28:18). As the One who has all authority in heaven, He is able to save us from sin and judgment and grant us eternal life. As the One who has all authority on earth, He is able to alleviate our pain; comfort us when we suffer; heal us when we are sick; and bless us with family, friends, jobs, shelter, food and so forth. The Christian witness therefore should present Christ to the unbeliever as He is—all powerful.

What is our goal? We want our Muslim friends to encounter Christ's majesty and glory and feel like doing what Moses did—take off their shoes in the presence of God, our Maker and Savior.

18 | *It's Happenning*

"In Africa alone, every year,
six million Muslims convert to Christianity."

(Inflated statistic given by Muslim leader Sheikh Ahmad al-Qataani, in an interview on Al-Jazeera TV, in December 2000.)

"Ever since I was a young lady, I have seen dreams and visions of things and events that I never heard of in Islam. I was wondering what all that meant. Then I saw a movie about Jesus. There on the screen I watched many of the things I saw in my dreams over the years! God spoke to me and I accepted Christ as my Savior and King. He has washed my sins away. He has given me new life. He is my Master and Lord."

(From an interview with a Muslim woman from the Middle East.)

Yes, Muslims are coming to Christ. We are seeing a fairly significant exodus into the freedom of Christ, but we shall see more. In this concluding chapter we give brief stories, testimonies and reports of some who dared to make the move.

A Medical Doctor

"My grandfather was an imam. I saw inconsistencies in Islam that bothered me. People prayed, fasted… on the outside, but on the inside there was lying, stealing, cheating, and immorality. Once as an innocent child I asked the muezzin why he was not giving the call to prayer louder. His voice was so soft. He said: 'I raise my voice according to the pay they give me!' I had a Christian friend in school who told me about Jesus... but I didn't pay much attention... I thought that Jesus was only a prophet like other prophets... I did not allow myself to think much about it....

"After I became a doctor, I had a chance to study other ideas and cultures besides my own. I found that many of my questions about the problems of everyday life, woman's role, marriage, polygamy, disparity between rich and poor... had no answers in the Qur'an. In the past, I posed these questions to the imams, but they had no answers either. Rather, they ridiculed me and threatened me, saying that I was going over the limits even by merely asking.

"More importantly, there were deeper questions not answered by the Qur'an: Who is God? Where is He? How did He create everything? What is the meaning of life? At this point, I started to study the Christian gospel. I also became acquainted with a Christian nurse at the hospital where I worked. She kept saying that Jesus Christ was the answer in different ways—through His miracles, knowledge, and teaching. But still her answers did not make an impression on me. I still thought that Jesus was only a prophet and didn't know much about His teachings.

"One time a pregnant woman needed a Caesarean section to save her and the baby... The closest hospital to us was forty kilometers away. All I had was my hands and the stethoscope. She was in danger. I found myself unintentionally saying, 'Lord, help me.' Then I felt the baby's position changing... both mother and baby were now safe. But I did not change my ideas. I continued to believe in Marxism. I asked my colleagues if any of them had a Bible. I couldn't find even one.

"Later, a young lady gave me a copy of the Bible. It said that Jesus is the only way to God. I put my faith in Him. I became a new creation! The Bible said that I should be baptized. I asked several pastors to baptize me. They all turned me down. They did not want to endanger themselves. As a Muslim convert in a Muslim country, baptism could mean imprisonment and death for me and the baptizer. Finally, I found someone who baptized me in his own home.

"I was frank with my family. I told them about my experience in Christ. Some members accepted what I did, others ridiculed me. My friends abandoned me. I was fired from my job because of that. I felt totally rejected. But I am reminded of the words of Jesus about those who confess Him or deny Him before men, and about those who put their hand to the plow who must not look back (Matthew 10:32–33; Luke 9:62). Later, I married a Christian woman. After my marriage, I had a vision which greatly deepened my faith... I saw someone with white clothes come to me. This person told me that He was Jesus Christ. He said, 'Follow Me.' He took my hand and started to lead me. He washed my hands in pure water and we sat down at one table and ate together. The food was delicious! Then I opened my eyes to find my wife right beside me. I told her the vision. We were both touched by it, and we knelt down together and prayed and worshiped God... Now I live away from my own country and cannot go back because I accepted Jesus... I have faith that Jesus will provide something good for me."[1]

An Indian Muslim

"I was impressed with the high ethical teachings of the gospel. If the Christians were to corrupt their book, the standard of its ethical teachings would have been lowered. The narratives of the gospel studied under this light suggested no motive for alteration or corruption in the text.

"The story of the crucifixion was an outstanding event in all the narratives concerning the life of Jesus, which completely contradicted the idea of the gospel being corrupted. No follower of religion would intentionally invent a narrative which would attribute to his leader or founder such a shameful treatment at the hands of his enemies. It is no matter of pride to be a follower of one who was shamefully put to death.

"The appearances of Jesus subsequent to His death were confined to His disciples only, and hence they made no redeeming feature of His ignominious death. The enemies remained triumphant over his death. Why? If the Christians were to alter or expurgate anything from the gospel, the account of the crucifixion would have been the first thing to be removed or modified."[2]

An Egyptian Sheikh

As a young boy, Muhammad Mansour entered the village qur'anic school. He was an intelligent lad, and in a few years he had memorized the whole Qur'an. Afterwards, he went on to study Islamic sciences and the Shari'a under one of the most famous educators in the area. Again Muhammad showed a great ability to learn, and he excelled in all he did. He later became the imam and preacher at the most famous mosque in his city and opened a school devoted to Islamic education.

As a zealous Muslim, Sheikh Muhammad started to investigate Christianity to find out how to "defeat Christians." His inquiries led him to meet with a "Christian" tanner. But when he asked the tanner about Christianity, the man said, "I do not know anything about Christianity... go to the priest." The priest did not know much about the Bible either, but he took Muhammad to a blind church deacon who knew the Bible. The deacon refused to talk with the Muslim sheikh, though, advising him to go to the evangelical pastor in the village instead.

After a long talk with the evangelical pastor, Sheikh Muhammad was convinced of the superiority of Islam. But just as he was leaving, the pastor made a final remark. "Everyone should ask God to lead him in the right path," he said, "and I advise you to ask Him to guide you to the truth." Muhammad protested: "Do you think I doubt my faith? God forbid! All of us Muslims ask God five times a day to guide us to the truth."

But later Muhammad Mansour started thinking: "How do I know that I am right? Maybe I am walking down the wrong path." He started to study Christianity again. He attended a few meetings at the evangelical church and obtained a Bible and began to read it. It was not long before he became distraught and anxious as he realized that he had been wrong. But soon all his doubts were replaced with joy and peace as he accepted Jesus.

The news of Mansour's conversion to Christ spread like wildfire, throwing the Muslim community in the village into great shock and turmoil. Mansour left the village to be baptized somewhere else, and the family discovered this. His father went to where he was, trying to convince him to come back to Islam—but to no avail. His uncle secretly monitored him for a few days and lay in ambush for him at a street corner to kill him with a butcher knife. But Muhammad felt what was happening just seconds before the fatal thrust. He hit his uncle with his staff, the knife dropped, and Muhammad took hold of him. Instead of punishing his uncle, Muhammad witnessed to him about Christ's love and forgiveness and let him go.

For twenty-five years, Sheikh Muhammad Mansour served his Lord and Savior. He preached Christ among his Muslim brothers until he went to be with the One who died and rose again for his sake.[3]

An African Muslim

Ali is an African Muslim from a country that is 100 percent Muslim. He is the very first convert to Christ in his country. After accepting Christ, Ali attended Bible school in another country. Upon his return home, he was arrested at the airport and imprisoned for three months. He was locked up in a small cell, able only to sit and lean on the wall or stand up part way. He was given one meal a day—a handful of rice filled with salt. Then he was told that he could choose his own punishment. Three penalties were offered: to be shot dead, imprisoned for life, or deported from his country. It was a very hard situation. What could he choose? He had a large family to care for, including eight children.

So, in front of his accusers and judges, Ali knelt in the courtroom and prayed out loud to Jesus, the Lord, King, Savior, and Redeemer. When the people heard his prayer, they thought he had gone insane. They immediately dismissed him from the court and set him free. Later Ali led his first convert to Christ—the police inspector sent to his village to spy on his Christian activities.[4]

An Albanian Muslim

A young Albanian Muslim whom we shall call Khaled had a friend who became a Christian. This caused Khaled to be hostile to him. But although Khaled's heart was filled with nationalistic pride and hatred toward all Christians, he decided to go with his friend to a Christian meeting. There, he was overwhelmed with the love of the Christians. But still he told his friend, "You're crazy to go to the Christians' meeting." Yet Khaled could not stay away. On his second visit to the meeting, he decided to follow Christ.

Khaled was rejected by his family as a result of becoming a Christian. That was not his only problem. He also had no job, and unemployment was high in the area where he lived. But the church was not indifferent to Khaled's situation. They prayed that God would supply employment for Khaled, as well as for three other young converts. God answered, and all four were hired to work at good jobs. Khaled then wanted to return to his family. They accepted him back, which certainly made him happy. But his days of peace were not to last.

One day the police stopped Khaled on the street, and took him away to the police station. There they locked him up for some hours. "What are you," they demanded, "Muslim or Christian?" "I am a Christian," Khaled said. Hearing this, the police beat him badly and left him battered and bruised, saying that they'd be back to beat him again. At two o'clock in the morning they came back. When Khaled saw them, he was terrified. He had a letter opener and cut himself with it in several places. When he did this, the police got worried and rushed him to the hospital. There a doctor took care of him, and the police let him go. After his release, Khaled went to his pastor who led him to ask forgiveness from God. Following this terrible experience, Khaled's family started pressuring him to revert to Islam. Again, he had to leave home.

Khaled has been baptized in water and in the Holy Spirit. At the time of writing this story, he needs permanent housing and employment.[5]

A Sheikh's Daughter

Sheikh M. F. was the top religious leader in his populous Muslim country. All of a sudden his daughter became sick. She was taken to the doctor. But the doctor's report was bleak. Blood analysis, X-rays, and other close investigation showed cancer. The family was informed that the medical science in that country would not be of much help. They were advised to take their daughter to France.

In France the young lady was taken to one of the most advanced hospitals in Paris and put under the care of a team of top specialists. But that did not help either. The reports were getting worse. Her health rapidly deteriorated, and she became unable to tend to her basic needs.

One night while things in that hospital room were quiet and she was asleep, Jesus came to the room. She woke up and asked what was happening. Jesus spoke with compassion and love. He said to her: "I'm Jesus. I came to heal you and make you live. But I want also to be your Lord and Savior." He touched her, and she felt power go through her body. The girl immediately worshiped Jesus.

In the morning the father came to visit his daughter. He saw the great change in her health but did not want to believe the story about Jesus. The following night, Jesus came to the father and confirmed what the daughter said.[6]

A Nigerian Muslim

"My name is D. B. and I am twenty-five years old. I was a Muslim from a family that had been Muslim for many generations. I was brought up in the Islamic faith… without any knowledge of Christianity… My father is a very devout Muslim who always prays five times a day, fasts every Ramadan… and has even performed the hajj to Mecca on three occasions. He married nineteen wives… I do not even know some of my half-brothers and sisters…

"From birth I was taught Islamic ways. Our home was like a mosque with my father as the Imam. He would lead…with a stick by his side. All my brothers and I would line up facing the kibla and if we made any mistakes my father would hit us with the stick or slap us on our faces. With heavy beatings and floggings I learned to pray in the correct Muslim way, saying prayers in the Arabic language that made no sense to me as I did not know the meaning…

"In January 1984, I was on my way to play soccer… Someone with a Bible in his hand stopped me and preached the Good News to me and I gave my life to Christ. This was the greatest day in my life! The man of God spoke to me in a gentle way, yet he spoke with power and authority. He did not condemn me although there was much sin and wrong in my life and heart…

"Two very important things stick out in my mind about what he said to me and about what he read. The first had to do with love and the fact that this stranger really loved me and was genuinely interested in my well-being and in the condition of my eternal soul. More than that, this kind man told me that God loved me and wanted to take care of me. That was very strange to me, since I had never been taught that God loves me. I thought God was unknowable and that He would not be concerned with my problems or needs. I thought of Allah as a very strict master who was quick to punish my wrong deeds but who cared very little about me as a person since I was not worthy of His attention, since I had never done anything great for Him to win His admiration or concern.

"The second thing that I remember had to do with the power and authority of Jesus. The man of God who ministered to me spoke with authority and power as he told me of Jesus the Messiah who came to earth as God in the flesh. He told me that Jesus has all authority in heaven and earth and that He could and would help me find solutions to my problems and supply my needs. That was extremely good news for me. I had never seen any demonstration of power in Islam. All I had seen in Islam was fear and threats.

"After I gave my life to Christ, my father and all my relatives were very much against me. Some cursed me while others mocked me mercilessly. My father was very furious… He hired a qur'anic teacher to tutor me in the Qur'an and he would schedule those lessons on the same days and at the exact times that my church would have its… services… When that did not dampen my spirit because the Lord gave me peace and joy and grace, my father threatened to kill me with "black medicine" of the voodoo and other evil spirits… but I did not fear the evil spirits because I knew that Jesus was greater than Satan and his evil hosts. My father's pride and reputation as a respected hajji were jeopardized by my confession that Jesus is Lord. I continued to respect my father and to submit to the qur'anic teacher until I finished my education. I then left home and had the liberty to attend the church meetings that are so precious to me.

"I found a job as a storekeeper in the northern part of [my country] and I settled there for a while and joined a small church that now has grown to be very large and powerful by God's Holy Spirit. I came under attack there by Muslims who threatened my life and… I was attacked by Satan who would speak to me and tell me that I was going to die. At times late at night (one or two o'clock in the morning), his voice would wake me up and tell me that I must die. From 1984 to 1986, this problem from Satan nearly took my life but I continued serving Jesus. In April 1986 after Sunday services, I went back to the church alone. I prayed earnestly pleading the blood of Jesus Christ, and that was the end of this oppression by Satan and his evil forces! So Jesus set me free and I'm free forever, Amen!

"I was obedient to the Lord's command to be baptized in water... At the same time that I was baptized in water, the Lord Jesus baptized me in His Holy Spirit... This very special blessing has given me a special closeness to God... God has allowed me to minister healing in Jesus' name... On one occasion I was ministering healing in the mighty name of Messiah Jesus to a small Muslim boy who was crippled in his legs, arms, and hand. I prayed for his hand to be healed and God immediately healed it, all praise and glory be to Him. There was a large crowd of Muslims who saw me praying to God for this little boy. They chased me into my home where they were unable to harm me. The boy's hand was completely healed and the Muslims could not deny this miracle from God.

"I have worked as a merchant marine and have sailed to many places... God has always supplied my needs... He has given me opportunities to witness to many who are bound by Satan in alcohol and drug abuse and prostitution and demon possession and oppression. I try always to give a witness for the Lord Jesus the Messiah who has the power to set people free from all these things.

"Very late in the evening while at port... some of us were playing soccer, trying to get some exercise for our legs that were quite weak from our time at sea... the ball went into the water... I dived into the water after the ball... I threw it back to someone on the dock but then I started to struggle with the water... I could not make it to the ladder. I thought that I would surely die... All the people on the ship and dock thought I was going to die since most of them worshipped the sea and thought it was an angry god who would punish me for jumping into it in such a manner. Just as I thought that I would die, someone threw me a line and the Lord gave me strength to hold on...

I know that the Lord saved me from the sea that night and I praise Him that He has something for me to do for Him before I am called home to heaven.

"I have forgiven [my father] for all the things that he did to me wrongly and I love him with a supernatural love, a special love that can only be given to us by a loving God... Praise God my mother has come into the kingdom of God... She, as well as two of my siblings are living victoriously for Him. God is supplying my needs... I study His word daily and I enjoy praising Him in songs and hymns... He is my true Father and I am extremely fortunate to have been snatched from the bondage of Satan.

"In conclusion, right from the time I was saved, God taught me that the devil and his evil spirits are powerless by the blood of Christ. I praise God for His wonderful love and His tremendous power. My Muslim brother, I am not condemning you... I challenge you to investigate the things I have claimed in this testimony. Find out for yourself if they will work in your life."[7]

A Photographer

"I am twenty-eight years old. I come from a devout Muslim family. When I was a teenager, a friend in school accepted Christ. I tried to dissuade him. I persecuted him so harshly. When he withstood the persecution, returning love for hatred and kindness for mistreatment, I thought that the Bible had to be more than just a trivial book as I had been taught as a Muslim. 'The Bible that changed my friend must be a powerful unclean book,' I thought. So I decided to kill him.

"I got together with some friends and secretly planned to kill the Christian boy. But just before our plot was to be executed, he seemed so calm, smiling and loving. He read a Psalm to me. It touched my fanatic heart. It sent a great light that shone in my dark soul. My wickedness became so clear to me. I could not sleep that night. The Holy Spirit began to reveal my sins to me. I confessed that I needed Jesus to change my heart. I accepted Him as my Lord and Savior. My heart was filled with joy. Peace filled my soul. My life was changed."[8]

Muhammad

Sleeping on an unsmoothed, concrete floor in mid-winter with no mattress, pillow, or covers other than his own clothing was new to Muhammad. The great-grandson of an influential and wealthy politician, he had always had whatever he needed. Then, just a couple of years before, he had come to know what it meant to have his sins forgiven through believing in Christ. He had become one of those "others"—followers of Christ—a forbidden change in a Muslim society. It was winter now—cold and damp; and the space between the roof and the walls of his solitary confinement prison cell was big enough to let strong currents of cold air invade the small, lonely room.

It happened on December 19, 1981. Muhammad caught a taxi home. He chatted with fellow passengers a few moments and discovered that everyone in the taxi claimed to be a Christian. So he joyfully told them how he a Muslim had come to believe in Christ. They asked for his church's address, declaring that they wanted to attend. That same evening they appeared at the church, bringing the secret police with them. The police arrested Muhammad, shaved his head, beat him, and tried threats and even bribery to get him to renounce his faith in Christ. When he refused, they confined him to a solitary jail cell for five days. He asked if he could call his family or friends to tell them where he was, but the police refused. Then they transferred him to the prison where they kept the country's most dangerous criminals. Muhammad would spend the next eight months in solitary confinement although there had never been a warrant for his arrest and he was never brought to trial. When a Christian attorney asked to take his case and represent him, the refusal was flat and final.

Muhammad spent the entire winter of 1981–82 with no bed or covers, although all other prisoners had beds and by law each inmate was to have two blankets. When he asked for covers, the guards said: "No. You are a Christian. You're not going to get any." For a month and a half all he had was the clothes he was wearing when he was arrested; so he was not able to change. (But he says that during that time the Lord kept him from having any rash or skin sores.) He received only one meal a day made of lentils.

After Muhammad's arrest, his family did not know where he was for a month and a half. When they asked the police where he was, they claimed they didn't know. During the first few weeks Muhammad got to know another prisoner who agreed to send letters to his family and friends to tell them where he was. But when Muhammad's family came to the prison where he was being held, the officials denied that he was there. His brother, an officer in the army, asked the secret police if he could visit Muhammad, saying that maybe he could get him to renounce his faith in Christ. The police finally agreed. Later they permitted three family members to see him, but denied visiting rights to all his friends.

For the first two months of his confinement the police forbade anyone to give Muhammad extra food, clothes, or even money although all other prisoners used bribes to get the basic things—hot water in the winter, extra food, and so forth. They wanted to make it hard on him. Eventually, another prisoner who had extra privileges was able to quietly give him two covers.

Muhammad was confined to his cell all day except for five minutes when he was allowed to go out to use the toilet. Even then, the soldiers would push and hit him, ordering, "Go quickly." All the other prisoners were allowed to leave their rooms freely from 9:00 in the morning to 4:00 in the afternoon.

Every so often the secret police would send a man to ask Muhammad, "Will you renounce your faith in Jesus Christ now and be a good Muslim again?" When he refused, the man would try to tempt him by offering him money, a car, freedom, or even a job with the secret police. He always answered "No." The prison director told Muhammad not to speak with anyone for fear that others would become Christians. Once when he was speaking with a prisoner who had asked him for a Bible, the prison director pushed him, slapped him, and then got a whip and beat him.

After eight months, the authorities, with no explanation, decided to release Muhammad on bail. (We believe it was the result of the prayers and fasting of God's people!) As he left prison, the secret police warned him that if they saw him go to church they would arrest and kill him.

A few months after his release, Muhammad married a beautiful Christian girl and left the country. Since then he and his wife have been in full-time ministry.

Praise God for Muhammad and many other converts like him who have been willing to face persecution, imprisonment, and sometimes even death to follow Jesus Christ.[9]

* * *

To help Muslims make the exodus from darkness into the light and freedom of Christ is one of the greatest opportunities the Church has today. God so loved the world, including Muslim peoples. God humbled Himself and became man to save whoever believes, including those from among the Muslims. Jesus identified Himself with human beings to show needy, miserable, fallen, sinful people the Father's love. There is no lack of opportunity for the Church to bring Muslims to Christ. They are there—everywhere around us—about 1.3 billion—hungry, thirsty, needy, disillusioned, and lost.

As gospel witnesses let us be aggressive and loving. Let us enter all the open doors and lead many Muslims to freedom, joy and new life in Jesus Christ! In the words of J. N. D. Anderson, "The world has yet to see what would happen if the gospel of the living Christ was adequately presented to the millions of Islam."[10]

Let Kedar Rejoice!

A song of hope and victory resounds in the book of Isaiah about Kedar. Kedar was one of the nations that emerged from the line of Ishmael, the forefather of the Arab nations. It was among the Arabs that Islam started and through them that it spread throughout the world. Let us claim this promise for all Muslim peoples and hold on to it by faith. Let its fulfillment be our constant prayer:

Let the desert and its cities raise their voices,

the encampments where Kedar lives.

Let the inhabitants of the Rock cry aloud for joy

and shout from the mountain tops.

Let them give glory to Yahweh

and, in the coasts and islands, let them voice his
praise . . .
I shall lead the blind by a road they do not know,
by paths they do not know I shall conduct them.
I shall turn the darkness into light before them
and the quagmires into solid ground.
This I shall do—without fail (Isaiah 42:11, 12, 16, New Jerusalem Bible).

GLOSSARY

Word	Meaning
Abbasid	Branch of the Quraysh tribe (named after al 'Abbas, one of Muhammad's uncles) which was the ruling Muslim dynasty from 750 to 1258.
Abd	Slave, servant; all humans are slaves of God.
Ablution	Ritual washing of one's body or part of it in preparation for prayer.
Abrogation	Cancellation of a previous statement or action.
Adjuration	Solemn oath; an earnest urging or advising.
Ahmadiyyahs	Islamic sect which believes that although Jesus was crucified, He did not die but revived and went to live in India.
Allah	Arabic name for God. (Note: Allah was used before Islam and is not an exclusively Muslim term. Today even Christian Arabs use it. It is related to the Hebrew terms for God, Eloah and Elohim.)
Amulet	Charm (as in ornament) often inscribed with a magic incantation or symbol to protect the wearer against evil (such as disease or witchcraft) or to aid him or her.
Analogy	The notion that if two (or more) things agree with one another in some respects, they will probably agree in others.
Anthropomorphic	Attributing human characteristics to God such as having hands or eyes, and so forth.
Apocryphal	Of doubtful authenticity.
Apologist	One who speaks or writes in defense of a faith or a cause.
Barakah	Supernatural, transempirical influence of blessedness and spiritual force.

Bismellah	"In the name of God."
Byzantine	Name of the empire ruled by the Eastern Orthodox Church whose existence lasted from around 330 to its final destruction by the Ottoman Turks in 1453.
Caliph	A successor of Muhammad as temporal and spiritual ruler/leader of Islam.
Carnal	Bodily, corporeal; relating to or given to crude bodily pleasures and appetites.
Colonialism	Control by one power over a dependent area or people.
Communal	Characterized by collective ownership or use of property; participated in, shared, or used in common by members of a group or community.
Companions	The key assistants to Muhammad during his lifetime.
Coptic	Of or relating to the Copts (members of the traditional Monophysite Christian church originating and centering in Egypt).
Creedal	Pertaining to an authoritative formula of fundamental beliefs.
Crusades	Any of the military expeditions undertaken by Christian powers in the eleventh, twelfth, and thirteenth centuries to win the Holy Land from the Muslims.
Dar al-Harb	"House of war;" refers to all people who are not Muslim.
Dar al-Islam	"House of Islam (or peace);" refers to all Muslims anywhere in the world.
Diacritical	Marks and points that determine how to pronounce a letter.
Din	Religion encompassing all of life's beliefs and practices as ordained by God.

Djamaa	Mosque.
Donatism	A view held by the North African church from the fourth to the seventh century which taught (in opposition to Rome) that the sacraments were valid only if they were administered by a priest in "correct standing" with the church according to how the North African church defined "correct."
Existentialism	A philosophy which places emphasis on the experience of existence.
Ethnic Christian	Member of an indigenous Christian group in a land now dominated by Islam or another religion, such as the Copts in Egypt or Armenians in Turkey.
Fatwa (or Fatwah)	Decree based on the Shari'a and issued by the highest religious authorities in the land.
Fundamentalism	A movement or attitude emphasizing strict and literal adherence to a set of basic principles.
Ghul	A female cannibalistic spirit of a bestial, diabolical, and treacherous nature.
Gnostic	Related to the thought and practice of various pre-Christian and early Christian cults who believed that matter is evil and salvation comes through a special kind of knowledge (gnosis); an adherent of gnosticism.
Gospel	The message concerning Christ, the kingdom of God, and salvation.
Hadith	Collection of stories of what Muhammad said and did.
Hajj	The formal pilgrimage to Mecca prescribed as a religious duty for Muslims.
Hajji	One who has made a pilgrimage to Mecca.
Hanif	Title by which pre-Islamic monotheists were known.

Hijra	The migration of Muhammad from Mecca to Medina in A.D. 622 which marked the beginning of Islam as an identifiable religion.
Houri	One of the beautiful virgins that a Muslim will marry in paradise.
Huda	God's guidance; also refers to salvation and being on the right path.
Hypostasize	To attribute real identity to (a concept).
Id al-Adha	Feast of sacrifice commemorating Abraham's obedience to sacrifice his son.
Id al-Fitr	Feast of breaking the month-long fast.
Ijtehad	Diligent judgment regarding a theological issue based on the interpretation of Islamic law.
Illusion position	The view which holds that the Jews were made to only imagine that they had crucified Jesus, thus that the crucifixion was a mere illusion.
Imam	Prayer leader; any of various rulers that claim descent from Muhammad and exercise spiritual and temporal leadership over a Muslim region.
Immutability	The quality of not being susceptible to change.
Incantation	A use of spells or verbal charms spoken or sung as part of a ritual of magic.
Indigenous	Having originated in, and being produced, growing, and living, or occurring naturally in a particular region or environment.
Individualistic	Characterized by an emphasis on the freedom and independence of the individual and a stress on individual initiative, action, and interests.
Islam	Submission to the will of God; the religious faith of Muslims including belief in Allah as the sole deity and in Muhammad as His prophet.
Jacobites	The Monophysites of Syria who have been traditionally named after Jacob Baradaeus (died A.D.

	578), a proponent of Monophysitism.
Jama'at	Islamic fundamentalist groups which try to impose the Shari'a on everyone as the only legitimate law.
Jihad	Holy war waged on behalf of Islam as a religious duty.
Jinn	One of a class of spirits that according to Muslim belief inhabit the earth, assume various forms, and exercise supernatural power.
Judaizer	One who advocates conformity to Jewish rites, ceremonies, and practices.
Ka'aba	A small stone building in the court of the Great Mosque in Mecca that contains a sacred black stone and is the goal of Islamic pilgrimage.
Qiblah	The direction toward which Muslims turn in prayer.
Kufic	A highly angular form of the Arabic alphabet used especially for costly copies of the Qur'an.
Legalism	Strict, literal, or excessive conformity to the law or to a religious or moral code.
Liberal	One who is not bound by authoritarian, orthodox, or traditional forms.
Linear logic	Reasoning which leads in a straight line from a premise to a conclusion.
Logos	Word of God that became Man; Jesus Christ.
Magi	Traditionally, the wise men from the East who came to pay homage to the infant Jesus.
Maktub	Fate; that which is decreed.
Masjed	Mosque, place of worship.
Matn	Part of a hadith that is Muhammad's statement.
Melkites	Christians in Egypt and Syria who accepted the decrees of the council of Chalcedon (A.D. 451) affirming that Jesus Christ is both God and man, two

perfect natures in one divine Person, which affirmation was against the views of the Nestorians and Monophysites.

Monophysitism   The view which holds that the incarnate Christ had only a single divine nature, clad in human flesh (thus denying the orthodox doctrine of the two natures of Christ).

Muezzin   Someone who shouts the call to Muslim prayer.

Muslim   One who surrenders to God; an adherent of Islam.

Nazarenes   Thought to be an early sect of Jewish Christians who held that Christians of Jewish descent should observe the Jewish law; in Arabic called "Nasara."

Nestorians   Followers of Nestorius, patriarch of Constantinople (A.D. 428), who taught that the unity between Christ's human and divine natures was one of will rather than one of essence, which view was judged to be a denial of the orthodox doctrine of the union between Christ's human and divine natures.

Nominal   Existing or being something in name or form only.

Ottoman   Turkish empire which lasted from 1300 to 1924, reaching the peak of its power from 1481–1566; the early Ottomans were leaders of the Turkish ghazis, fighters for the faith of Islam.

Papal   Of or relating to the pope or to the Roman Catholic Church.

Paraphernalia   Articles of equipment.

Polytheism   Belief in or worship of more than one god.

Power encounter   The confrontation between opposing forces, good and evil.

Preexist   Precede or exist before someone ar something else.

Qarin   Spirit-companion or familiar spirit which Muslims believe is born with each individual and accompanies him or her throughout life.

Qur'an	The book composed of sacred writings accepted by Muslims as the supreme and final revelation "sent down" by Allah through the angle Gabriel "on" Muhammad.
Rabbinical	Relating to Jewish teachers or their writings.
Ramadan	The ninth month of the Islamic year observed as sacred with fasting practiced daily from dawn to sunset.
Reincarnation	Rebirth in new bodies or forms of life.
Rightly Guided Caliphs	The first four caliphs to succeed Muhammad and whose caliphates lasted from A.D. 632 to 661 (Abu Bakr, Omar, Othman, and Ali).
Risalah	Prophethood; the office of a messenger sent from God.
Salaf	The forefathers of Islam.
Sanad	Chain of authorities or names which carries a hadith on from the first person who heard Muhammad say it.
Seal of the Prophets	Descriptive phrase used of Muhammad which indicates the Muslim belief that he is God's final messenger to the world.
Shabih	Resemblance; likeness.
Shari'a	Fundamental law which covers the whole of the religious, political, social, domestic, and private life of those who profess Islam.
Sharif	A descendant of the prophet Muhammad through his daughter Fatima; or an object that is holy or sacred.
Sheikh	An Arabic term of reverence for a religious leader. Even a Christian can be called sheikh.
Shi'a	The second largest Muslim branch which was formed by the partisans of Ali, the fourth caliph, and whose imam is considered to be infallible. Also a member of that branch.

Shirk	Partnership or association and relates to the fact of accepting partners or associates with God; that is, worshipping others along with God.
Stigma	A mark of shame or discredit.
Subhan Allah	"Praise be to God."
Subsist	To have existence.
Substitute position	The view which holds that a substitute was crucified and killed instead of Jesus because God miraculously hid Him.
Sunna	The custom and example of the Prophet—his teachings and statements regarding different situations and experiences.
Sunni	The largest Muslim branch that adheres to the orthodox tradition and recognizes the Rightly-Guided Caliphs as legitimate successors of Muhammad. Also a member of that branch.
Sura (or Surah)	Chapter of the Qur'an.
Syllogism	A deductive method of argument consisting of a major premise ("All dogs have four feet"), a minor premise ("Fido is a dog"), and a conclusion ("Therefore, Fido has four feet").
Syncretism	The combination of different forms of beliefs or practices.
Talisman	An object held to act as a charm to avert evil and bring good fortune.
Taqiya	The fact that Muslims, when facing threat or injury, have the freedom to suspend their convictions and hide their true feelings and pretend to accept other beliefs or practices forced on them.
Tawhid	From the root wahid meaning one; this is the act of worshipping only one God.
Textual variation	A wording in one copy of an original which is slightly different from the wording in another copy.

Transcendental	Relating to the philosophy which asserts that the spiritual (that which lies beyond the ordinary limits of experience) has primacy over the material.
Ummah	Group of people; community; nation which as a unit is the object of salvation and is liable to judgment.
Verbum Dei	The Word of God; Jesus Christ.
Vicarious	Serving instead of someone or something else.
Zar	Ritual which includes group dancing, singing, swaying to the rhythms of drums, and feasting on special foods; participants often experience abnormal states of consciousness, which are viewed as proof of having entered into communication with the spirits.
Zoroastrianism	A Persian religion founded in the sixth century B.C. which is characterized by worship of a supreme god Ahura Mazda who requires men's good deeds for help in his cosmic struggle against the evil spirit Ahriman.

NOTES

Chapter 1

1 *Hadith*: Bukhari, Volume 6, p. 128.

2 One cannot help but reflect on how the Jews rejected Jesus but accepted Muhammad. In fact they invited Muhammad to Medina. They welcomed him with open arms and gave him refuge in their city. But within a very short time after he moved to Medina, Muhammad drove out or slaughtered all the Jews of that city. Today the very existence of Jews is threatened by Muslims. It is ironic that they rejected Christ but welcomed Muhammad.

3 Embedded in the eastern wall of the Ka'aba, this black stone is about ten inches across and twelve inches high. It was worshipped by pre-Islamic Meccans for many generations. Muslims believe that it descended from heaven. It is probable that it is a meteorite. In some cultures, the worship of meteorites was not unusual. It seems that the Ephesians in Paul's time believed that a meteorite had come to them from heaven (Acts 19:23 – 36). Muslims believe that when it came down from heaven, this stone was white, but over time it became black because it absorbed the sins of the pilgrims who touched it. As a matter of fact, this change of color is consistent with known meteorites which are white and change hues over time because they oxidize. Today, as Muslim pilgrims go around the Ka'aba, they attempt to kiss the Black Stone if they can get close to it. This is veneration that borders on worship.

4 Mohammed Marmaduke Pickthall. *The Meaning of the Glorious Koran*. New York: The New American Library, 1961, p. XXIII.

5 Ahmad Ibn Taimiyya. *Repentance*. Batna, Algeria: Shahab Publishing, n.d., p. 71; and *Al-Watan Al-Arabi*, no. 1148, March 5, 1999, p. 67.

6 Jalal-u-Din Seyouti. *Rules of Jinn*. Cairo, Egypt: Islamic Turath Library, 1989, p. 205.

Chapter 2

1 Some suggest that perhaps the Greek church in the eastern Mediterranean and John of Damascus in particular played a role in forming early Islamic thought.

2 http://grahamlester.typepad.com/point2point/2004/07/reconstructing_.html.

3 Yassa Mansour. *Evidence of the Truth*, Vols. 3 and 4 1966, p. 39.

4   B. Lewis et al, eds. *The Encyclopedia of Islam*. New Edition. Leiden, Nether-
    lands: E. Brill, 1975, p. 1206.

5   **What if?** Muslims claim that "Pastor Waraqa" told Muhammad that God
    must have chosen him to be a prophet to the Arabs and that what he had
    heard was the angel Gabriel sent with an inspiration. I often wonder: *Why
    would Waraqa so mislead Muhammad? What kind of "pastor" was that man?
    What if Muhammad had received godly council from someone who really knew
    Christ and knew His Word?* Yet, no amount of conjecture can change the sev-
    enth-century history and what followed. Yet, my musing is not useless. Today,
    many young people come from all parts of the world to the West for educa-
    tion and training. Some of these will go on to be leaders in their countries.
    What kind of Christians are they meeting in the West? I have a clipping from
    an international news magazine that lists kings, presidents, prime ministers
    and cabinet ministers from all over the world who have studied in the United
    States. Their countries of origin include Argentina, Chile, Czech Republic,
    Denmark, Egypt, France, Israel, Japan, Liberia, Mexico, Norway, Philippines,
    Qatar, Saudi Arabia, Sudan, Sweden, Taiwan and Turkey. If Waraqa failed to
    present the gospel to Muhammad, it looks like we have no lack of opportuni-
    ties today to send tens of thousands of expatriate young people back to their
    countries with the gift of eternal life in Christ.

6   For a fuller treatment of this subject see Rev. W. St. Clair-Tisdall. *The Sources
    of Islam*. New Delhi: Amorko Book Agency, 1901.

7   Seyouti citing ibn Merdawiyya as quoted in Klein, 1971, p.17; also al-Ward-
    ani, 1997 p. 24.

8   As quoted in Hussein M. Yusef and M. Attia Khamis. *Stop Destroying Islam
    from the Inside*. Cairo: Dar al-E'tesam, 1979, p. 20.

9   Even today, before Muslims recite qur'anic verses they are required to make a
    statement to seek protection against Satan during their recitation. Muham-
    mad was told: "When you recite the Quran, seek refuge in Allah from the
    cursed Satan" (Sura 16:98).

10 Abu-Mousa al-Hariri. *The World of Miracles*, 1986, p.123.

11 Abu-l Qasem b. Omar Al-Zamakhshari. *Kashaf*. Cairo: Muhammad Mus-
    tafa: 1354 A.H., Vol. 3, p. 19.

12 W. Montgomery Watt. *Muhammad, Prophet and Statesman*. New York: Ox-
    ford University Press, 1961, p. 61.

13 Alfred Guillaume. *Islam*. London: Penguin Books, 1954, p.187.

14 Abu-Mousa al-Hariri. *The World of Miracles*. Lebanon: For Knowledge
    House, 1986, p.124

15 Seedbed. XVIII No. 2. West Sussex, UK: 2004, p. 21.

16 *Hadith*: Ahmad, 18–16.

17 Ibn Taimiya. *Sword Withdrawn Against the Insulter of the Apostle*. p. 221.

18 See also H. A. R. Gibb and J. H. Kramers. *Shorter Encyclopaedia of Islam*. New York: Cornell University Press, 1953, p. 361.

19 Compare this with Psalms 28:3.

Chapter 3

1 M. A. A. Baghdadi. *Terrorism and the Second Islam*. Beirut: Arab Knowledge Publishers, 2003, p. 46.

2 Gustave E. Von Grunebaum. *Modern Islam: The Search for Cultural Identity*. Westport: Greenwood Press, 1962, p. 111.

3 http://hadith.al-islam.com/Display/Display.asp?Doc=0&ID=42304&Searc hText=%CE%E3%D3%20%D5%E1%E6%C7%CA%20%DD%ED%2 0%DF%E1%20%ED%E6%E3%20%E6%E1%ED%E1%C9&SearchTy pe=exact&Scopc-0&Offset=0&SearchLevel=Allword.

4 *Hadith*: Abu Hurayrah, Askalani, 16.

5 http://www.islamicity.com/hadith/Bukhari, 008.073.049

6 Ibid., Bukhari, 008.075.319.

Chapter 4

1 See for example A. K. Touati. *The Tragic Decline of Arab Presence in Andalu-sia*. Casablanca: Edition Librairie Rachad, 1967, pp. 33-38.

2 For a fuller treatment of this subject in Arabic see the two volumes on the Companions by Khalil Abd al-Karim.

3 G. K. Chesterton. *St. Francis of Assisi*. New York: Image Books, 1957, p. 123.

4 Ahmad ibn Taimiya. *Repentance*. Algeria: Shahab Publishing, 1987, p. 54.

5 *Huda-l-Islam*. Jerusalem: January, 1984.

6 Jan Goodwin. *Price of Honor: Muslim Women Lift the Veil of Silence on the Islamic World*. Boston: Little, Brown and Company, 1994, p. 345.

7 In Arabic: أينما وجدت قلبك فخيم An English equivalent is: Home is wherever your heart resides.

8 Muhammad Ahmad Khalaf-Allah. *Muhammad and the Antagonizing Powers*. Cairo: Anglo-Egyptian Books, 1973, p. 237.

9 Von Julius Wellhausen. *History of the Arab State*. Cairo: Thousand Books, 1958.

10 Alfred Guillaume. *Islam*. London: Penguin Books, 1973, p. 19.

11 Will Durant. *The Story of Civilization*. Vol. 4, *Age of Faith*. New York: Simon and Schuster, 1950, p. 49.

12 Von Julius Wellhausen, ibid., p. 291.

13 Michael Youssef. *Making Christ Known to Muslims*. Atlanta, Georgia: Haggai Institute, 1980, p. 83.

14 Ishak Ibraham. *Black Gold and Holy War*. New York: Thomas Nelson, 1983, p. 83.

15 http://www.cnn.com/2005/WORLD/meast/10/26/ahmadinejad/.

Chapter 5

1 *Ten Great Religions*. Vol. II, p. 68. As quoted in Samuel Zwemer. *The Moslem World*. New York: Student Volunteer Movement, 1908, p. 60.

2 Hadith: Bukhari, (Hadith Qudsi) http://www.fordham.edu/halsall/source/misc-hadith.html; and Sami Khartabil. *The Legend of Al-Hallaj*. Beirut, Lebanon: Ibn Khaldoun, 1979, p. 73.

3 Some suggest that this was done to satisfy the polytheistic pagan Arabs who worshiped the many daughters of God which were all dethroned by Muhammad.

4 Kenneth Cragg. *The Call of the Minaret*. New York: Oxford University Press, 1964, p. 43.

5 *The Story of Dr. Saied, the Iranian*. Cyprus: Logos, 1971, p.184. Also compare these statements of famous Muslim leaders with what Adoniram Judson said: "God has not led me so tenderly thus far to forsake me at the very gate of heaven!" (As quoted in C. H. Spurgeon. *The Treasury of David*. Vol. III. p. 24.).

6 Ishak Ibraham, Ibid, p. 63.

7 A. W. Tozer. *The Knowledge of the Holy*. New York: Harper and Row, 1961, p. 9.

8 G. Campbell Morgan. *An Exposition of the Whole Bible*. Westwood, NJ: Fleming H. Revell, 1959, p. 43.

9 George W Peters. *A Biblical Theology of Missions*. Chicago: Moody Press, 1984, p. 101.

10 Ray G. Register, Jr. *Dialogue and Interfaith Witness with Muslims*. Kingsport, TN: Moody Books, 1979, p. 25.

11 Tor Andrae. *Mohammed, the Man and His Faith*. London: George Allen and Unwin, 1956, p. 35.

12 Kenneth Cragg and Marston Speight. *Islam from Within: Anthology of Religion*. Belmont, CA: Wadsworth, 1980, p. 67.

13 Abdulateef Mushtahari. *This Is Our Call.* هذه دعوتنا Cairo: Dar al-E'tesam, 1979, p. 256.

14 Andrew Rippin and John Knappert. *Textual Sources for the Study of Islam*. Chicago: University of Chicago Press, 1986, p. 99.

15 This celebration was to be held at Jamia Ghausia Masjid in London on Sunday May 2, 2004.

16 http://biphome.spray.se/isllam/WAHABYA.htm.

17 www.submission.org/hajj/idolatrous.html.

18 http://www.islamset.com/encyclo/muhammad.html.

19 Bill A. Musk. *The Unseen Face of Islam*. Eastbourne, UK: Monarch Publishing Company, 1989, p. 233.

20 Musk, ibid., p. 233.

21 Some qur'anic statements give us the impression that Muhammad is equal to God. Sura 33:36 talks about decrees made by God and Muhammad together: "If God and his Apostle decree something... anyone disobeying God and his Apostle will go terribly astray." Sura 3:132 says, "Obey God and the Apostle; perhaps you might receive mercy." However later on in Sura 4:56 we find God is not even mentioned: "Obey the Apostle; perhaps you might receive mercy"!

22 *Hadith*: Bukhari, http://hadith.al-islam.com/Display/hier.asp?Doc=0&n=235 and F. A. Klein, The Religion of Islam, Curzon Press, London, 1971, p. 121.

23 Muhammad al-Ghazali. *The Muslim's Creed*. Cairo: al-Da'wah, 1990, p. 236.

24 For a fuller treatment of this subject see Robert Peter Coenradi. *Continuity and Discontinuity in Conversion from Islam to Christ: An Examination of Salat*. Unpublished Master's Thesis. Bible College of New Zealand, 1998.

25 Sandra Mackey. *The Saudis: Inside the Desert Kingdom*. Kent, UK: Coronet Books, Hodder and Stoughton, 1990, pp. 140–142.

26 Muhammad Metwalli Sha'rawi. *Fatwas*. Vol. 1. Cairo: Qur'an Library, 1981, pp. 26–27; and F. A. Klein, ibid., p. 131.

27 Fatima al-Zahraa Azrouel. *Prostitution: Permissible Bodies*. Beirut: Afrique Orient, 2000, p. 10.

28 Farag Fouda. *The Absent Truth*. Cairo: Dar al-Fikr, 1988, pp. 127-128.

29 Ali B. Hadyah, et al. *New Dictionary*. Tunis: STD, 1979 p. 898.

30 Edward Fitzgerald, trans. *Rubaiyat of Omar Khayyam*. New York: Barnes & Noble, 1993, p. LXXI.

31 Abdel Mon'em Al-Hofni. *Omar Khayyam and the Ruba'iyat*. Cairo: Al-Rashad House, 1992, p.105.

32 Fouda, ibid., p. 88.

33 Alan Palmer. *The Decline and Fall of the Ottoman Empire*. New York: Barnes & Noble, 1992, p. 103.

34 Michael Tomkinson. *Tunisia*. London and Tonbridge: Earnest Benn, Limited, 1970, p. 25.

35 Stephen Neill. *A History of Christian Missions*. New York: Penguin Books, 1964, p. 385.

36 Elizabeth Warnock Fernea and Basima Qattan Bezirgan, Eds. *Middle Eastern Women Speak*. Austin: University of Texas Press, 1977, pp. 71-73.

37 Jean Sasson. *Daughters of Arabia*. London: Bantam Books, 1997, pp. 62, 63.

38 Jean Sasson. *Princess*. London: Bantam Books, 1993, p. 181.

39 Fatima Mernissi. *The Social Dynamics of Sex*. Casablanca: Fennec, 1996, p. 27.

40 Mernissi, ibid., p. 30.

41 Mernissi, ibid., p. 28.

42 As quoted in Ibrahim A'rab. *Political Islam and Modernism*. Casablanca: Afrique Orient, 2000, p. 137.

43 In Arabic: المرأة كالضلع إن أقمتها كسرتها وإن استمتعت بها، استمتعت بها وفيها عوج
Hadith Bukhari, Book 9, 253; and http://hadith.al-islam.com/Display/Display.asp?Doc=0&ID=42782&SearchText=%C7%E1%E3%D1%C3%C9%20%E3%E4%20%D6%E1%DA&SearchType=root&Scope=0,1,2,3,4,5,6,7,8&Offset=0&SearchLevel=QBE

44 *Hadith*: Muslim, Book 2, 603.

45 *Hadith*: Bukhari, Book 1, 28.

46 Emily J Van Dalen. "Raising Radiant Daughters in Dark Places." *Seedbed*. Vol. XV, No. 4–2001. West Sussex, UK: 2001, p. 16.

47 Jalal al-Mukh. A. *Qassem al-Shabbi and the Crown of Thorns*. Sousse, Tunisia: Dar al-Ma'aref 1998, p. 61.

48 Imam al-Ghazali. *Ihya' Ulumn al-Din*. Cairo, n.d., p.56 and *Rules of Marriage*, p. 86.

49 Jean Sasson. *Desert Royal*. London: Bantam Books, 1999, p. 186.

50 Mernissi, Ibid., p. 35.

51 Goodwin, Ibid., p.333.

52 *Al-Jadidah*, No. 791. 22 August 2001, p. 20.

53 Ibid., p. 21.

54 Tehmina Durrani. *My Feudal Lord, A Devastating Indictment of Women's Role in Muslim Society*. Great Britain: Corgi Books, 1995, p. 77.

55 Bernard Lewis. *What Went Wrong?* New York: Harper Collins, 2003, pp 67, 69.

56 Goodwin, ibid., p. 44.

57 Lewis, ibid., p. 73.

58 http://www.memri.org/bin/opener_latest.cgi?ID=SD68804.

59 *Hadith*: Muslim, Book 008, Number 3253.

60 Emad Nassef. *Sex in the University*. Cairo: Hadaf Publishing, 1999, p.47.

61 Saleh al-Wardani. *Mut'a Marriage Allowed to Sunnis*. Cairo: Little Madbouli, 1997, p. 136.

62 Fazlur Rahman. *Major Themes of the Qur'an*. Chicago: Bibliotheca, 1980, p. 18.

63 Muhammad al-Ghazali. *The Muslim's Creed*. Cairo: Al-Da'wah, 1990, p. 119.

64 *Hadith*: Muslim according to Muhammad al-Ghazali, Ibid., p. 119.

65 Abd al-Masih. *Why Is It Difficult for a Muslim to Become a Christian?* Schorndorf, Germany: Ev. Karmel Mission, n.d., p. 10; and www.intervarsity.org/ism/article/14).

66 Francis Schaeffer. *Death in the City*. L'Abri Fellowship, 1969, p. 80.

67 Sandra Mackey, ibid., p. 281.

68 Sasson, *Desert Royal*, ibid., p. 90.

69 Ibid., p. 90.

70 Abdurrahman al-Jezeery. *The Sure Proof*. Cairo: Irshad Press, 1934, p. 24.

71 Serge Trifkovic. *The Sword of the Prophet*. Boston, Mass: Regina Orthodox Press, 2002, p. 63. In my estimation Trifkovic's book is one of the most insightful on Islam.

Chapter 6

1 Touati, ibid., p. 401.

2 *Hadith*: Bukhari, Muslim and Termidhi.

3 January 8, 1982.

4 Muhammad A. Samman. *Belief and Militancy Together*. Beirut: Dar al-Jil, 1974, p. 381.

5 Name withheld. Lecture to a gathering of missionaries in Missouri, 13 July 1992.

Chapter 7

1 Paul Fregosi. *Jihad in the West: Muslim Conquests from the 7th to the 21st Centuries*. New York: Prometheus Books, 1998, p. 20.

2 Some try to equate the Crusades with Jihad. Yet the Crusades were not a biblical teaching, while jihad is a qur'anic teaching. Let us compare the two.

Jihad	Crusades
Muhammad practiced warring and killing.	Jesus never fought and never killed.
When Muslims kill "infidels" because they do not convert to Islam, they act in harmony with the teachings of the Qur'an and the Hadith.	The Crusaders' campaigns were out of step with the teachings of the Bible and Jesus.
Islam does not require regeneration or a change of heart. Thus, forcing non-Muslims to convert to Islam is an acceptable means of expanding the House of Islam.	Biblical Christianity involves a change of heart; a new birth. No military force can bring people to experience this new life. War is not a biblical means of bringing souls to the Kingdom of God.

3 Trifkovic, ibid., p. 205.

4 Naser Ben Hamad al-Fahd. *An Essay in the Use of Weapons of Mass Destruction*. Manuscript, dated 1424 A.H. [A.D. 2003–2004], p. 6.

5 Naser Ben Hamad al-Fahd, ibid., p. 6.

6 Gibb, H. A. R. and J. H. Kramers, eds. *Shorter Encyclopaedia of Islam*. New York: Cornell University Press, 1953, pp. 272–273.

7 Wismar, Adolph L. *A Study in Tolerance*. New York: AMS Inc., 1966, p. 43.

8 Caesar E. Farah. *Islam: Beliefs and Observances*. Woodbury, NY: Barron's, 1968, p. 158.

9 Alan M. Dershowitz. *Why Terrorism Works: Understanding the Threat, Responding to the Challenge*. Yale University Press, 2002, p. 225.

10 Ergun Mehmet Caner and Emir Fethi Caner. *Unveiling Islam: An Insider's Look at Muslim Life and Beliefs*. Grand Rapids, MI: Kregel, 2002, p. 184.

11 http://books.google.com/books?vid=ISBN1844675289&id=uySTXcBPEE kC&pg=PA43&lpg=PA43&dq=Ramadan+Shalah&sig=wLTWcs2Am5n5j b0mqrcMYPsSK_Q#PPA280,M1

12 *L'Express*, Paris: 31 January 1991, p.62.

13 John Laffin. *The Dagger of Islam*. London, UK: Sphere Books, Limited, 1979, pp. 54–55. These statements were made during the proceedings of the Fourth Conference of the Islamic Research Academy in October 1968.

14 J. Dudley Woodberry, quoting *Hadith al-Tirmidhi*, in *The War on Terrorism: Reflections of a Guest in the Lands Involved*. Manuscript, n.d., p. 2; and http://jmm.aaa.net.au/articles/119.htm.

15 Caesar Farah, ibid., p. 158.

16 Kenneth Cragg. "A Tale of Two Cities." *Mission Frontiers*. Pasadena, CA: US Center for World Mission, December 2001, p. 21.

17 In Arabic: مرحلة الاستضعاف

18 M. J. Akbar. *The Shade of Swords: Jihad and the Conflict Between Islam and Christianity*. London: Routledge, 2003, p. xvi.

19 H. A. R. Gibb. *Whither Islam? A Survey of Modern Movements in the Moslem World*. London: Victor Gollancz, Ltd., 1932, p. 24.

20 A. A. Abdel-Hakam. *The Conquest of Africa and Andalusia*. Beirut: Dar al-Ketab, 1964, p. 109.

21 Trifkovic, ibid., p. 65.

Chapter 8

1 Samuel M. Zwemer. *The Influence of Animism on Islam: An Account of Popular Superstitions*. New York: Macmillan, 1920, p. 8.

2 Donald A. McGavran. *How Churches Grow*. New York: Friendship Press, 1976, p. 51.

3 Phil Parshall. *Bridges to Islam*. Grand Rapids, MI: Baker Book House, 1983, p. 71.

4 Abdulateef Mushtahari. *This Is Our Call*. Cairo: Dar al-E'tesam, 1979. The entire book comes out against such "heresies."

5 Jalal-u-Din Seyouti. *Rules of Jinn*. Cairo: Turath, 1989, pp. 95–96 and 211–212.

6 Muhammad Metwalli Asha'rawi. *The Fatwas*. Vol. 1. Cairo: Qur'an Library, 1981, p.59.

7 Andrew Rippin and John Knappert. *Textual Sources for the Study of Islam*. Chicago: University of Chicago Press, 1986, pp. 162–163. See also similar incidents in Jalal-u-Din Seyouti. *Rules of Jinn*. Cairo: Turath, 1989, pp. 113–117.

8 1895, p. 479.

9 Jalal-u-Din Seyouti. *Rules of Jinn*. Cairo: Turath, 1989, p. 97 and Samuel M. Zwemer. *Studies in Popular Islam*. New York: Macmillan, 1938, p. 57.

10 Zwemer, 1920, ibid., p. 21.

11 See Larry G. Lenning. *Blessing in Mosque and Mission*. Pasadena, CA: William Carey Library, 1980, pp. 65–66.

12 *Sira*, Ibn Ishaq. P. 47.

13 *Hadith*: Bukhari. Book 76, p. 36.

14 Zwemer, 1920, ibid., p. 85.

15 Osama Al-Karm. *A Dialogue with Jinn*. Cairo: Madbouli, 1990, p. 208 and *Al-Muslimun*. (12 August 1982), p. 20.

16 Phil Parshall. *Bridges to Islam*. Grand Rapids, MI: Baker Book House, 1983, pp. 41-42. It seems that these were cases known medically as microcephalies. Medical science states that the brains of such babies are not developed properly or are altogether lacking. By mentioning this fact, I am not ruling out the possibility that Shah Dawla was casting magic spells against the mothers or utilizing other forms of folk practices and dabbling with the underworld.

17 *Hadith*: Muslim. Book 035, Number 6581, and http://www.usc.edu/dept/MSA/fundamentals/hadithsunnah/muslim/035.smt.html#035.6581.

18 Nasr H. Abu Zeid. *Muhei-ddin Ibn Arabi's Philosophy of Interpreting the Qur'an*. Casablanca, Morocco: Arab Cultural Center, 1998, pp. 70, 86, 115, 412.

19 Abdel Halim Mahmood. The Case of Sufism. Cairo: Dar al-Ma'aref, 1988, p. 41.

20 Mahmood, ibid., p. 42.

21 For the six preceding quotes see: Mahmood, ibid., pp. 43–45.

22 See for example, Nasr Hamed Abu Zeid. *Muhei-ddin Ibn Arabi's Philosophy of Interpreting the Qur'an*. Casablanca: Arab Cultural Center, 1998, pp. 113–131 and 177–193.

23 For the three preceding quotes see: Sami Khartabil. *The Legend of Al-Hallaj*. Beirut: Ibn Khaldoun, 1979, pp. 45 and 68–70; F.A. Klein. *The Religion of Islam*. New York: Humanities Press, 1971, p. 234; Carl Brockelmann, Ed. *History of the Islamic Peoples*. London, Routledge and Kegan Paul, 1982, p. 150.

24 Nasr Hamed Abu Zeid. *Muhei-ddin Ibn Arabi's Philosophy of Interpreting the Qur'an*. Casablanca, Morocco: Arab Cultural Center, 1998, p. 206. Ibn Arabi also said that he was one of those assigned to carry God's throne. Ibid., p. 117.

25 Mustafa al-Shak'ah. *Islam with No Sects*. Cairo: al-Masriah al-Lubnaniah, 1989, p. 499.

26 http://home.infionline.net/~ddisse/rabia.html.

27 Sadeq, Hassan. *Roots of Dissension among Islamic Groups*. Cairo: Madbouli, 1991, pp. 202–209.

28 Khalil Abd al-Karim. "The Problem of Sectarianism." In: *Where Is Sectarianism Taking Us?* Cairo: Dar al-Masri al-Jadid, 1987, p. 107.

29 Tehmina Durrani. *My Feudal Lord*. London: Corgi Books, 1995, p. 283.

30 Phil Parshall. *Bridges to Islam*. Grand Rapids, MI: Baker Book House, 1983, p. 44.

31 H.A.R. Gibb and J.H. Kramer, eds. *Shorter Encyclopedia of Islam*. Ithaca, NY: Cornell University Press. 1953, p. 629.

32 Richard J. Foster. *Prayer: Finding the Heart's True Home*. New York: Harper-Collins Publishers, 1992, p. 49.

33 Idries Shah. *The Sufis*. New York: Doubleday & Co., Inc., 1971, p. 192; and Abdel Mon'em Al-Hofni. *Omar Khayyam and the Ruba'iyat*. Cairo: Al-Rashad House, 1992, p. 123.

34 See Chris Horri and Peter Chippindale. *What is Islam?* London: Virgin Books, 1991, pp. 19–20; and Ghulam Sarwar. *Islam: Beliefs and Teachings*. London: The Muslim Educational Trust, 1984, pp. 102–103. It is interesting to note that the story of the Mirâj or Ascent to Heaven (Night Journey) is found in the writings of religions other than Islam. For example, a Pehlavi book called Artâ Vîrâf nâmak records the story of a Zoroastrian named Mahomet who was sent to heaven to bring back news of the events that were happening there.

35 David Burnett. *Unearthly Powers*. Nashville, TN: Nelson, 1988, p. 29.

36 Myrtle S. Langley. "Spirit-Possession, Exorcism and Social Context: an Anthropological Perspective with Theological Implications." In: *Churchman*. Vol. 94, no. 3, pp. 227-228.

37 Bill A. Musk. *The Unseen Face of Islam*. Eastbourne, UK: Monarch Publishing Company, 1989, p. 124.

Chapter 9

1 Hadith: *Muslim*. Book 004, Number 1885. Note also such voices as Seyyed Hossein Nasr who said: "Despite serious encroachments upon the body of Islam by modernism and by the confusion caused within the mind and soul of certain Muslims caught between the pull of their tradition and Western ideologies and values, Islam remains very much a living tradition on both the exoteric and the esoteric levels" (*Islam and the Plight of Modern Man*. London: Longman, 1975 p. 86).

2 Ahmad ibn Taimiya, ibid., p. 59.

3 http://www.faithfreedom.org/forum/viewtopic.php?t=8104.

4 *International Herald Tribune*, 30–31 October 2004, p. 6.

5 Mark A. Gabriel. *Islam and Terrorism*. Lake Mary, FL: Charisma House, 2002, p.48.

6 Sayyed Qutb. *Landmarks on the Road*. Cairo: Dar al-Shoroq, 1991, pp. 150–151.

7 Fox News. 10 August 2006.

8 *Financial Times*, 28 July 2003, D8523A.

9 In a statement from President Zine El Abidine Ben Ali to his Minister of Religious Affairs on Oct. 11, 2006: http://www.magharebia.com/cocoon/awi/xhtml1/en_GB/features/awi/newsbriefs/general/2006/10/12/newsbrief-04.

10 M. Jamil Hanifi. *Islam and the Transformation of Culture*. New York: Asia Publishing House, 1974 pp 143–144.

11 *Al-Yum* (newspaper in Saudi Arabia). 26 August 1992, p. 20.

12 Taha Hussein. *Pre-Islamic Poetry*. Cairo: Dar al-Kutub, 1926, p. 38.

13 Hussein M. Yusef and M. Attia Khamis. *Stop Destroying Islam from the Inside*. Cairo: Dar al-E'tesam, 1979, p. 19.

14 Ibid., p. 19, and http://debate.org.uk/topics/history/interprt.htm.

15 Ibid., p. 20.

16 *Time International*, July 11, 1994, p. 36.

17 Ibid., Dec. 13, 1993, p. 27.

18 Toby Lester. *The Atlantic Monthly*. January 1999.

19 http://grahamlester.typepad.com/point2point/2004/07/reconstructing_.html.

20 http://www.truthbeknown.com/islamquotes.htm.

21 http://www.truthbeknown.com/islamquotes.htm.

22 Yusef and Khamis, ibid., p. 16.

23 Muhammad Al-Ghazali. *The Bitter Reality*. Cairo: Dar al-Shoroq, 1990, p. 148.

24 Hisham Sharabi. *Arab Intellectuals and the West: The Formative Years, 1875–1914*. Baltimore: Johns Hopkins Press, 1970, p. 94.

25 Reported to me by a friend after her talk with the professor, March 2001.

26 Al-Hofni, ibid., p. 117.

27 Sasson, *Desert Royal*, ibid., p. 184.

28 Nabil Abdel Fattah. *The Qur'an and the Sword.* Cairo: Madbouli, 1984, p.48.

29 http://www.memri.org/bin/opener_latest.cgi?ID=SD68804.

30 http://www.muslim-refusenik.com/thebook.html.

31 Nawal Sa'dawi is a prolific author and a psychiatrist. She is well known both in the Arab world and in many non-Arab countries. She is a courageous reformist. Her novels and other books on women in Islam have provoked severe hatred from Muslim fundamentalists. She spent time in prison; and some of her books are banned. http://www.nawalsaadawi.net/bio.htm.

32 Sayyid Amir Ali, as quoted by H. A. R. Gibb, in *Whither Islam*. London: Victor Gallancz, 1932, p. 201.

33 *Time*. June 10, 1991, p. 7.

34 Abdel-Jalil Shalabi. *Islam and the Battle of Evangelism*. Cairo: Arabian Gulf Est. 1989, p. 85.

35 Abu al-A'la Mawdudi. *Political Theory of Islam*. Karachi: Maktaba-e Islami, 1976, p. 160.

36 Ibid., p.30 and http://www.messageonline.org/2002aprilmay/editorial.htm.

37 John Esposito, ed. *Voices of Resurgent Islam*. New York: Oxford University Press, 1983, p. 244.

38 Hurst, David. "The Democratic Move in Iran after Khomeini." In *Political Islam*. Rabat, Morocco: Tareq b. Ziad Center, 2000, pp. 146–148.

39 Jan Goodwin, ibid., p.127.

40 Naguib Mahfouz. *Heart of the Night*. Cairo: Misr Library, 1981, p. 122.

41 Muhammad Saied al-Ashmawi. *Political Islam*. Cairo: Sina Publishing, 1987, pp. 130–134.

42 In Arabic: الضرورات تبيح المحظورات. See for example Farabi in *Al Magalla*, No. 590, pp. 12–15 but particularly p. 13.

43 These points are drawn from various sources, but see in particular: Esam Amer. *Fundamentalism, Violence and Terrorism*. Cairo: Nahdat Misr, 2000, pp. 76–77, 92; and Dr. Abd-al Ghani Emad. The Rule of God and the Authority of the Faqih. Beirut: Taliaa, 1997, pp. 63–65.

44 Hussein Ahmad Amin. *Islam in a Changing World*. Cairo: Atlas, 1988, p. 207.

45 http://www.help-for-you.com/news/Nov2002/scripts/375e6b4c.html, and other sites.

46 See for example Nabi Abd al-Fattah. *The Qur'an and the Sword*. Cairo: Madbouli, 1984, p. 40.

47 Amir al-Taheri. *Holy Terrorism*. Cairo: Arabi Publishing, 1989, p. 27.

48 Ibid., p. 45.

49 Phil Parshall. Newsletter, Dec. 2001, p.2.

50 http://www.brentmorrison.com/030728Koran.htm.

51 Mark Gabriel, ibid., p. 182.

52 Dr. Ramadan Shalah, Secretary-General of the Palestinian Islamic Jihad: http://books.google.com/books?vid=ISBN1844675289&id=uySTXcBPEE kC&pg=PA43&lpg=PA43&dq=Ramadan+Shalah&sig=wLTWcs2Am5n5j b0mqrcMYPsSK_Q.

53 For a detailed treatment of how politicians should react to violence, see Alan M. Dershowitz. *Why Terrorism Works: Understanding the Threat, Responding to the Challenge*. New Haven and London: Yale University Press, 2002.

54 Sayyed Qutb. *This Religion*. Cairo: Dar al-Shoroq, 1989, p. 36.

55 Sayyed Qutb. *The Future is for this Religion*. Cairo: Dar al-Shoroq, 1988, p. 86.

56 John Esposito, ibid., pp. 241, 243.

57 For a fuller treatment of this subject see George Otis, Jr. *The Last of the Giants*. New York: Chosen Books, 1991, pp. 31–42.

58 Richard Kriegbaum. *Leadership Prayers*. Wheaton, IL: Tyndale, 1998, p. 106.

Chapter 10

1 Sasson. *Princess*. Ibid., pp 224–225.

2 John B. Nielson. *The Epistle to the Colossians. Beacon Bible Commentary*. Kansas City, MO: Beacon Hill Press, 1965, p. 369.

3 Fahmi Huwaidi. *Citizens, Not Dhimmis*. Cairo: Dar al-Shoroq, 1990, p. 7.

4   Ergun Mehmet Caner and Emir Fethi Caner. *Unveiling Islam: An Insider's Look at Muslim Life and Beliefs.* Grand Rapids, MI: Kregel, 2002, p.174.

Chapter 11

1   Hadith: Sunan al-Drami, Introduction, http://hadith.al-islam.com/Display/Display.asp?Doc=8&ID=50770&SearchText=%C7%E1%CA%E6%D1%C7%C9&SearchType=root&Scope=0,1,2,3,4,5,6,7,8&Offset=0&SearchLevel=QBE

2   See for example Yusef Durrah al-Haddad. *Introduction to Islamic-Christian Dialogue.* Junieh, Lebanon: Pauline Publications, 1986, pp.391–398.

3   Josh McDowell and John Gilchrist. *The Islam Debate.* San Bernardino, CA: Here's Life Publishers, 1983, p. 90.

Chapter 12

1   Abdul-Haqq. Ibid., pp. 13–14.

2   Muhammad Zafrulla Khan. *Islam, Its Meaning for Modern Man.* New York: Harper and Row, 1962, p. 91.

3   Austryn Wolfson. *The Philosophy of the Kalam.* Cambridge, Massachusetts: Harvard University, 1976, p. 133.

4   David Brown. *The Divine Trinity.* London: Sheldon Press, 1969, p. 60.

5   Karl Rahner. *The Trinity.* New York: Herder and Herder, 1970, p. 35.

6   Rahner. Ibid., p. 29.

7   Justin Martyr (ca. A.D. 100–165). *Dialogue with Trypho.*,n.d., p. 127.

8   H. Orton Wiley. *The Epistle to the Hebrews.* Kansas City: Beacon Hill Press, 1984, pp. 33-34.

9   Thomas O'Shaughnessy. *The Koranic Concept of the Word of God.* Rome: Pontifico Instituto Biblico, 1948, pp. 56-57.

10 Alister E. McGrath. *Understanding the Trinity.* Grand Rapids, MI: Zondervan, 1990, p. 146.

11 Karl Barth. Church Dogmatics. Vol. 1, Part 1. *The Doctrine of the Word of God.* Edinburgh: T. and T. Clark, 1936, p. 495.

12 Thomas F Torrance. *God and Rationality.* London: Oxford University Press, 1971, p. 175.

13 Rahner. Ibid., p. 66.

14 Torrence. Ibid., pp. 173-174.

Chapter 13

1 Henry Bettenson quoting Irenaeus in: *Documents of the Christian Church*. Oxford: Oxford University Press, 1967, p. 36.

2 Bettenson. Ibid., p. 35.

3 Mahmoud M. Ayoub. "Toward an Islamic Christology, II: The Death of Jesus, Reality or Delusion?" *The Muslim World* 70, no. 2. April 1980, p. 106.

4 Flavius Josephus (A.D. 37–97). *The Wars of the Jews*. 5.11.1.

5 Marcus Tullius Cicero (106–143 B.C.). *Against Verres*. 2.64.165.

6 Marcus Tullius Cicero. *In Defence of Rabirius*. 5.16.467.

7 Martin Hengel. *Crucifixion in the Ancient World and the Folly of the Message of the Cross*. Philadelphia: Fortress Press, 1977, p. 64.

8 Muhammad Din, 1924, 24.

9 Abdullah Yusuf Ali. *The Meaning of the Holy Qur'an. Text, Translation, and Commentary*. Lahore, Pakistan: Ashraf Press, 1934, p. 30.

10 Muhammad Din. "The Crucifixion in the Koran." *The Muslim World* 14, no. 1. January 1924, p. 25.

11 Cornelius P. Tacitus (A.D. 55–120). *The Annals*. 15.44.

12 Flavius Josephus (A.D. 37–97). *The Antiquities of the Jews*. 18.3.3.

13 I. Epstein, trans. *The Babylonian Talmud. Sanhedrin 43a*. London: Soncino Press, 1935, p. 281.

14 Gary R. Habermas. *Ancient Evidence for the Life of Jesus*. Nashville: Thomas Nelson, 1977, p. 100.

15 Habermas. Ibid., p.100.

16 Kenneth Bailey. *Finding the Lost*. St Louis: Concordia, 1992, p. 75.

17 Hengel. Ibid., pp. 19-20.

18 Hengel. Ibid., p. 10.

19 Kenneth Bailey. Unpublished class notes. School of World Mission, Fuller Theological Seminary. ca. 1976, p. 2.

20 Such as Maghazi and Ibn Ishaq. See Mohammed Marmaduke Pickthall. *The Meaning of the Glorious Koran*. New York: The New American Library, 1961, p. 23.

21 Kenneth Cragg. *Operation Reach*. The Near Eastern Christian Council Study Program in Islam, September and October, 1959, p. 11.

22 Abbas Mahmood al-Aqqad. *The Genius of Christ*. Cairo: Nahadat Misr, n.d., pp. 148–149.

23 Calvin as quoted by Sanders 1971, p. 165.

Chapter 14

1   Is it possible that the continual lament by some Western Christians over the injustices of centuries past is due to an exaggerated sense of guilt? To overindulge in such remorse at the expense of evangelism is biblically unwarranted and certainly a waste of spiritual energy!

2   Paul B. Smith. *Jesus by John.* Toronto: G. R. Welch, 1980, pp. 18-19.

3   Alexander Balmain Bruce. *The Training of the Twelve.* Grand Rapids, MI: Kregel Publications, 1971, p. 14.

4   Alan R. Tippett. *Solomon Islands Christianity.* London: Lutterworth Press, 1967, p. 363.

Chapter 15

1   Raymond Davis. *Fire on the Mountains.* Grand Rapids, MI: Zondervan, 1975, p. 241.

2   Donald K. Smith. *The Basis in Communication Theory for Effective Christian Ministry.* Nairobi, Kenya: Daystar Communications, n.d., p. 1.

3   Here is an example of Goha's stories: Goha sold a house. But one of the conditions he gave to the buyer was that he would retain possession of one nail in a wall of the house; and he wanted that clearly stated in the sales contract. This sounded strange to the buyer, but he thought that it should not stop him from buying the house. A short while after the deal was finished, Goha knocked at the door of his old house. The new buyer answered. Goha informed him that he wanted to check on his nail. The contract stated his right to do so. The new owner accepted the visit and would have to accept all such visits in the future. This story is an example of someone who wants to keep control of things that are no longer under his power—someone who cannot let go.

4   *Lausanne Occasional Papers, No. 4: The Glen Eyrie Report—Muslim Evangelization.* Wheaton, IL: Lausanne Committee for World Evangelization, 1978, p. 4.

5   For a more detailed treatment of this subject see Lester Fleenor, *God Almighty! His Word for Christians, Jews, and Moslems.* Evangel Press, 2005.

6   Loewenthal, Isidor. *The Muslim World.* September, July 1911. Loewenthal was a missionary to Afghanistan. He wrote this in 1860 and it was reprinted in 1911.

7   Eugene Peterson. *Eat this Book.* Grand Rapids, MI: Wm. B. Eerdmans, 2006, pp. 154–155.

8 See Webster's 1913 Dictionary, http://www.newadvent.org/cathen/06608x. htm and http://www.hyperdictionary.com/dictionary/god.

9 Consider the contents of his address:
   a. He commended them as very religious (v. 22).
   b He built a bridge to communicate the message to them: He proclaims the God they already worship (v. 23).
   c. He described God from his own perspective with some detail: He is the supreme creator of all and cannot be confined to temples (v. 24), He is not like pagan gods, He does not need anything from us (v.25). He is the source of our life and holds our destiny in His hand (vv. 25–26). He is not far from each one of us, and He wants us to seek Him, reach out for Him to find Him (v. 27). In him we live and move and have our being... We are His offspring (v. 28).
   d. He tried to correct their misconceptions about God: We should not think that the divine being is like gold or silver or stone—an image made by man's design and skill (v. 29).
   e. He challenged them to repent and place their faith in Jesus Christ: In the past God overlooked such ignorance, but now he commands all people everywhere to repent (v. 30). He is the just judge of the world through Jesus Christ (v. 31).

10 A slave who lived around 550 B.C. and whose fables are well-known in many places around the world for their moral lessons.

11 Lesslie Newbigin. *The Open Secret*. Grand Rapids, MI: Wm. B. Eerdmans, 1995, p. 142.

12 *Lausanne Occasional Papers, No. 4*, 1978, p. 4.

13 *Lausanne Occasional Papers, No. 1: The Pasadena Consultation-Homogeneous Unit Principle*. Wheaton, IL: Lausanne Committee for World Evangelization, 1978, p. 3.

14 *Lausanne Occasional Papers, No. 3: The Lausanne Covenant—An Exposition and Commentary by John Stott*. Wheaton, IL: Lausanne Committee for World Evangelization, 1978, p. 25.

15 *Lausanne Occasional Papers, No. 2: The Willowbank Report—Gospel and Culture*. Wheaton, IL: Lausanne Committee for World Evangelization, 1978, p. 19.

Chapter 16

1 From Ahmad's personal testimony, given in a Christian meeting two days after his discharge.

2 Burnett, David. *Unearthly powers*. Nashville: Thomas Nelson, 1988, p. 252.

3 I have written about this in other publications. See for example: "Islam Encountering Gospel Power" in *Called and Empowered*. Peabody, MA: Hendrickson, 1991; and "Overcoming Resistance Through the Paranormal" in *Reaching the Resistant*. Pasadena, CA: William Carey Library: 1998.

4 See for example Gibb. *Whither Islam*, 1932, 24.

5 Guy P. Duffield, and Nathaniel M. Van Cleave. *Foundations of Pentecostal Theology*. Los Angeles: L. I. F. E. Bible College, 1983, p. 507.

6 Lesslie Newbigin. *Foolishness to the Greeks. The Gospel and Western Culture.* Grand Rapids, Michigan: Wm B. Eerdmans, 1986. p. 126.

7 Anton Wessels. *Images of Jesus*. John Vriend, trans. Grand Rapids, MI: Wm. B. Eerdmans, 1990, p.94.

8 Arthur F. Glasser. "The Powers and Mission." Manuscript. Fuller Theological Seminary, 1983, p. 163.

9 John Bright. *The Kingdom of God*. Nashville, Tennessee: Abingdon-Cokesbury Press, 1963, p., 218.

10 Timothy Warner. "Teaching Power Encounter." In *Evangelical Missions Quarterly* 22, no. 1, January 1986, p. 69.

11 Quoted by Glasser, ibid., p. 171.

12 John Calvin. *Institutes*. Ibid., p. 192.

13 Timothy Warner. Ibid., p. 70.

14 Karl Friedrich Keil and F. Delitzsch. *Commentary on the Old Testament*. Vol. 3. Trans. from German by James Martin. Peabody, MA: Hendrickson. 1989, pp. 245, 249.

15 Kenneth Scott Latourette. *A History of Christianity*. Vol. l. New York: Harper and Row, 1975, p. 105.

16 Latourette. Ibid., p. 348; and Sabine Baring-Gould. *The Lives of the Saints*. London: J. S. Nimmo, 1897, p. 47.

17 A. O. Igenoza "African Weltanschauung and Exorcism: The Quest for the Contextualization of the Kerygma." *Africa Theological Journal* 14, no. 3, 1985, p. 181.

18 Alan R. Tippett. *Solomon Islands Christianity*. London: Lutterworth Press, 1967, p. 110.

19 Ajith Fernando. *The Supremacy of Christ*. Wheaton, IL: Crossway Books, 1995, p.83.

20 Richard J. Foster. *Prayer: Finding the Heart's True Home*. New York: Harper Collins Publishers, 1992, p. 204.

21 Ajith Fernando. Ibid., p. 82.

Chapter 17

1 Walter Houston Clark, et. al. *Religious Experience: Its Nature and Function in the Human Psyche*. Springfield, Illinois: Charles C. Thomas, 1973, pp. 8-11.

2 Kenneth Nolin. "A Christian Pilgrimage Into Islam." Manuscript, 1976, p. 86.

3 «C'est le cœur qui sent Dieu, et non la raison. Voilà ce que c'est la foi, Dieu sensible au cœur, non à la raison. «(Blaise Pascal. *Pensées*. Paris: Librairie Hachette, 1950, p. 107, #278.)

4 «Si on soumet tout à la raison, notre religion n'aura rien de mystérieux et de surnaturel. Si on choque les principes de la raison, notre religion sera absurde et ridicule.» (Blaise Pascal. *Pensées*. Paris: Librairie Hachette, 1950, p. 106, #273.)

5 Paul G. Hiebert. *Cultural Anthropology*. Philadelphia: J. B. Lippincott Co., 1976, p. 372.

6 Oswald chamber. *My Utmost for His Highest*. December 22. http://www.myutmost.org/12/1222.html

7 Edward Westermarck. *Pagan Survivals in Muhammedan Civilization*. London: Macmillan Press, 1933, p. 121.

8 Aida Barkan. "Evangelism and Colonialism in Our Islamic East." In *Huda-'l-Islam*. Jerusalem: January 1984, p. 7.

9 Muhammad Jalal Kishk. *When Horses Entered Al Azhar*. Beirut: Elmiyah, n.d.

10 Sandra Mackey. *The Saudis*. London: Coronet Books, Hodder and Stoughton. 1990, p. 281.

11 Angus Kinnear. *The Story of Watchman Nee: Against the Tide*. Wheaton, IL: Tyndale House. 1973, pp. 151, 152.

Chapter 18

1 From a letter to the author.

2 From the testimony of J. A. Subhan in Mark Hanna. *The True Path*. Colorado Springs: International Doorways, 1975, p. 40.

3 Condensed from: Kamel Mansour. *Sheikh Mikhael Mansour*. Cairo: Al-Muhit Printing, n.d. Mikhael is the name Muhammad acquired for himself after he came to Christ. Kamel was his brother. The book has a beautiful introduction by Samuel Zwemer.

4 Name of country withheld. I wrote this story after I listened to Ali give his testimony in a large Christian meeting. Later, I received the news that Ali had started eight home cell groups in surrounding villages, and that believers in his country were suffering persecution.

5 Khaled was brought to Christ by the powerful love of the Christians he met. Pray that God's love will continue to flow through them to him as their brother and that God will meet his needs.

6 Most Muslims who heard this story maintained that both father and daughter either lost their minds or were bewitched by Christians.

7 From a letter from D. B. to the author.

8 This young man told his story in an interview with the author on radio.

9 As told to Jeri S. Malek, missionary to Muslims.

10 J. N. D. Anderson. *The World's Religions*. Grand Rapids, Michigan: Wm. B. Eerdmans, 1960, p. 98.

BIBLIOGRAPHY

Abd Al-Bari, Jamal. *The Islamic Alternative to Undue Magic* البديل الإسلامي لفك السحر Cairo: Egypt, Leqa, 1990.

Abd Al-Fattah, Nabil. *The Qur'an and the Sword* المصحف والسيف Cairo: Madbouli, 1984.

Abd Al-Karim, Khalil. *The Historic Roots of the Islamic Shari'a* الجذور التاريخية للشريعة الإسلامية No country, no publisher, no date indicated.

——. "The Problem of Sectarianism." In *Where Is Sectarianism Taking Us ?* الطائفية إلى أين ؟ Cairo: Dar al-Masri al-Jadid, 1987.

——. "Political Islam and the Problem of Sectarianism." In *The Problem of Sectarianism in Egypt* المشكلة الطائفية في مصر Cairo: Center for Arab Research, 1988.

——. *Singing with the Rababah about the Group of Companions. Book I: Muhamamd* شدو الربابة بأحوال مجتمع الصحابة، الكتاب الأول: محمد Cairo: Sina, 1998.

——. *Singing with the Rababah about the Group of Companions. Book II: The Companions* شدو الربابة بأحوال مجتمع الصحابة، الكتاب الثاني: الصحابة Cairo: Sina, 1997.

——. *The Foundational Text and its Society* النص المؤسس ومجتمعه Cairo: Misr al-Mahrousa, 2002.

Abd Al-Maqsood, A. F. *Crusades Forever* صليبية إلى الأبد Beirut, Lebanon: Irfan, n.d.

Abd Al-Masih. *Why Is It Difficult for a Muslim to Become a Christian?* Schorndorf, Germany: Ev. Karmel Mission, n.d.

Abdul-Haqq, Abdiyah Akbar. *Sharing Your Faith with a Muslim.* Minneapolis: Bethany House Publishers, 1980.

Abu-l Futouh, A. Ma'ati. *The Inevitability of the Islamic Solution* حتمية الحل الإسلامي Guiza, Egypt: Al-Andalus, 1987.

Abu-Zeid, Nasr Hamed. *Muhei-ddin Ibn Arabi's Philosophy of Interpreting the Qur'an* فلسفة التأويل عند محي الدين بن عربي Casablanca, Morocco: Arab Cultural Center, 1998.

Adeney, Miriam. *Daughters of Islam: Building Bridges with Muslim Women.* Downers Grove, IL: InterVarsity, 2002.

Ahmad, Khurshid. *Islam, its Meaning and Message.* London: Islamic Council of Europe, 1975.

Akbar, M.J. *The Shade of Swords, Jihad and the Conflict Between Islam and Christianity.* London: Routledge, 2003.

Al-Amrousi, Fayed. *Concubines Who Were Singers* الجواري المغنيات Cairo: Dar al-Maaref, 1984.

Al-Aqqad, Abbas Mahmoud. *The Genius of Christ* عبقرية المسيح Cairo: Nahadat Misr, n.d.

Al-Ashmawi, Muhammad Saied. *Political Islam* الإسلام السياسي Cairo: Sina Publishing, 1987.

Al-Asqalani, Ahmad Ibn Hajar. *Reaching the Goal* بلوغ المرام من أدلة الأحكام (15th Century). This printing, Beirut: Al-Elmiyah, n.d.

———. *Magic, Sorcery and the Evil Eye* السحر والكهانة والحسد (15th Century). This printing, Cairo: Turath, 1990.

Al-Banna, Hassan. *The Call and the Caller* الدعوة والداعية Cairo: Azzahra, 1990.

Al-Baydawi, Imam Naser al-Din. *Anwar Al-Tanzil* أنوار التنزيل وأسرار التأويل Cairo: Dar al-Fikr, n.d.

Al-Bukhari, Imam Abdullah. *Sahih Al-Bukhari* صحيح البخاري Beirut: Al-Elmiyah, n.d.

Al-Ghazali, Imam. *Ihya' Ulum Al-Din* إحياء علوم الدين.

———. *Rules of Marriage* (excerpts from Ihya') آداب الزواج Tunis, Tunisia: Shahmi Press, n.d.

Al-Ghazali, Muhamamd. *The Bitter Reality* الحق المر Cairo: Dar al-Shoroq, 1990.

Al-Haddad, Yusef Durrah. *Introduction to Islamic-Christian Dialogue* مدخل إلى الحوار الإسلامي المسيحي Junieh, Lebanon: Pauline Publications, 1986.

——. *The Qur'an and the Book,* 4 volumes القرآن والكتاب Beirut: Paulist Publications, 1986.

Al-Hariri, Abu Musa. *Nusayrian Alawites* العلويون الناصريون Beirut: 1980.

——. *Was He an Arab?* أعربي هو ؟ Lebanon: Ma'refah, 1984.

——. *The Prophet of Mercy and the Muslims' Qur'an, A Study in Mecca's Society* نبي الرحمة وقرآن المسلمين Lebanon: Ma'refah, 1985.

——. *The World of Miracles, A Study in the History of the Qur'an* عالم المعجزات Lebanon: Ma'refah, 1986.

——. *Priest and Prophet, A Study in the Origins of Islam* قس ونبي Lebanon: Ma'refah, 1991.

Al-Hofni, Abdel Mon'em. *Omar Khayyam and the Ruba'iyat* عمر الخيام والرباعبات Cairo: Al-Rashad House, 1992.

Ali, Abdullah Yusuf. *The Meaning of the Holy Qur'an. Text, Translation, and Commentary.* Lahore, Pakistan: Ashraf Press, 1934.

Ali Ben Hadyah, Belhassan Balishand, and Jilani B.H. Yahya, eds. *Al Jadid Dictionary* القاموس الجديد Tunis: STD, 1979.

Al-Jezeery, Abderrahman. *The Sure Proof* أدلة اليقين Cairo: Irshad Press, 1934.

Al-Karm, Osama. *A Dialogue with Jinn* حوار مع الجن Cairo: Madbouli, 1990.

Al-Shak'ah, Mustafa. *Islam with No Sects* إسلام بلا مذاهب Cairo: Al-Masriah Al-Lubnaniah, 1989.

Al-Sha'rawi, Muhammad Metwalli. *The Fatwas,* Vol. 1, 3 الفتاوي Cairo: Qur'an Library, 1981.

———. *This Is Islam* هذا هو الإسلام Cairo: Turath, 1990.

Al-Taheri, Amir. *Holy Terrorism.* الإرهاب المقدس Cairo: Arabi Publishing, 1989.

Al-Wardani, Saleh. *Mut'a Marriage Allowed to Sunnis* زواج المتعة حلال عند أهل السنة Cairo: Little Madbouli, 1997.

———. *Dialogues Between Sunni and Shi'a Experts* المناظرات بين فقهاء السنة وفقهاء الشيعة Beirut: Al-Ghadeer, 1999.

Al-Zamakhshari, Abul-Qasem b. Omar. *Al-Kashaf* الكشاف عن حقائق التنزيل وعيون الأقاويل فى وجوه التأويل 4 Volumes. Cairo: Muhammad Mustafa: 1354 A.H.

Amin, Hussein Ahmad. *The Sad Muslim's Guide* دليل المسلم الحزين Cairo: Madbouli, 1987.

———. *The Call to Apply the Islamic Shari'a* الدعوة إلى تطبيق الشريعة الإسلامية Cairo: Madbouli, 1987.

———. *Islam in a Changing World* الإسلام في عالم متغير Cairo: Atlas, 1988.

Anderson, J. N. D. *The World's Religions.* Grand Rapids, MI: Wm. B. Eerdmans Publishing Co., 1960.

Andrae, Tor. *Mohammed, the Man and His Faith.* London: George Allen and Unwin, 1956.

A'rab, Ibrahim. *Political Islam and Modernism* الإسلام السياسي والحداثة Casablanca: Afrique Orient, 2000.

Arkoun, Muhammad. *Islamic Thought* الفكر الإسلامي Casablanca: Arab Cultural Center, 1996.

Arselan, Prince Shakib. *Why Muslims Went Backward and Others Went Forward* لماذا تأخر المسلمون ولماذا تقدم غيرهم Cairo: Al-Bashir, n.d.

Ayoub, Mahmoud M. "Toward an Islamic Christology, II: The Death of Jesus, Reality or Delusion?" In *The Muslim World* 70, no. 2 (April 1980).

Azrouel, Fatima Al-Zahraa. *Prostitution: Permissible Bodies* البغاء أو الجسد المستباح Beirut: Afrique Orient, 2000.

Baghdadi, Jalal Al-Din. *The Devil's Deception* تلبيس إبليس Beirut: Dar al-Jil, n.d. (Originally written about AD 1200).

Baghdadi, M. A. A. *Terrorism and the Second Islam* الإرهاب والإسلام الثاني Beirut: Arab Knowledge Publishers, 2003.

Bahgat, Ahmad. In *Al-Ahram* الأهرام Cairo: May 26, 1983.

Bailey, Kenneth. *Finding the Lost.* St Louis: Concordia, 1992.

——. Unpublished class notes. School of World Mission, Fuller Theological Seminary. ca.1976.

Baring-Gould, Sabine. *The Lives of the Saints.* London: J. S. Nimmo, 1897.

Barkan, Aida. "Evangelism and Colonialism in Our Islamic East" التبشير والاستعمار في شرقنا الإسلامي In *Huda-'l-Islam.* Jerusalem: January 1984.

Barth, Karl. *Church Dogmatics.* Vol. 1, Part 1, *The Doctrine of the Word of God.* Edinburgh: T. and T. Clark, 1936.

Barth, Markus. "Was Christ's Death a Sacrifice?" In *Scottish Journal of Theology. Occasional Papers, No. 9.* Edinburgh and London: Oliver and Boyd Ltd, 1961.

Bettenson, Henry. *Documents of the Christian Church.* Oxford: Oxford University Press, 1967.

Betts, Robert Brenton. *Christians in the Arab East.* London: SPCK, 1979.

Breghish, M. H. *The Phenomenon of Backsliding in Early* Islam ظاهرة الردة في المجتمع الإسلامي الأول Beirut: Risalah, 1974.

Bright, John. *The Kingdom of God.* Nashville, TN: Abingdon-Cokesbury Press, 1963.

Brockelmann, Carl, ed. *History of the Islamic Peoples.* London: Routledge & Kegan Paul, 1982.

Brown, David. *The Divine Trinity.* London: Sheldon Press, 1969.

Bruce, Alexander Balmain. *The Training of the Twelve.* Grand Rapids, MI: Kregel, 1971.

Calvin, John. *The Institutes of Christian Religion.* Translated by John Allen. Philadelphia: Presbyterian Board of Christian Education, 1936.

Caner, Ergun Mehmet and Emir Fethi Caner. *Unveiling Islam: An Insider's Look at Muslim Life and Beliefs.* Grand Rapids, MI: Kregel, 2002.

Chesterton, G. K. *St. Francis of Assisi.* New York: Image Books, 1957.

Cicero, Marcus Tullius (106-43 B.C.). *Against Verres.*

———. *In Defence of Rabirius.*

Clark, Walter Houston, et. al. *Religious Experience: Its Nature and Function in the Human Psyche.* Springfield, IL: Charles C. Thomas, 1973.

Cragg, Kenneth. "Operation Reach." *The Near Eastern Christian Council Study Program in Islam* (September and October, 1959).

———. *The Call of the Minaret.* New York: Oxford University Press, 1964.

———. *Muhammad and the Christian.* London: Darton, Longman and Todd, 1984.

———. "A Tale of Two Cities." In *Mission Frontiers.* Pasadena, CA: US Center for World Mission, December 2001.

Cragg, Kenneth and Marston Speight. *Islam from Within: Anthology of Religion.* Belmont, CA: Wadsworth, 1980.

Davis, Raymond. *Fire on the Mountains.* Grand Rapids, MI: Zondervan Publishing House, 1975.

Dershowitz, Alan M. *Why Terrorism Works: Understanding the Threat, Responding to the Challenge.* New Haven and London: Yale University Press, 2002.

Din, Muhammad. "The Crucifixion in the Koran." In *The Muslim World* 14, no. 1 (January 1924).

Duffield, Guy P. and Nathaniel M. Van Cleave. *Foundations of Pentecostal Theology.* Los Angeles: L. I. F. E. Bible College, 1983.

Durant, Will. *The Story of Civilization.* Vol. 4, *Age of Faith.* New York: Simon and Schuster, 1950.

Durrani, Tehmina. *My Feudal Lord, A Devastating Indictment of Women's Role in Muslim Society.* London: Corgi Books, 1995.

Emad, Abd Al-Ghani. *The Rule of God and the Authority of the Faqih* حاكمية الله وسلطان الفقيه Beirut: Taliaa, 1997.

Epstein, I., trans. *The Babylonian Talmud, Sanhedrin 43a.* London: Soncino Press, 1935.

Esposito, John L., ed. *Voices of Resurgent Islam.* New York: Oxford University Press, 1983.

Farabi, Abd Al-Latif. In *Al Magalla,* no. 590. London: Arab Press, May 29-June 4, 1991.

Farah, Caesar E. *Islam: Beliefs and Observances.* Woodbury, NY: Barron's Educational Series, Inc., 1970.

Fernando, Ajith. *The Supremacy of Christ.* Wheaton, IL: Crossway Books, 1995.

Fernea, Elizabeth Warnock. *A Street in Marrakech.* Garden City, N.Y.: Anchor Books, 1980.

Fernea, Elizabeth Warnock and Bezirgan, Basima Qattan, eds. *Middle Eastern Women Speak.* Austin: University of Texas Press, 1977.

Fitzgerald, Edward, trans. *Rubaiyat of Omar Khayyam.* New York: Barnes & Noble, 1993.

Foster, Richard J. *Prayer: Finding the Heart's True Home.* New York: HarperCollins Publishers, 1992.

Fouda, Farag. *The Absent Truth* الحقيقة الغائبة Cairo: Dar al-Fikr, 1988.

Fregosi, Paul. *Jihad in the West: Muslim Conquests from the 7th to the 21st Centuries.* New York: Prometheus Books, 1998.

Fry, C. George and James Roy King. *The Middle East: Crossroads of Civilization.* Columbus, OH: Charles Merrill, 1973.

Gabriel, Mark. *Jesus and Muhammad.* Lake Mary, FL: Charisma House, 2004.

Geisler, Norman L. and Abdul Saleeb. *Answering Islam: The Crescent in the Light of the Cross.* Grand Rapids, MI: Baker Books, 1993.

Gibb, H. A. R. *Whither Islam? A Survey of Modern Movements in the Moslem World.* London: Victor Gollancz, Ltd., 1932.

Gibb, H. A. R. and J. H. Kramers, eds. *Shorter Encyclopaedia of Islam.* New York: Cornell University Press, 1953.

Glasser, Arthur F. "The Powers and Mission." Manuscript, 1983.

Goha, Mustafa. *The Crisis of Mind in Islam* محنة العقل في الإسلام *No publisher indicated, 1982.*

Goodwin, Jan. *Price of Honor: Muslim Women Lift the Veil of Silence on the Islamic World.* Boston: Little, Brown and Company, 1994.

Guillaume, Alfred. *Islam.* London: Penguin Books, 1973.

Habermas, Gary R. *Ancient Evidence for the Life of Jesus.* Nashville: Thomas Nelson, 1977.

Hamada, Louis Bahjat. *Understanding the Arab World.* Nashville: Thomas Nelson, 1990.

Hammoudah, Adel. *Sayyed Qutb: from Village to Scaffold* سيد قطب: من القرية إلى المشنقة Cairo: Sina Publishing, 1990.

Hanna, Mark. *The True Path.* Colorado Springs, CO: International Doorways Publications, 1975.

Hausfeld, Mark and Lynda with Ken Horn. *Silk Road Stories.* USA: Onward Books, 2005.

Hengel, Martin. *Crucifixion in the Ancient World and the Folly of the Message of the Cross.* Philadelphia: Fortress Press, 1977.

Hiebert, Paul G. *Cultural Anthropology.* Philadelphia: J. B. Lippincott Co., 1976.

Hindawi, Farid Amin. *Ibn Taimiya's Fatwas About Marriage and Sex* فتاوي الزواج وعشرة النساء Cairo: Turath, 1988.

Horner, Norman A. *A Guide to Christian Churches in the Middle East.* Elkhart, IN: Mission Focus, 1989.

Horri, Chris and Peter Chippindale. *What is Islam?* London: Virgin Books, 1991.

Hourani, Albert. *A History of the Arab peoples.* Cambridge, MA: Harvard University Press, 1991.

Hughes, Thomas Patrick. *A Dictionary of Islam.* London: H. A. Allan and Company, 1895.

Hurst, David. "The Democratic Move in Iran After Khomeini." In *Political Islam.* Rabat, Morocco: Tareq b. Ziad Center, 2000.

Huwaidi, Fahmi. *Citizens, Not Dhimmis* مواطنون لا ذميون Cairo: Dar al-Shoroq, 1990.

Ibn Arabi, Muhei-Din. *Pearls of Wisdom,* vol. 1 فصوص الحكم Beirut: Dar al-Ketab al-Arabi, n.d.

Ibn Kathir, Abu-lfeda Ismael. *The Sira of the Prophet (abbreviated)* مختصر السيرة النبوية Beirut: Masirah, 1987.

Ibn Taymiyya, Ahmad. *Repentance* التوبة Algeria: Shahab Publishing, n.d.

Ibraham, Ishak. *Black Gold and Holy War.* New York: Thomas Nelson, 1983.

Igenoza, A. O. "African Weltanschauung and Exorcism: The Quest for the Contextualization of the Kerygma." In *Africa Theological Journal* 14, no. 3 (1985).

Josephus, Flavius (A.D. 37-97). *The Wars of the Jews.*

———. *The Antiquities of the Jews.*

Justin Martyr, Saint (A.D. 100-165). *Dialogue with Trypho.* n.d.

Keil, Karl Friedrich and F. Delitzsch. *Biblical Commentary on the Old Testament,* Vol.1. Translated by James Martin. Edinburgh: T. and T. Clark, 1866.

Khalaf-Allah, Muhammad Ahmad. *Muhammad and the Antagonizing Powers* محمد والقوى المعارضة Cairo: Anglo-Egyptian Books, 1973.

Khaled, K. Muhammad. *Men Around The Apostle*, 5 Volumes رجال حول الرسول Cairo: Dar al-Kutub al-Hadithah, 1966.

Khan, Muhammad Zafrulla. *Islam, Its Meaning for Modern Man*. New York: Harper and Row, 1962.

Khartabil, Sami. *The Legend of Al-Hallaj* أسطورة الحلاج Beirut: Ibn Khaldoun, 1979.

Kinnear, Angus. *The Story of Watchman Nee: Against the Tide*. Wheaton, IL: Tyndale House, 1973.

Kishk, Muhammad Jalal. *When Horses Entered Al Azhar* ودخلت الخيل الأزهر Beirut: Al-Elmiyah, n.d.

——. *Thoughts of a Muslim About Sex* خواطر مسلم في المسألة الجنسية Cairo: Turath, 1992.

Klein, F.A. *The Religion of Islam*. New York: Humanities Press, 1971.

Kriegbaum, Richard. *Leadership Prayers*. Wheaton, IL: Tyndale, 1998.

Laffin, John. *The Dagger of Islam*. London: Sphere Books Limited, 1979.

Langley, Myrtle S. "Spirit-Possession, Exorcism and Social Context: an Anthropological Perspective with Theological Implications." In: *Churchman*, Vol. 94, No. 3.

Latourette, Kenneth Scott. *A History of Christianity*, Vol.1. New York: Harper and Row, 1975.

Lausanne Committee for World Evangelization. *Lausanne Occasional Papers, No. 1: The Pasadena Consultation-Homogeneous Unit Principle*. Wheaton, IL: Lausanne Committee for World Evangelization, 1978.

——. *Lausanne Occasional Papers, No. 2: The Willowbank Report—Gospel and Culture*. Wheaton, IL: Lausanne Committee for World Evangelization, 1978.

——. *Lausanne Occasional Papers, No. 3: The Lausanne Covenant—An Exposition and Commentary by John Stott.* Wheaton, IL: Lausanne Committee for World Evangelization, 1978.

——. *Lausanne Occasional Papers, No. 4: The Glen Eyrie Report—Muslim Evangelization.* Wheaton, IL: Lausanne Committee for World Evangelization, 1978.

Lenning, Larry G. *Blessing in Mosque and Mission.* Pasadena, CA: William Carey Library, 1980.

Lewis, Bernard. *The Political Language of Islam.* Chicago: The University Of Chicago Press, 1991.

——. *What Went Wrong? The Clash Between Islam and Modernity in the Middle East.* New York: HarperCollins, 2003.

——. *From Babel to Dragomans.* New York: Oxford University Press, 2004.

Lewis, B., et al, eds. *The Encyclopedia of Islam.* New Edition. Leiden, Netherlands: E. Brill, 1975.

Loewenthal, Isidor. In *The Muslim World.* July- September, 1911.

Lunde, Paul. *Islam: Faith, Culture, History.* London: DK Publishing, 2002.

Mackey, Sandra. *The Saudis.* London: Coronet Books, Hodder and Stoughton, 1990.

Mahfouz, Naguib. *Heart of the Night* قلب الليل Cairo: Misr Library, 1981.

Mahmood, Abdel Halim. *The Case of Sufism* قضية التصوف Cairo: Dar al-Ma'aref, 1988.

Mahmood, Mustafa. *Muhammad* محمد Cairo: Dar al-Maaref, 1977.

Manji, Irshad. The Trouble with Islam الخلل في الإسلام Internet book at http://www.muslim-refusenik.com/arabic.html

Mansfield, Peter. *The Arabs.* New York: Penguin Books, 1983.

Mansour, Kamel. *Sheikh Mikhael Mansour* الشيخ ميخائيل منصور Cairo: Al-Muhit Printing, n.d.

Mansour, Yassa. *Evidence of the Truth,* 4 Volumes بيان الحق No publisher indicated, 1966.

Marwah, Hussein, et al. *Studies in Islam* دراسات في الإسلام Beirut: Farabi, 1985.

Mawdudi, Abu Al-A'la. *Political Theory of Islam.* Karachi: Maktaba-e Is-lami, 1976.

———. *The Rights of Dhimmis* حقوق أهل الذمة Cairo: Mukhtar Books, n.d.

McDowell, Josh and Gilchrist, John. *The Islam Debate.* San Bernardino, CA: Here's Life Publishers, 1983.

McGavran, Donald A. *How Churches Grow.* New York: Friendship Press, 1976.

McGrath, Alister E. *Understanding the Trinity.* Grand Rapids, MI: Zon-dervan, 1990.

Mernissi, Fatima. *The Forgotten Queens of Islam.* Cambridge: Polity Press, 1994.

———. *Women's Rebellion and Islamic Memory.* London: Zed Books, 1996.

———. *The Social Dynamics of Sex* الجنس كهندسة اجتماعية Casablanca: Fen-nec, 1996.

———. *Are You Immune Against Women?* هل أنتم محصنون ضد الحريم Casa-blanca: Fennec, 2000.

Metwalli, Nahed Mahmoud. The Qur'an in Pre-Islamic Poetry القرآن في الشعر الجاهلي Internet Book: http://www.alkalema.net/alquran/index.htm?

Morgan, G. Campbell. *An Exposition of the Whole Bible.* Westwood, NJ: Fleming H. Revell, 1959.

Mushtahari, Abdulateef. *This Is Our Call* هذه دعوتنا Cairo: Dar al-E'tesam, 1979.

Nassef, Emad. *Sex in the University* الجنس في الجامعة Cairo: Hadaf Publishing, 1999.

Newbigin, Lesslie. *Foolishness to the Greeks. The Gospel and Western Culture.* Grand Rapids, MI: Wm B. Eerdmans, 1986.

———. *The Open Secret.* Grand Rapids, MI: Wm. B. Eerdmans, 1995.

Neill, Stephen. *A History of Christian Missions.* New York: Penguin Books, 1964.

Nielson, John B. *The Epistle to the Colossians.* Beacon Bible Commentary. Kansas City, MO: Beacon Hill Press, 1965.

Nolin, Kenneth. "A Christian Pilgrimage into Islam." Manuscript, 1976.

O'Shaughnessy, Thomas. *The Koranic Concept of the Word of God.* Rome: Pontifico Instituto Biblico, 1948.

Otis, George, Jr. *The Last of the Giants.* New York: Chosen Books, 1991.

Palmer, Alan. *The Decline and Fall of the Ottoman Empire.* New York: Barnes & Noble, 1992.

Patai, Raphael. *The Arab Mind.* New York: Scribner's, 1983.

Peters, George W. *A Biblical Theology of Missions.* Chicago: Moody Press, 1984.

Pickthall, Mohammed Marmaduke. *The Meaning of the Glorious Koran.* New York: The New American Library, 1961.

Qamni, Sayyed M. *The Hachemite Party* الحزب الهاشمي Cairo: Sina, 1990.

Qutb, Muhamamd Ali. *Imam Nisaai's Book on Sex* عشرة النساء للإمام النسائي Beirut: al-Asriyah, 1992.

Qutb, Sayyed. *The Future is for this Religion* المستقبل لهذا الدين Cairo: Dar al-Shoroq, 1988.

———. *This Religion* هذا الدين Cairo: Dar al-Shoroq, 1989.

———. *Landmarks on the Road* معالم في الطريق Cairo: Dar al-Shoroq, 1991.

Raban, Jonathan. *Arabia: A Journey Through the Labyrinth.* New York: Simon Schuster, 1979.

Rahman, Fazlur. *Major Themes of the Qur'an.* Chicago: Bibliotheca, 1980.

Rahner, Karl. *The Trinity.* New York: Herder and Herder, 1970.

Register, Ray G., Jr. *Dialogue and Interfaith Witness with Muslims.* Kingsport, TN: Moody Books, 1979.

Riddell, Peter G. and Peter Cotterell. *Islam in Context.* Grand Rapids, MI: Baker Academic, 2003.

Rippin, Andrew and John Knappert. *Textual Sources for the Study of Islam.* Chicago: University of Chicago Press, 1986.

Rudolph, Barbara. "Still Aboil About Nasrin." In *Time International,* July 11, 1994.

Sadeq, Hassan. *Roots of Dissension Among Islamic Groups* جذور الفتنة في الفرق الإسلامية Cairo: Madbouli, 1991.

Samman, Muhammad Abdullah. *Belief and Militancy Together* العقيدة والقوة معا Beirut: Dar al-Jil, 1974.

Sanders, J. Oswald. *The Incomprehensible Christ.* Chicago: Moody Press, 1971.

Sarhan, Samir. *Egypt Between the Religious and Secular State* مصر بين الدولة الدينية والمدنية Cairo: al-Misriyah, 1992.

Sasson, Jean. *Princess.* London: Bantom Books, 1993.

———. *Daughters of Arabia.* London: Bantam Books, 1997.

———. *Desert Royal.* London: Bantam Books, 1999.

Schacht, Joseph and C. E. Bosworth, eds. *The Legacy of Islam.* London: Oxford University Press, 1979.

Schaeffer, Francis. *Death in the City.* L'Abri Fellowship, 1969.

Seyouti (or Suyuti), Jalal-u-Din. *Rules of Jinn* أحكام الجان Cairo: Turath, 1989.

Shah, Idries. *The Sufis.* New York: Doubleday & Co., Inc., 1971.

Shalabi, Abdel-Jalil. *Islam and the Battle of Christianization* الإسلام ومعركة التنصير Cairo: Arabian Gulf Est., 1989.

Shaltut, Mahmood. *Islam, Creed and Law* الإسلام عقيدة وشريعة Cairo: Dar al-Shoroq, 1988.

Sharabi, Hisham. *Arab Intellectuals and the West: The Formative Years, 1875-1914.* Baltimore: Johns Hopkins Press, 1970.

Shoebat, Walid. *Why I Left Jihad.* USA: Top Executive Media, 2005.

Smith, Donald K. *The Basis in Communication Theory for Effective Christian Ministry.* (Unpublished Notes). Nairobi, Kenya: Daystar Communications, n.d.

Smith, Paul B. *Jesus by John.* Toronto. G. R. Welch, 1980.

Spencer, Robert. *The Myth of Islamic Tolerance.* Amherst, New York: Prometheus, 2005.

——. *The Truth about Muhammad.* Washington, D.C.: Regnery Publishing, Inc., 2006.

St. Clair-Tisdall, Rev. W. *The Sources of Islam.* New Delhi: Amorko Book Agency, 1901.

Tacitus, Cornelius P. (A.D. 55-120). *The Annals.*

Tippett, Alan R. *Solomon Islands Christianity.* London: Lutterworth Press, 1967.

Tomkinson, Michael. *Tunisia.* London & Tonbridge: Earnest Benn, Limited, 1970.

Torrance, Thomas F. *God and Rationality.* London: Oxford University Press, 1971.

Touati, A. K. *The Tragic Decline of Arab Presence in Andalusia* مأساة انهيار الوجود العربي في الأندلس Casablanca: Librairie Rachad, 1967.

Tozer, Aiden Wilson. *The Knowledge of the Holy.* New York: Harper and Row, 1961.

Van Dalen, Emily J. "Raising Radiant Daughters in Dark Places." *Seedbed,* Vol. XV, No. 4, 2001. West Sussex, UK.

Vander Werff, Lyle L. *Christian Missions to Muslims—the Record.* South Pasadena, CA: William Carey Library, 1977.

Von Grunebaum, Gustave E. *Medieval Islam: A Study in Cultural Orientation.* Chicago: University of Chicago Press, 1953.

———. *Modern Islam: The Search for Cultural Identity.* Westport: Greenwood Press, 1962.

Warner, Timothy. "Teaching Power Encounter." In *Evangelical Missions Quarterly* 22, no. 1 (January 1986).

Watt, W. Montgomery. *Muhammad, Prophet and Statesman.* New York: Oxford University Press, 1961.

Weekes, Richard V. *Muslim Peoples: A World Ethnographic Survey.* Westport, CT: Greenwood Press, 1978.

Wellhausen, Von Julius. *History of the Arab State* تاريخ الدولة العربية Cairo: Thousand Books, 1958.

Westermarck, Edward. *Pagan Survivals in Muhammedan Civilization.* London: Macmillan Press, 1933.

Wiley, H. Orton. *The Epistle to the Hebrews.* Kansas City: Beacon Hill Press, 1984.

Wismar, Adolph L. *A Study in Tolerance.* New York: AMS Inc., 1966.

Wolfson, Harry Austryn. *The Philosophy of the Kalam.* Cambridge, MA: Harvard University, 1976.

Yafe'i, Abdullah b. Asa'ad. *A Garden of Scents* روض الرياحين في حكايات الصالحين Cyprus: Emad, n.d.

Youssef, Michael. *Making Christ Known to Muslims.* Atlanta, Georgia: Haggai Institute, 1980.

Yusef, Amre. *Exciting Facts about Jinn and Ghosts* حقائق مثيرة عن الجن والعفاريت Cairo: Arabic Publishing Center, 1990.

——. *Exciting Facts about Magic* حقائق مثيرة عن السحر Cairo: Arabic Publishing Center, n.d.

Yusef, Hussein M. and M. Attia Khamis. *Stop Destroying Islam from the Inside* لكي لا تتحطم حصون الإسلام من الداخل Cairo: Dar al-E'tesam, 1979.

Zamakhshari. See Al-Zamakhshari.

Zwemer, Samuel M. *The Moslem Doctrine of God.* New York: American Tract Society, 1905.

——. *The Influence of Animism on Islam, An Account of Popular Superstitions.* New York: Macmillan, 1920.

——. *Studies in Popular Islam.* New York: Macmillan, 1938.

CPSIA information can be obtained
at www.ICGtesting.com
Printed in the USA
LVHW041544151120
671756LV00001B/111